KEITH SOKO

A MOUNTING EAST–WEST TENSION

BUDDHIST-CHRISTIAN DIALOGUE ON HUMAN RIGHTS, SOCIAL JUSTICE, & A GLOBAL ETHIC

MARQUETTE
UNIVERSITY

PRESS

MARQUETTE STUDIES IN THEOLOGY
NO. 66
ANDREW TALLON, SERIES EDITOR

LIBRARY OF CONGRESS CATALOGING-IN-PUBLICATION DATA

Soko, Keith, 1957-
A mounting East-West tension : Buddhist-Christian dialogue on human rights, social justice & a global ethic / Keith Soko.
 p. cm. — (Marquette studies in theology ; No. 66)
Includes bibliographical references and index.
ISBN-13: 978-0-87462-743-5 (pbk. : alk. paper)
ISBN-10: 0-87462-743-5 (pbk. : alk. paper)
 1. Human rights—Religious aspects—Buddhism. 2. Human rights—Religious aspects—Catholic Church. 3. Buddhism—Relations—Catholic Church. 4. Catholic Church—Relations—Buddhism. 5. Human ecology—Religious aspects—Buddhism. 6. Human ecology—Religious aspects—Catholic Church. I. Title.
BQ4570.H78S65 2009
261.7—dc22

2009030242

COVER DESIGN AND ART BY COCO CONNOLLY

♾The paper used in this publication meets the minimum requirements of the
American National Standard for Information Sciences—
Permanence of Paper for Printed Library Materials, ANSI Z39.48-1992.

Association of American
University Presses

MARQUETTE UNIVERSITY PRESS
MILWAUKEE

The Association of Jesuit University Presses

A MOUNTING EAST—WEST TENSION

TABLE OF CONTENTS

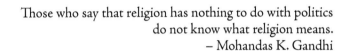

Those who say that religion has nothing to do with politics
do not know what religion means.
– Mohandas K. Gandhi

PREFACE

The initial motivation for this study can be traced back to my undergraduate years in religious studies, where, intent on finding answers to "the big question" of God's existence, I felt "sidetracked" by having to take courses in other world religions. Those courses eventually altered the question from "Does God exist?," although always a healthy nagging doubt, to the question "What is God like?" Primarily, Hinduism and Buddhism offered Eastern worldviews which often contrasted, yet also often complemented, my own Roman Catholic upbringing. My own fascination with Buddhism stems from its radically different religious concepts, on one hand, (no God, no soul, no self, no personal afterlife, at least at first glance), to its often similar ethical insights with Christianity, on the other hand. Life, even if the answer to the "God question" was "Void" or "Emptiness," was not nihilistic, but was ethical.

This interest in Buddhism and in comparative ethics was put into sharper focus by my dissertation director's suggestion for an earlier study to focus on "human rights." This initial comment provided the direction for this study as well, which includes multiple interests of mine. The concept of "human rights" combines religious aspirations with political ramifications. An intellectual and spiritual interest in comparative religions, along with a practical and moral concern in comparative ethics, was now wed to global concerns for social activism and justice. Thus, one is reminded that religion has never been merely an intellectual endeavor, but is a way of life, as in the Eastern concept of *dharma*.

Despite the prominence of the concept of "human rights" in this study, by its completion the "secondary" issue of "ecological duties" was looming larger and larger. It is one of my hopes that this study will aid in bringing the concept of human rights into greater dialogue with overall concerns for the environment. In addition, by reviewing the past and present work of Roman Catholic authors involved in human rights advocacy and interreligious dialogue, I hope to acknowledge the Catholic, and in that sense "universal," contribution in these endeavors. May the spirit of these earlier authors continue on in this study in seeing Christianity as a sometimes radical and world transforming religion, in dialogue with and as an advocate for justice among the world's religions.

ACKNOWLEDGMENTS

M any people have contributed toward the completion of this study, first as a dissertation and now as a book, and I would like to express my sincere gratitude for their assistance. First, I am deeply indebted to my dissertation committee for being with me on this project initially, including Christine Firer Hinze, my academic advisor, who was there from the beginning of my doctorate program with advice and guidance on a number of levels and to all of the faculty in the Theology Department at Marquette University.

But I would probably have not considered graduate work had it not been for two key mentors in my Master's program at Mount St. Mary's College in Los Angeles: Alexis Navarro and Marie Egan. For their collegial attitude and approach to religious studies, social justice and Catholicism, and their continual support and friendship, I am extremely grateful. Stemming from these years as well is a close friend and colleague, Maurice Hamington, who as a fellow traveler along this academic path has been invaluable to me for his sincere advice and his sense of humor, which has helped to keep my sanity. In regard to that sanity, I am especially grateful to my wife, Jane, and my children, Jessica, Stephen, and Luke, for their patience and understanding during the dissertation process when Dad was "in the study," and during writing of this book when Dad was "in the study" again.

Finally, I would like to express my sincere gratitude, appreciation, and admiration to my dissertation director at the time, Daniel C. Maguire, for his support of my research interests and pursuits. But most importantly, for his overall attitude and approach to ethics, politics, religion, and Catholicism, and for his openmindedness, outspokenness, and vision, I am deeply indebted. My studies, and this book, would not have been the same without his presence.

INTRODUCTION

The concept of "human rights" is an important political tool in the current discussion and legislation of global concerns. In recent years, it has also received growing attention as a common focus for world religions, acting as a linchpin for common ethical and social justice concerns. As Robert Traer affirms, the "support for human rights is global, cutting across cultures as well as systems of belief and practice"(Traer 1991, 1).

Current human rights abuses and ecological devastation necessitate more than ever the involvement of religions within these discussions. Describing "religion" as a "response to the sacred"(Maguire 1993, 9), Daniel C. Maguire observes that these "powerful symbol systems"(Maguire 1998, 20) "will be a major player in the planetary crisis ... *for good or for ill*"(ibid. 36 [italics in original]). Hans Küng further asserts that "religions which in themselves do not make human rights a reality are no longer credible today"(Küng 1990, 118).

In this book, I focus primarily on the concept of human rights and argue for the importance of that concept and the role which religion can and must play in its articulation. Secondarily, I argue for the necessity of ecological duties as a correlate to human rights. Thirdly, I emphasize that both of these concepts contribute to, and are aided by, a global ethic. In doing so, I am implicitly arguing against a general postmodernist cultural relativism, and instead argue for some type of "universals," some type of "moral core," in which the concept of human rights plays a role.

In particular, I examine these concepts from the current point of view of two diverse religious traditions: Buddhism and Roman Catholicism. Buddhism and Roman Catholicism offer radically different views of the individual, the human being, the "person." (In this study, I use the terms "individual," "human being," and "person," somewhat interchangeably throughout. However, I acknowledge that these terms, particularly "person," may be problematic in regards to Buddhism.)

This can be seen in the notions of anatta (nonself) and impermanence in Buddhism compared with the Catholic concept of a unique individual person created in God's image and destined for eternal life. Yet, their ethical emphasis is often similar. In examining their often contrasting views of the individual human being, I argue that, despite these differences, both traditions affirm the sacredness and *value* of the individual. This text examines current discussions of the term "human rights" in Roman Catholicism and in Buddhism and argues that the term can be used by both traditions to express common human aspirations, concerns, and ethical paths of action. In addition, it cautions against an approach to human rights which is laden with ego and anthropocentrism, and argues in favor of a concept of human rights which contains a corresponding ecological duty to other species and the environment. The concept of the common good, as seen in Roman Catholicism, can include ecological concerns, and these ecological concerns are seen in Buddhism in the concept of interconnectedness.

The importance of this study, therefore, is primarily to affirm the value of the individual, in Buddhism and Roman Catholicism, as exemplified in the language of human rights. Secondarily, it affirms the connectedness of that individual with other living beings and the environment, and emphasizes a corresponding ecological duty. Yet, the importance of this study extends beyond Buddhist-Roman Catholic dialogue. As the world emerges as a global village, the necessity of a global ethic becomes more apparent for many, especially in light of injustices, human rights violations, and neglected duties toward the environment. Hans Küng has argued, and the Parliament of the World's Religions has affirmed, for example, that there can be "no new global order without a new global ethic" (Küng and Kuschel 1995, 18). And Paul Knitter observes that talk of liberation is one-sided unless it contains dialogue among the world religions (Knitter 1987, 180). In arguing that the term "human rights" can be used fruitfully in and between such diverse systems as Buddhism and Roman Catholicism, I conclude that the term can form a key component in dialogue among world religions in the development of a global ethic.

Therefore, the central thesis guiding this book is that the language and concept of "human rights" can be applied within the current traditions of Buddhism and Roman Catholicism, and that "ecological duties" form a necessary component in the discussion of human rights. An implication of this is that, if "human rights" can be applied, and be useful, in such radically different systems of belief, it can also be used as a basis for a global ethic between systems which are less diverse. Hence, it is a "test case" for a global ethic.

One fundamental issue running throughout this study involves the differences between the worldviews of Eastern and Western religions. While the concept of "human rights" receives growing attention in religious studies, debate remains as to what extent the term can be applied at all within Eastern traditions and to what extent between East and West. Does the term contain the elements of common aspirations and hopes for all people, or is it a form of Western imperialism upon the East?

Although some argue that no moral common ground exists between religions, or that no social ethic exists in some Eastern religions, many would argue for some sort of moral common ground. And, while the actual term "human rights" does not traditionally exist within religions, historically or scripturally, is it an expression of the aspirations and core beliefs of these traditions, East as well as West? Others argue that to define the term as a completely Western term is to define it too narrowly, and that one must look at the intentionality behind other concepts in the religions, not just the terms themselves.

While most arguments here generally do favor at least some consensus between East and West, the concept of *human* rights becomes even more problematic in Buddhism. Arguments within Buddhism itself are widespread even on the general concept of a social ethic, ranging from no social ethic to a profound social ethic. The specific issue of "human rights" presents problems because of the general Buddhist view of the individual human being as anatta (nonself), and different interpretations of it. Therefore, while a growing number argue favorably for the use of the term "human rights" within Buddhism currently, others argue that the radically different nature of the individual human being in Buddhism makes the term foreign to Buddhism. Still others argue that it *is* the radically different notion of the human being in Buddhism which *adds* to the concept of human rights, avoiding the ego-centeredness lurking behind the term itself. Therefore, given the fact that the term "human rights" does not exist historically or scripturally within Buddhism, the task at hand is to discern whether it is in keeping with general Buddhist concerns, aspirations, and intents.

On the other hand, the Roman Catholic tradition *has* stressed the importance and the value of the individual created in God's image, although it saw that individual as a part of a larger social and cosmic whole. The notion of human dignity was articulated more precisely with Vatican II, and the actual term "human rights" has found growing support within Church teaching within the last century, leading to Roman Catholicism's current involvement as an advocate for human rights on a global scale.

Therefore, while the East-West problem has been generally debated, a specific Buddhist-*Roman Catholic* discussion of human rights has not been analyzed in great detail. These two traditions, Buddhism and Roman Catholicism, may make up two of the most extreme poles of the East-West debate on the issue of human rights.

In addition, while the ecological contribution of Buddhism is generally acknowledged, along with a growing Catholic concern for environmental issues, studies on human rights often exist independently of ecological ones. An additional contribution of this text, I feel, is to bring the wealth of ecological concerns more sharply into dialogue with the issue of human rights.

My approach historically is engaged primarily with the work of scholars currently and within the past century in both traditions. Thus, while both traditions draw on the historical traditions, texts, and scriptures of their respective religion, the study will be a "current state of the question" in Buddhism and Roman Catholicism, not a historical or scriptural analysis per se. In line with this, my approach to the term "human rights" focuses on the *intentionality* of the concept of human rights, not the actual language of human rights historically or scripturally. This follows from the fact that the term "human rights" does not exist within traditional religions historically, including Buddhism. However, concepts such as the value and preciousness of the person and of all living beings, the oneness of the human family and its connectedness to all of creation, and ethical standards similar with the West do exist within Buddhism. Hence, what modern Westerners intend for the welfare of the individual when the term "human rights" is used can also be said to apply in Eastern traditions such as Buddhism.

Buddhism can be broken down into such divisions as Theravada, Mahayana (including Zen), Vajrayana, etc., and then into numerous other subdivisions. My approach in using the term "Buddhism" rather than one school of Buddhism is that current scholars themselves on this issue of human rights do not make a rigid differentiation in this regard. While scholars come from various schools within Buddhism, and sometimes note this, overall there seems to be a general Buddhist worldview which these scholars concern themselves with. I focus initially on general Buddhist concepts before delineating differences as they present themselves. On the other hand, I focus on a specific form of Christianity, that of Roman Catholicism, as a Catholic moral theologian noting the growing advocacy of the Catholic Church over recent years on the issue of human rights.

Throughout this study, the focus is on the issue of *human* rights. I will not be arguing for the rights of other living beings. However, I do argue that the concept of human rights becomes too ego-centered and anthropocentric if it does not also recognize an ecological duty. This related issue is necessitated because of Buddhist views of the human being, other living beings, and the interconnectedness between them, and from Catholic notions such as the stewardship of creation and the common good.

Chapter One raises some of the fundamental issues in the current discussion of human rights. These include the relationship of the concept of human rights to religion in general, its relationship to Eastern and Western religious worldviews in particular, the relationship of rights and duties, and the debate over universal moral norms. It begins by examining the current use of the term in U.N. documents and in the political arena, and gives a brief historical overview of the concept of human rights in Western civilization. It examines the issue of human rights and religions in general, asking whether the concept even belongs within religious systems. It also focuses on a comparison of Eastern and Western religions in regard to human rights, noting similarities and differences. In the West, the concepts of "human rights" and "the poor" are examined in the Judaeo-Christian tradition and Islam. These concepts are looked at within Hinduism as the Eastern worldview out of which Buddhism historically develops. This general contrast between Eastern and Western worldviews in regard to the concept of human rights sets the stage for the more specific examination of the differences and similarities between the two traditions of Buddhism and Roman Catholicism.

Chapter Two examines how the individual human being is perceived within Buddhism, and how human rights language fits in with or contradicts these views. Buddhist concepts such as anatta (nonself), paticca-samuppada (dependent co-arising), Buddha-nature, and Sunyata (emptiness), are presented. Dissenting views with the concept of human rights are examined along with those scholars who argue that the term can and must be applied within Buddhism currently. In addition, the concept of "the poor" within Buddhism is examined in light of human rights and current Buddhist social activism.

Chapter Three examines current Roman Catholic thought on the issue of human rights, noting Catholicism's general affirmation of the individual throughout its history in the concepts of the "image of God," the concern for human dignity and the poor and marginalized, and in natural law. It also notes Roman Catholicism's general opposition to the concept of human rights in the modern era. Given this backdrop, it explores more closely the development over the past century of Catholicism's acceptance of the concept of human rights to its current advocacy for it. This includes, for example, Leo XIII's *Rerum Novarum*, John XXIII and *Pacem in Terris*, the documents of Vatican II such as the *Pastoral Constitution on the Church in the Modern World* and the *Declaration on Religious Freedom*, the U.S. bishops' Pastoral Letter *Economic Justice for All*, and the pontificate of John Paul II. This examination of Church documents and leading figures and theologians within Catholicism over the past century emphasizes that human rights is currently a central concept, and not a fringe issue, within Catholicism.

Having established the importance and compatibility of the concept of human rights within Buddhism and Roman Catholicism, Chapter Four deals with the related issue of avoiding an ego-centered, selfish view of "human rights" which neglects the concept of "duty," specifically an ecological duty. Ecological duties are seen as a necessary correlate to the concept of human rights. Ecological duties in religions in general are examined before specifically noting concepts within Buddhism and Roman Catholicism which contribute toward ecological concerns.

Finally, Chapter Five raises the concept of a global ethic, as articulated in the Declaration of the Parliament of the World's Religions. It notes the connection between the concept of human rights and a global ethic, and looks at Buddhist and Roman Catholic perspectives on a global ethic. It also offers the example of Engaged Buddhism as a religion in transition, remaining true to its tradition yet refocusing itself in light of global concerns.

In conclusion, having established that the term "human rights" can be used fruitfully within Buddhism and Roman Catholicism, I argue for its necessity and compatibility between the two traditions. I conclude that the concept of human rights operates in both traditions as an affirmation of the value of the individual, as a recognition of a duty toward other living creatures and the environment, and as a cornerstone toward a global ethic.

Given that most Christians who are interested in Buddhist meditation and dialogue are either Roman Catholic or Orthodox (McDaniel 1990, 244), and given the growing social justice concerns of both traditions, a specific Buddhist-*Roman Catholic* discussion on human rights and ecological duties seems imperative. Yet, I maintain that the importance of this study applies not only to Catholic and Buddhist scholars and activists but to all citizens concerned with issues of justice on a global scale.

In *Renewing the Earth*, a Pastoral Statement of the United States Catholic Conference in 1991, the U.S. bishops called "upon Catholic scholars to explore the relationship between this tradition's emphasis upon the dignity of the human person and our responsibility to care for all of God's creation" (United States Catholic Conference 1996, 241). This book attempts to contribute toward that end. For, as Maguire points out, "*religion* in the general sense, as the experience of sacredness, *is at the core of ecological ethics and human rights thinking*" (Maguire 1998, 48 [italics mine]).

CHAPTER I

THE CONCEPT OF HUMAN RIGHTS AND
ITS IMPORTANCE

I.I: INTRODUCTION

This chapter introduces general issues and concerns which are raised in the current discussion of the concept of "human rights." It examines how the term is currently used politically and in U.N. documents, and offers a brief sketch of some key points in its historical development. Next, it raises the issue of how the concept of human rights relates to religion in general, noting that while some argue that human rights are at the core of religious ethical understanding, and that some traditions led to the development of the concept, others observe that human rights were generally denounced by religions during their development in the modern era. Having examined the relationship between human rights and religion in general, this chapter points out problems and possibilities with the concept of human rights within particular Eastern and Western traditions, and between those Eastern and Western worldviews in general. Particularly, can the term human rights be used within Eastern traditions, or is it a form of modern Western imperialism upon these Eastern traditions? This also necessitates a discussion of the concept of duties as it relates to the concept of rights. Thus, the concept of human rights as it is used politically, as it develops historically, as it relates to religion in general, and as it relates to Eastern and Western religious traditions, is the broad focus of this chapter. This sweeping overview raises the scope of the human rights discussion as it currently stands, before proceeding onward to two specific traditions.

I.2: THE CURRENT CONCEPT OF HUMAN RIGHTS IN UNITED NATIONS DOCUMENTS AND POLITICAL USE

A. UNITED NATIONS DOCUMENTS

Any discussion of human rights, religion, and a global ethic would be incomplete without acknowledging the contemporary use of the term "human rights" in international discourse, as seen primarily in the United Nations documents. John Kelsay and Sumner Twiss point out that the term "human rights" can be understood as

> the set of rights articulated in the thirty articles of the Universal Declaration of Human Rights, a statement of principles proclaimed by the United Nations in 1948, and in related international treaties. These treaties include the two international human rights covenants, which the United Nations adopted in 1966 and which give legal form to the Universal Declaration.

They remind us that "together, the Universal Declaration and the international Covenants with the Optional Protocols are known as 'The International Bill of Rights'" (Kelsay and Twiss, 1994, iii).

The Universal Declaration of Human Rights, approved by the U.N. General Assembly on December 10, 1948, includes in its Preamble that "whereas recognition of the inherent dignity and of the equal and inalienable rights of all members of the human family is the foundation of freedom, justice and peace in the world," and "whereas the peoples of the United Nations have in the Charter reaffirmed their faith in fundamental human rights, in the dignity and worth of the human person and in the equal rights of men and women" ... "now, therefore, the General Assembly proclaims this Universal Declaration of Human Rights as a common standard of achievement for all peoples and all nations" (United Nations 1993, 4).

Some samples from the document which exemplify its importance for this book on human rights and a social justice context in general include Article 1: "All human beings are born free and equal in dignity and rights. They are endowed with reason and conscience and should act towards one another in a spirit of brotherhood." Article 16 states that "The family is the natural and fundamental group unit of society and is entitled to protection by society and the State." Article 18 affirms that "everyone has the right to freedom of thought, conscience and religion. . . ." Article 23 observes that "everyone who works has the right to just and favourable remuneration ensuring for himself and his family an existence worthy of human dignity, and supplemented, if necessary, by other means of social protection." Article 25 includes the statement that "motherhood and childhood are entitled to special care and assistance," noting that "all children, whether born in or out of wedlock, shall enjoy the same social protection." Article 26 notes that "everyone has the right to education" and that "education shall be directed to the full development of the human personality." Finally, Article 29 of the thirty article Declaration acknowledges the role of duty corresponding to rights and the importance of community in observing that "everyone has duties to the community in which alone the free and full development of his personality is possible" (ibid. 5-9).

The concept of human rights is integral to the United Nations and its documents. Kathleen Teltsch observes that, in regard to the United Nations, "from the beginning, the concept of the world organization having responsibility for safeguarding human rights was accepted as a commitment by the big powers" (Teltsch 1981, 6). She notes that, while the covenant of the earlier League of Nations had no provisions on human rights, the U.N. Charter had seven references to them (ibid. 7). She explains that "the first article of this historic document affirmed that one of the main purposes of the world organization was the achievement of cooperation in promoting and encouraging respect for human rights, fundamental freedoms for all without distinction as to race, sex, language, or religion" (ibid.).

The 1948 Universal Declaration of Human Rights, then, interpreted and elaborated on the general references to human rights in this earlier U.N. Charter. Teltsch explains that the wording of the Declaration "suggested that it was intended primarily as a statement of principle, backed by moral authority rather than binding laws." However, she continues that "the wide recognition given to the Universal Declaration for ... years has led many legal experts to insist that it has acquired another dimension and has become a part of the customary law of nations" (ibid. 9). Thus, she concludes that "the declaration has gained acceptance by usage and secured the status of international law without formal ratification" (ibid.). Therefore, if religions are to enter this discussion at the U.N. and other international forums, the concept of "human rights" provides the entree.

Christina M. Cerna agrees, noting that "in 1948, when the Universal Declaration was adopted, Eleanor Roosevelt, as chair of the

Commission on Human Rights, stated that the Declaration 'is not and
does not purport to be a statement of law or of legal obligation,' but
rather that it is 'to serve as a common standard of achievement for all
peoples of all nations.'" Cerna continues that, however, "in 1968, at the
first World Conference on Human Rights, the international community proclaimed: 'The Universal Declaration of Human Rights states
a common understanding of the peoples of the world concerning the
inalienable and inviolable rights of all members of the human family
and constitutes an obligation for the members of the international community'" (Cerna 1994, 745 [Emphasis added, Cerna]).

Two later covenants, the Covenant on Civil and Political Rights and
the Covenant on Economic and Social Rights, both approved by the
U.N. General Assembly in 1966, *were drafted as legally binding documents* whose language is more precise than the more generally word-
ed Universal Declaration of Human Rights (Teltsch 1981, 11). The
United States Catholic Conference notes that "the *U.N. Covenant on
Civil and Political Rights* and the *U.N. Covenant on Economic, Social
and Cultural Rights* stand as the most comprehensive international
effort to establish a common minimum standard for human rights"
(*Human Rights, Human Needs* 1978, 6).

Both covenants begin with the following:

> *Considering* that, in accordance with the principles proclaimed
> in the Charter of the United Nations, recognition of the inherent
> dignity and of the equal and inalienable rights of all members of the
> human family is the foundation of freedom, justice and peace in the
> world,
> *Recognizing* that these rights derive from the inherent dignity of
> the human person ...
> Realizing that the individual, having duties to other individuals
> and to the community to which he(/she) belongs, is under a re-
> sponsibility to strive for the promotion and observance of the rights
> recognized in the present Covenant,
> *Agree* upon the following articles. ... (ibid. 6 and 13 [The USCC
> text adds the female pronoun "in the spirit of equality"]).

The two Covenants, and later documents, have been instrumental in expanding the concept of human rights from the original U.N.
Declaration. Sumner B. Twiss acknowledges the work of Burns
Weston and others in observing a history of human rights development. He explains that "that history is marked by at least three

distinctive generations or types of human rights, with each successive generation not supplanting the earlier one(s) but rather adding to as well as nuancing the earlier" (Twiss 1996, 364). The first generation, Twiss describes, "emerging most definitively in the aftermath of World War II, is generally comprised of civil-political rights and liberties." The second generation, he continues, "emerging most definitively in the human rights covenants of the 1970's, adds a new emphasis on the importance of social and economic rights to certain crucial goods and services and their just allocation." And, the third generation, which Twiss explains "is now most definitively emerging amid Third and Fourth World claims for global redistribution... adds yet another new emphasis on developmental-collective rights of people's self-determination and development" (ibid.).

Thus, *critique of the concept of human rights as too individualistic or too political often does not take into account this development of human rights beyond this first generation.* The next section of this chapter offers a brief history of this first generation of human rights in Western thought which leads up to the U.N. Declaration in 1948.

Twiss observes that this first generation of civil-political rights was "also touching on certain social and economic rights, as influenced by the background of Franklin Roosevelt's 'Four Freedoms' and the identification of 'freedom from want'" (ibid.). Louis Henkin points out that Roosevelt, in 1941, "delivered a famous address in which he spoke about Four Freedoms, which became a rallying cry during the Second World War and an agenda for peace to follow." He explains that "Roosevelt's Four Freedoms were: freedom of speech, freedom of religion, freedom from want (then a very progressive idea), and freedom from fear (by which he meant freedom from invasion by people such as Hitler)." Henkin continues that "those who drafted the Universal Declaration doubtless had the Four Freedoms in mind" (Henkin 1995, 13).

As noted earlier, Eleanor Roosevelt was chair of the commission that drafted the Universal Declaration. Given the Roosevelts' involvement, many are surprised by the document's lack of reference to religion. Some see the omission as a practical step by the Western countries in forging a working document with the Communist countries as the Cold War era was beginning. But Richard Falk sees this omission as more than a practicality. He observes that "the Declaration was very much a product of a secular humanist sensibility," and that "the place of religion was deliberately kept at the margins of its statements" (Falk cited in ibid. 17). Falk explains that "religion in general was also subsumed under a wider humanist ethos, one derived primarily from the Enlightenment and the emergence of a liberal-democratic, scientific civilization that placed its hopes for human progress on the material capacities of society, whether Marxist or Capitalist" (ibid. 18).

However, many would argue that this modern view of political rights is rooted within ancient religious traditions, most notably the Judeo-Christian tradition, as well as being influenced by Western political ideas and developments. I would now like to offer a very brief history of this Western concept of human rights which led up to the U. N. Declaration in 1948.

B. HISTORICAL BACKGROUND ON THE IDEA OF HUMAN RIGHTS

Leonard Swidler observes that the concept of human rights "has its foundations in the two pillars of Western civilization: Judeo-Christian religion and Greco-Roman culture" (Swidler 1990, 12).[1] In regard to the development of the Hebrew religion, Carl F. H. Henry observes that "the ancient Near Eastern religions offer three distinctive conceptions of law and human rights: Mesopotamian, Egyptian and Hebrew," and that "the basic contrast lies in the irreducible monotheism of biblical religion and its unique cosmological, ethical and legal consequences" (Henry 1986, 28).

Henry notes that "the Israelites recognized law as a revelation of Yahweh's will and not as a distillation only of a cosmic order to which gods also were answerable. Yahweh transcends not only part of the universe but the whole" (ibid.). Swidler agrees, noting that "the two elements of the Judeo-Christian root source of the modern notion of human rights" are "ethical monotheism and the image of God" (L. Swidler 1990, 14).

Swidler observes that "because there was only one Source of all reality, the order encoded into all reality would also be one, and that included humankind" (ibid. 13). He continues that, unlike polytheistic

---

1   It is for this reason that I am using the phrase "Judaeo-Christian tradition," although I realize that it may be problematic for some in its combination of two Western religions. Its use is also not meant to slight Islam, which is also dealt with in this study and which is acknowledged as one of the three Abrahamic traditions.

religions, which had one set of rules for how to treat their own people and another set for other peoples, "the Hebrews were committed, at least in theory, to treating all human beings by the same ethical rules" (ibid. 14).

Henry explains that "the biblical creation account makes only one distinction within humankind, that between the sexes, and it does so to stress that both male and female are created equally in God's image" (Henry 1986, 32). Hence, the Hebrew creation account's belief in one God as the source of all humans and of all creation, and the belief of all humans created in the "image of God," are central to Western theories of human rights.

Henry also observes that the Old Testament avoids some key features of Hammurabi's code. For example, it "prohibits bodily mutilation – such as cutting off arms, legs and noses – and limits flogging to 40 strokes." But more importantly, it also avoids "communal responsibility by kin for an individual's acts of crime, and compensation to victims of crime by money" (ibid.). Henry explains that, in the account of Cain and Abel, the divine penalty "falls on Cain alone and not collectively on his family," thus emphasizing the role of personal responsibility for one's moral life and actions. In addition, he observes that "Hebrew law sharply distinguished crimes against human life and those against property." In contrast to nonbiblical religions, including the later Qur'an, which permitted monetary compensation for the taking of human life, "the Bible places human life-including that of the stranger-beyond monetary valuation" (ibid.).

In addition to the creation story, the role of the Hebrew prophets is pivotal to discussions of human rights, particularly in their concern for the marginal and the poor. Max L. Stackhouse observes that, in the prophets, "we can see the reaffirmation of covenantal concerns, the ancient creedal foundations of human rights." He articulates that "there is a universal moral order, rooted in the righteousness of God, which is other than ordinary experience yet directly pertinent to ordinary experience" (Stackhouse 1984, 33).

* Daniel C. Maguire explains that "this innovative, biblical justice (commonly called *sedaqah*) is the foundation of the reign of God, the secret of the humanity that could have been and could yet be" (Maguire 1993, 126). Maguire emphasizes that "Biblical literature drums incessantly on this central category" (ibid. 127). This points to its pivotal and seminal role in shaping Western thought on human rights.

In addition, these Hebrew concepts were complemented by elements within Greco-Roman culture. Stackhouse explains that

> as Jews and Christians believed in an 'otherness' that was also 'present,' the Greeks had discovered 'theory.' There is, they held, a 'realm of ideas' where one can grasp matters of universal importance, where one can learn about the form of existence, even if the situation in which one empirically lives is not just (Stackhouse 1984, 38).

He continues that "both traditions understand all humans both as having a unique individuality – an 'image of God' for Jews and Christians, a 'soul' for Greeks – and as being social creatures." He concludes that "in both traditions humanity has a capacity to know and discern an 'other' world, and to attempt to enact it in this life, in both private and public life" (ibid.).

Henry observes that "the human rights tradition that emerged in the West ... was nurtured and shaped also by Athenian democracy and Roman jurisprudence" (Henry 1986, 32). Swidler points out that "the Romans found many fundamentals of law which applied across all nations, a *ius gentium*, or 'common law of all humans' (*commune omnium hominum ius*), as the third-century Roman jurist Gaius phrased it." He continues that "here indeed is a basis for claiming a right simply on the grounds of one's humanity, for at the foundation of all there lies nature, which can be discovered by reason – and only humans have that" (L. Swidler 1990, 13). Henry also adds that "Greek and Roman sages held that deity is immediately accessible to human reason" (Henry 1986, 33). Hence, the importance of the concept of "nature" and of "reason" in the Western development of human rights. There is a "human nature," common to all humans, which is rooted in the natural order of the universe. And, we can generally discern what is in accord with that nature through reason.

* Swidler observes that "Plato, Aristotle, the Stoics and others in Hellenistic civilization developed the notion of a natural law, under whose jurisdiction the human fell" (L. Swidler 1990, 12). Cicero himself wrote that "True law is right reason in agreement with nature; it is of universal application, unchanging and everlasting ... ." He continued that

> there will not be different laws now and in the future, but one eternal and unchangeable law will be valid for all nations and all times, and there will be one master and ruler, that is God, over us all for

he is the author of this law, its promulgator and its enforcing judge (Cicero cited in Hehir 1980a, 4).[2]

Stackhouse reminds us that, after Rome collapsed, "the church remained, preserving the universalistic values of both Greco-Roman and Hebraic belief, without which modern discussions of human rights would have been impossible" (Stackhouse 1984, 39). He continues that "during the Middle Ages these decisive roots of all modern discussions of human rights were deeply planted in the church: there is a universal moral law governing all human relations known by faith and reason" (ibid. 40).

Thomas Aquinas represents the hallmark of medieval scholasticism in his optimism toward human reason and his appropriation of natural law theory within Christianity. However, this discernment of the natural law through reason, and possibly apart from revelation, led to what Henry describes as a later secularization of natural law theory, "championed independently of any divine referent and solely on a foundation of human rationalistic determination" (Henry 1986, 33).

Henry describes Dutch jurist Hugo Grotius (1583) as the watershed in this secularization of natural law theory. He explains that "Grotius deduced natural law not from the divine mind or will, nor from a doctrine of creation, but from the human community" (ibid.). He explains that "creative human personality becomes the source of law and rights" and that "Grotius was the founder of the humanistic natural-law theory that dominated Western legal and political thought until early in the 19th century" (ibid.).

Jack Mahoney observes that Grotius' concern was in developing a doctrine of a just war, not only in terms of declaring a war but also in waging one. It was in the introduction to his *Law of War and Peace* that Grotius dealt with law and legal rights in general and natural law and natural rights in particular. Mahoney explains that "Grotius sought to establish rules for war to which all human beings would subscribe, not from Christian revelation, but from the power of human reason as it considered the nature of law and of rights" (Jack Mahoney 1990, 316). He continues that "Grotius drew upon the long tradition stemming from Aristotle that every human is kin and friend to every other

---

2   However, Hehir notes that Cicero, in his earlier works *On the Nature of the Gods* and *On Divination*, denied the truth of God's existence.

(*Ethics* VIII, 1)." Mahoney observes that "among the human characteristics, then, is a desire for society ... a society which is peaceful and
rationally structured with one's fellows" (ibid.). He concludes that, for
Grotius, "this conservation of society which is in accord with human
intelligence is the origin of *jus*, or natural law," which in effect served to
"'detheologize' natural law" (ibid. 317 [The term is Kohler's]).

Another key figure in the discussion on natural law and rights is
the English philosopher John Locke, who in the late 1600's wrote his
Two Treatises on Government, "which spoke at length about the natural
law, the separation of governmental powers, and the right of all to 'life,
liberty and property'"(L. Swidler 1990, 16). Bamidele Ojo notes the
importance of the

> Lockean concept of the state of nature in which the individual is in
> a 'state of perfect freedom to order their actions and dispose of their
> possession and persons as they think fit, within the bound of the
> law of nature, without asking leave or depending upon the will of
> any other sect' (Locke cited in Ojo 1997, 11).

 * Locke's influence can be seen in the 1776 Declaration of Independence
with "its paraphrase of Locke: 'All men are created equal ... with certain unalienable rights ... life, liberty, and the pursuit of happiness'" (L.
Swidler 1990, 16).

However, while Locke is commonly seen as the founder of the theory of modern, political, individual rights, this secular understanding of
Locke may belie his own religious influences and convictions. Richard
Ashcraft cautions that "all Lockean natural rights are premised upon
a religious belief in God" (Ashcraft 1996, 199). He explains that, for
Locke, "'the true ground of morality ... can only be the will and law of
a God' who exercises authority over individuals." He continues that

> as Locke states repeatedly throughout his writings, the Law of
> Nature, which is 'the decree of the divine will,' establishes the frame-
> work for any definition of moral action by human beings. Hence,
> for Locke, 'all obligation leads back to God,' and no moral claim
> could be advanced for which any independent justification can be
> provided (Locke cited in ibid.).

Thus, Ashcraft explains that "Locke has so structured his argument
that any notion of natural or human rights can be justified if, and only
if, it can be shown to be derivative from some obligation individuals
owe to God, as stipulated by natural law" (Ashcraft, 1996, 199). In

addition, in regard to reason, Locke stated that without a belief in God, the individual cannot be counted as a rational being and is no better than a dangerous wild beast (ibid. 201).

Mahoney suggests that Locke's belief in God, combined with his rejection of original sin, "lay at the root of his rejection of Hobbes' view of the state of nature as brutish and anarchical" (Jack Mahoney, 320). Locke wrote that "men living together according to reason, without a common superior on earth, with authority to judge between them, is properly the state of nature" (Locke cited in Jack Mahoney, 319).

The tie between "rights," "nature," and God can be seen in the documents of the American colonies. Henry explains that "the American political charter documents insisted on the Creator's role as the transcendent ground of unalienable rights," noting that "the appeal to natural rights emerged only after extensive colonial political debate" (Henry 1986, 38). He continues that "the Stamp Act Congress (1765) appealed not to laws of nature but only to God as a higher authority than the English Parliament" (ibid.) However, Swidler observes that, in the 1774 Declaration and Resolves of the First Continental Congress, "for the first time the law of nature was explicitly made the foundation of rights: 'By the immutable laws of nature ... the following RIGHTS ...'" (L. Swidler 1990, 16). Henry explains that "the decision to appeal to nature as a basis of rights influenced the draft of the Declaration of Independence (1776) as it did also the Constitution of Virginia (1776), although these both grounded rights in the Creator" (Henry 1986, 38).

Two other interrelated concepts which are important for the Western notion of human rights are freedom of conscience and freedom of religion. David Little emphasizes that

> there can be little question that [the] expressions of religious liberty and freedom of conscience developed by Jefferson and Madison, and done so against the background of the history of the doctrine of erroneous conscience in the West, provided the model for contemporary statements (Little 1988, 25.)[3]

He continues that "the formulations contained in Article 18 of the Universal Declaration of Human Rights and in the International Covenant on Civil and Political Rights ... are unthinkable apart from

---

3   In this article, Little discusses primarily the contributions of Aquinas and Calvin.

that tradition" (ibid.). Little explains that implicit in this view "is the
idea that human beings have implanted in them 'by nature' a set of
general requirements and standards of behavior, both formal and substantive, according to which the internal appraisal of one's own acts
and character is conducted" (ibid. 14).

Swidler agrees, noting that "the degree of religious liberty granted
is an important touchstone of the advance of the notion of human
rights" (L. Swidler 1990, 14). Tertullian (ca. 160-225) even used the
term himself, stating that "it is a fundamental human right, a privilege
of nature, that all human beings should worship according to their
own convictions" (Tertullian cited in ibid.).

✴ Additional key events include the Magna Carta of political and civil
liberties, granted by King John in England in 1215, where "here again
human reason was the foundation stone, thereby providing a solid basis for the building of the full-blown idea of human rights" (L. Swidler
1990, 15). The Protestant Reformation and Protestant Christianity in
general contributed by the emphasis which it placed on the individual
(Henkin 1995, 12). And the French Revolution, with the *Declaration
des droits des hommes et citoyens*, passed in 1789, was "a landmark document in the history of human rights … a French, but now for the first
time universalized, version of the Enlightenment's notion of human
rights" (L. Swidler 1990, 17).

This brief historical sketch attempts to lay out some of the key
Western concepts which have influenced the current discussion of
human rights and the formation of the U. N. documents on human
rights. As Ojo notes, "the purpose of the classical doctrine of universal inalienable human or natural rights was to rule out the conceptual
possibility of ever treating a person as if he had no intrinsic worth"
(Ojo 1997, 40).

Yet, questions still remain regarding various interpretations of the
historical development of the concept of human rights, the source or
ground of human rights, and how Western and/or individual the concept of human rights remains as stipulated in the U.N. documents.
The next section of this chapter examines issues that are raised in the
current political use and interpretation of the U.N. documents on human rights, and the resources that these documents offer in forming a
global ethic.

C. UNITED NATIONS DOCUMENTS, INTERNATIONAL LAW, AND A GLOBAL ETHIC

Although the historical development of the concept of human rights is framed within religious contexts, the U.N. documents do not address the subject of religion. Some object that, because of this, the documents offer no grounding for the validity of human rights. In addition, they focus less on "duty" than on rights. Henry argues that "the contrast between the biblical and the modern approaches to human rights could not be more pointed." He explains that "the Universal Declaration of Human Rights (1948) presents a panorama of human rights while it says very little about human duties and nothing at all about duties to God" (Henry 1986, 30).

This lack of emphasis on duty has caused many to argue that the concept of human rights presented in the U.N. documents is based far too much on the modern Western notion of the autonomous individual, and not enough on communal aspects. Hence, many argue that the concept as framed cannot apply to developing non-Western nations. P.J.I.M. de Waart echoes these sentiments in arguing that "in the wake of the American and French revolutions, the Western doctrine of human rights has viewed civil and political rights as a shield protecting the liberty of the individual from his or her state" (de Waart 1995, 50). He continues that "this may explain why little attention has been paid to human responsibilities" (ibid.).

While this is a common critique of the current concept of human rights in general and of the U.N. documents on human rights in particular, others argue that this critique is overly simplistic and unproductive. Twiss argues that, "in baldly characterizing ... civil-political human rights as the 'negative' freedoms from government intrusion advanced by liberal individualism, one might run the risk of deflecting attention away from the fact that these liberties are also properly understood as 'enablements' or 'empowerments' for persons to function as flourishing members of a polity or community where they work with others to advance their lives together in their society" (Twiss 1996, 365).

He emphasizes that

> the civil-political liberties of first-generation human rights are not simply ... the negative 'freedoms from' associated with a caricatured liberal individualism concerned with protecting the privacy

of radically autonomous, isolated, self-interested, ahistorical, and acultural selves, but rather are positive empowerments to persons' involvement in a flourishing community that are compatible with, for example, many communitarian traditions of moral and political thought and practice (ibid.).

The actual development of the Universal Declaration of Human Rights and later U.N. documents, their subsequent use, and the development of later generations of rights, seems initially to undermine the view that human rights documents are Western constructs. Twiss argues for the universality of the human rights documents on the practical grounds of the actual process of their development. He explains that "despite the common perception that international human rights are simply an outgrowth and entailment of Western assumptions about human nature and moral rationality, *it is a fact that the Universal Declaration of Human Rights (1948) was reached through a pragmatic process of negotiation among representatives of different nations and cultural traditions*" (ibid. 362 [italics mine]).

While acknowledging the influential role of the West in this process, he explains that "the simple fact remains that pragmatic negotiation between differing views about the subject matter was the process of choice, not theorizing about matters of moral knowledge, political philosophy, or even jurisprudence" (ibid. 363). He continues by noting that "this pragmatic approach has continued to characterize the drafting and adoption of subsequent human-rights covenants, conventions, and treaties" (ibid.).

Therefore, Twiss emphasizes that "far from preempting or replacing the moral teachings of various cultural traditions, specific expressions of human-rights concerns have arisen from the mutual recognitions by adherents of these traditions that they have a shared interest in the protection of certain important substantive moral values" (ibid.). He concludes that

> no one cultural tradition is the sole source of human-rights concepts and norms. Human rights are, from this point of view, the expression of a set of important overlapping moral expectations to which differing cultures hold themselves and others accountable (ibid. 364).

Robert Traer agrees, pointing out that the Universal Declaration "was declared to be not merely international, representing agreement among states, but universal in that it set forth a morality transcending that of any particular tradition or culture" (Traer 1991, 9).

Twiss' arguments, from the practical perspective of the actual composition of the U.N. documents, to their subsequent use, and the development of the more communal second and third generation of rights, are substantial. These arguments are raised here because of their examination of the U.N. documents, yet they will be raised throughout this study in the discussion of the universality of human rights. Unfortunately, the fact remains that some non-Western countries still *do* reject the documents, and the concept of human rights within them, as a Western construct with a hidden agenda. Thus, even today, the actual political acceptance of the U.N. documents on human rights is far from universal.[4] In addressing the fact that the U.N. doesn't have the financial resources for enforcing change, de Waart cites 1975 figures where "'the current United Nations expenditures barely equal the sum spent on armaments by Members in only 36 hours'" (Cited in de Waart 1995, 57).

Cerna observes that "today, a group of nations is seeking to redefine the content of the term 'human rights' against the will of the Western states." She explains that "this group sees the current definition as part of the ideological patrimony of Western civilization. They argue that the principles enshrined in the Universal Declaration reflect Western values and not their own" (Cerna 1994, 740). (These countries are primarily China, Colombia, Cuba, Indonesia, Iran, Iraq, Libya, Malaysia, Mexico, Myanmar, Pakistan, Singapore, Syria, Vietnam, and Yemen. They are all third world countries, and the Asian countries experiencing the strongest economic growth are the most outspoken advocates against the view of human rights put forth by the United Nations.)

Cerna describes the second U.N. World Conference on Human Rights, held in June 1993 in Vienna, Austria, where "this debate was center-stage." She explains that the Western states' "first priority was damage control to insure 'that the conference issue a strong endorsement of the universality of human rights and reject the idea that such rights can be measured differently in some countries." She notes that "the U.S. administration dismissed the argument that any definition

---

4   And this is to say nothing about accountability or actual enforcement. De Waart explains that "member states apparently were not really interested in improving the efficiency of the U. N. system for fear of creating a competing world government" (de Waart 1995, 58).

of human rights should consider regional, social and cultural differences," arguing that "such a position is a screen behind which authoritarian governments can perpetuate abuses" (ibid. 741).

The Vienna Declaration and Programme of Action, adopted by the World Conference on Human Rights on June 25, 1993, contained thirty-nine paragraphs and a programme of action, in which "the universality of human rights was affirmed repeatedly" (ibid.). Paragraph 1 states that: "The World Conference on Human Rights reaffirms the solemn commitment of all States to fulfill their obligations to promote universal respect for, and observance and protection of, all human rights. . . ." It continues that "the universal nature of these rights and freedoms is beyond question" (Cited in ibid.). Paragraph 5 states that "all human rights are universal, indivisible and interdependent and interrelated. The international community must treat human rights globally in a fair and equal manner, on the same footing, and with the same emphasis" (Cited in ibid.).

As noted, the developing Asian countries are the most outspoken critics of this view of human rights. Cerna observes that, while African and Latin American cultures were ravaged by colonialism, "the Asian civilizations maintained a direct link with the cultures and traditions of their ancestors." She explains that "it is, without doubt, this ancient cultural heritage, [plus] the region's enormous population, and its dramatic, relatively recent economic prosperity which provided the Asian governments with the confidence to challenge international human rights as a Western ideological imposition" (ibid. 743).

In addition, the strongest challenge to the universality of human rights from these developing nations comes in the area of "private rights." Cerna describes this private sphere as dealing with "issues such as religion, culture, the status of women, the right to marry and to divorce and to remarry, the protection of children, the question of choice as regards family planning, and the like" (ibid. 746). Thus, she explains that "certain societies are unwilling to assume international human rights in this private sphere – their own code of conduct, which is informed by their religious or traditional law, already covers this terrain" (ibid. 749). Therefore, religion may act as a hindrance in some cultures to the acceptance of the universality of human rights as stated in the U.N. documents. Cerna concludes that "international norms dealing with rights that affect the private sphere of human activity will take the longest time to achieve universal acceptance" (ibid. 752).

In cases such as this, and others, William P. George argues that international law may actually "call particular religions to a *higher* standard than current beliefs, practices, and even the inner disposition of individual believers allow" (George 1996, 368). He states that "occasionally, at least, international law forges ahead of one or another tradition." He explains that "if international law can challenge particular religious communities to transcend the boundaries of their own belief systems, to think and act more inclusively, to reassess their views of women, of cultures and races, ... of nonhuman species, of outer space, ... of future generations ... – all current or potential topics of international law -then this suggests that international law has a transformative, and in that sense a transcendental or religious, dimension or capacity" (ibid. 369). He continues that that "may even be construed as a move toward transcendence" (ibid.).

George's thinking runs counter to the conventional wisdom which sees religions as containing the higher norms, and law as being the more basic or minimal norm. His view is also noteworthy in signaling a convergence of a number of factors in looking at a "global ethic." On one hand, The International Bill of Human Rights, containing the Universal Declaration of Human Rights and other U.N. documents, which is examined in this first chapter, is seen by many as a sort of global ethic from a practical, political standpoint. On the other hand, there is the *Declaration Toward a Global Ethic* of the Parliament of the World's Religions from the 1993 meeting in Chicago, which was signed by representatives of the world's religions and drafted largely by Hans Küng, which acts as a global ethic from a religious standpoint (see Küng and Kuschel 1995). (This document will be examined more closely in Chapter 5 in the discussion of a global ethic.)

George is primarily addressing the Parliament's *Global Ethic* in stating that global ethicists, and religion in general, should be more conversant with international law in their attempt to formulate a global ethic. However, I would emphasize that it is important to acknowledge the convergence of, and the valuable assets contained within, the U.N. International Bill of Human Rights, international law, and the Parliament's *Declaration Toward a Global Ethic*, in arriving at a true global ethic.

George points out several concepts within international law which can contribute toward a global ethic. One of these is the notion of a "common heritage of humankind" which has emerged in contexts such as the Law of the Sea, outer-space law, international property rights, and governance of Antarctica (George 1996, 366). George explains that "common heritage has meant, among other things, that human-kind *as a whole,* including future generations, be regarded as a sub-ject of international law and that items identified as 'common heritage' should somehow benefit all humankind, especially the poorer nations" (ibid.). He continues that "common heritage of humankind is, in other words, a 'solidarist' principle par excellence" (ibid. 367).

Further, he observes that theological concepts, such as the "common good" in Roman Catholic social thought, have "reemerged in contem-porary international law in such notions as common heritage of hu-mankind or the 'common interest' frequently invoked in discussions of international environmental law" (ibid. 374). George also sees a com-mon critique of international law, its frequent lack of power to be en-forced, as a plus. He argues that it is this "more or less voluntary nature of international law" which "makes it especially worth considering as a carrier of moral meaning and value" (ibid. 367).

Therefore, a number of resources are available in the attempt to construct a viable global ethic. For the remainder of this chapter, I primarily focus on resources within religions as they address the topic of human rights. Yet the importance of the Universal Declaration of Human Rights and its subsequent documents in the movement to-ward a global ethic cannot be dismissed.

Henkin argues that "the Universal Declaration should be recognized by the religious world (and by the non-religious world) as an authentic foundation for a global ethic" (Henkin 1995, 14). He continues that "the commitment in the Declaration to the human dignity of every human being and to the principles of justice should be acceptable to all" (ibid.), and that it is necessary "to establish *rights* as the basis of a universal ethic" (ibid. 15 [italics mine]).

Falk observes that "there are a billion people who do not have the ba-sic needs of life satisfied, even unto food." He acknowledges that "one of the visionary elements of the global ethic embodied in the Universal Declaration as a text is the postulate of the human right of every per-son on the planet to have those basic needs satisfied" (Falk cited in ibid. 20). In addition, he points out that "what we need at this stage if we are to create a universally viable global ethic is to focus on economic and social rights as deserving priority and serious attention," noting that "unless this happens, it will always seem to most of the peoples of the world that human rights are little more than a luxury of the affluent" (ibid.). Thus, there is the necessity to view human rights as a dynamic concept, which has evolved into a second and third generation of rights, as Twiss has pointed out, and not to view human rights as a purely individual/political construct.

Falk concludes that "the great potential in world religions is that they can reach peoples around the globe more directly and more fully than any other societal institution." He argues that "if the religions of the world, despite their diversity, could begin to educate people based on their diverse interpretations of the Universal Declaration, it would eventually have an enormous impact on daily life" (ibid. 23). I will next examine how various world religions interpret the concept of "human rights" in general, within their own traditions, and in response to the Universal Declaration and the emerging vision of a global ethic, exploring the problems and possibilities involved with that concept as it relates to religion.

1.3 PROBLEMS AND POSSIBILITIES WITH THE CONCEPT OF HUMAN RIGHTS AND RELIGION IN GENERAL

A. PROBLEMS WITH THE CONCEPT OF HUMAN RIGHTS AND RELIGION

Differences of opinion abound as to whether the concept and language of human rights can be used in relation to religion in general and within specific religious traditions in particular. Some argue that the concept cannot apply to a religious worldview, while others argue that the concept itself *derives from* a religious worldview, primarily that of the Western Judaeo-Christian tradition. Others argue that, because of this, it does not apply within Eastern traditions. Along this line, arguments are made that *nothing* is universal, and that the concept of human rights comes from either particular religious or particular cultural circumstances. And while some argue that it is within the religious worldview of the Judaeo-Christian tradition that the concept of human rights originates, others argue that the institutions of this tradition continually fought against human rights until recent centuries, thus making human rights a secular concept.

Twiss observes three interrelated concerns that arise in international dialogues on human rights. The first concern is "the worry that international human rights represent a distinctively Western moral ideology intended to supplant the moral perspectives of diverse cultural traditions." The second concern is "the perception that human rights are principally or exclusively civil-political liberties ... that are incompatible with communitarian cultural traditions." And the third concern raised is that "international human rights embody or are otherwise grounded in problematic metaphysical-moral assumptions about human nature, personhood, and community" (Twiss 1996, 362). However, Twiss himself argues that these concerns "betray a serious misunderstanding of the nature, function, and source of international human rights"(ibid. 362).

Some objections to the concept of human rights come from philosophy and other disciplines, contributing to the overall critique of universal principles. Max Stackhouse and Stephen Healey reflect that, today, "the Enlightenment thinkers would surely have found it odd that some of the most serious arguments against human rights come not from religion or theology but from philosophy" (Stackhouse and Healey 1996, 503).

Stewart Sutherland argues that because the *intent* is different in different moral/religious systems, there is no common moral ground between these traditions" (Donovan 1986, 368-69). And Martin Prozesky claims that the concept of human rights is not even logically permissible in theistic religion. Prozesky argues that human rights in the Western liberal tradition "are not favours bestowed on us by a higher authority," and that theists cannot accept a "view which sees human beings as sovereign" (Prozesky 1989, 20). He contends that this belief in human rights "must logically be rejected by theists because they are obliged to consider its implicit anthropology as false" (ibid. 21). (He does admit, however, that process theology may be more open to the concept of human rights. See ibid. 23-24).

✳ Alasdair MacIntyre wrote that

> The truth is plain: there are no such rights, and belief in them is one with belief in witches and unicorns ... . The best reason for asserting so bluntly that there are no such rights is [the same] ... reason for asserting that there are no witches ... . [E]very attempt to give good reasons for believing that there *are* such rights has failed ... .

Natural or human rights ... are fictions (Cited in Stackhouse and Healey 1996, 488).

From other disciplines, Stackhouse and Healey point to Rhoda E. Howard and Jack Donnelly, who use sociological and anthropological theory as a basis for human rights. For them, human rights are "the cultural by-products of socio-evolutionary processes." They are a "historical artifact, pertinent only insofar as social conditions stand at a particular stage of development, and subject to disappearance if those conditions do not obtain or eventually pass away" (Stackhouse and Healey 1996, 489). (Stackhouse and Healey suggest that this view would be "a great comfort to those in closed societies who use torture as a policy of governance or allow slave labor, for they can claim that they are at a particular stage of development.")

They also note the work of Jean-Francois Lyotard and Richard Rorty, both of whom "believe that a theoretical defense or justification of human rights is neither possible nor desirable," since they are "opposed to all universalistic theory-religious, theological, or epistemological-that attempts to establish first principles" (ibid. 496). (Stackhouse and Healey point out the ambiguity they see in Rorty's and Lyotard's arguments, who reject this yet "want a world where the 'dignity' of each self, and of each unique locale, story, biography, and group identity is honored.") Stackhouse and Healey counter that "plurality without a larger sense of unity is tribalism" (ibid. 500), and that Rorty and Lyotard's "focus upon the smaller fragments of life leads them to ignore ... the world's increasingly unified economic, political, ideational, and legal global ethos" (ibid. 501).

Traer offers another example where lawyers "who embrace legal positivism hold that human rights are simply what the law says they are and are therefore justified by agreement among lawmakers and jurists" (Traer 1991, 85). He argues that this is the naturalistic fallacy, contending that "the 'ought' cannot be devised from the 'is.' The fact that people agree does not mean that they are right" (ibid. 86).

Yet, for this study, Raimundo Panikkar raises a stronger critique of human rights and their universality by judging "rights" as a Western concept which is not compatible with Eastern traditions. Panikkar asks whether "human rights are not observed because in their present form they do not represent a universal symbol powerful enough to elicit understanding and agreement?" (Panikkar 1982, 75) He argues that "that which is the foundation of one culture need not be the foundation for another" (ibid. 77), explaining that "human rights are one window through which one particular culture envisages a just human order for its individuals" (ibid. 78).

✳ Panikkar emphasizes that the philosophical assumptions behind the concept of human rights in general, and the Universal Declaration in particular, are Western. Is the concept of human rights a universal concept? For Panikkar, "the answer is a plain *no*" (ibid. 84). Although he admits that that "does not mean that it *should* not *become* so," he is leery of the culture which gave birth to human rights becoming the universal culture (ibid.). He argues that "there are no trans-cultural values, for the simple reason that a value exists as such only in a given cultural context" (ibid. 87).

Panikkar asserts that "to assume that without the explicit recognition of human rights life would be chaotic and have no meaning belongs to the same order of ideas as to think that without belief in one God as understood in the Abrahamic tradition human life would dissolve itself in total anarchy" (ibid.). He continues that "myriad examples from the past, especially regarding the West, are all too striking for one not to be wary of the danger of repeating what was done in the name of the one God, the one Empire, the one Religion, and what is nowadays being done under the aegis of the one Science and the one Technology" (ibid. 95).

Yet, while Panikkar argues that concepts and symbols are proper to a particular tradition, and are "as such not universal" (ibid. 93), he does admit that certain values "must have a certain universal meaning" (ibid. 92). Thus, he leaves the door open to the concept of human rights as being a helpful universal symbol, but is leery of the Western cultural baggage which may accompany that term.

Others assert that religion, in the form of the Judaeo-Christian tradition, is taking credit for a concept which it constantly fought against. Erich Weingartner suggests that "it is perhaps premature to speak of a 'Christian tradition' of human rights, especially in view of the fact that the Christian church has not historically been in alliance with the pioneers of human rights, whatever their tradition" (Cited in Traer 1991, 3). Hannah Arendt concurs, arguing that "the fact is that no revolution

was ever made in the name of Christianity prior to the modern age"
(Cited in Marty 1996, 11).[5]

Yet, even those who are convinced of the connection between religion and human rights may operate from different frameworks. Twiss
describes these two alternate frameworks as the "universalist" and the
"particularist." He explains that universalists "tend to emphasize the
universality of human rights as legal and moral norms that they see
grounded in some sort of foundationalist epistemology." He observes
that this framework is used "to make judgments about how the traditions measure up to universal human rights and to make recom-
mendations for social change" (Twiss 1996, 374). On the other hand,
Twiss notes that the particularists "tend either to deemphasize the legal status of human-rights norms or to stress their roots in Western
moral ideology" linked to the Enlightenment. He explains that this
framework tends to "stress the differences between cultural moral traditions and the regime of international human rights, ... contrasting
especially the communitarian moral visions of non-Western societies
and cultures with this ideological individualism" of the West (ibid.).

Twiss sees a weakness of the universalist position "in imposing human rights as a static framework on cultural traditions," and critiques
the particularist position for "the failure to take account of the fact
that there are three generations (not just one) of human rights" (ibid.).
Twiss himself is arguing here for what he describes as "a middle-way
framework that constructively combines aspirations to universality
with the realities of cultural particularity" (ibid. 375).

Mark Juergensmeyer describes the universalists, among which he
includes Twiss, as "trying to argue that you could conceive of a universalist ethics based upon categories of analysis developed under the
Western philosophic tradition, especially Kant." He contrasts those
with the "comparativists," to which he includes himself, who argue that
"you have to start where people are in their living traditions and try to
build up some sense of a collectivity of shared values" (Juergensmeyer
1995, 46-47). (Juergensmeyer here reflects on discussions between
both groups with the Berkeley-Harvard Program for the Comparative

---

5   Martin E. Marty observes that Arendt has politely suggested "that such
     religious spokespersons might at least send a card of thanks to modernity,
     to the Enlightenment, for having led them to the delayed-fifteen century
     late!-discovery of the latent pro-human rights, pro-religious rights, ele-
     ments in their treasury" (ibid.).

Study of Values, in which subsequent conferences addressed the questions: "Are there ethics in the Asian traditions?" and "Is there dharma in the West?" He describes "one poignant moment" in which the group was discussing suttee, the tradition within Hinduism where the widow throws herself on the funeral pyre of her dead husband. After realizing that there was not a single one of them who would not try to save the woman from the fire, the project "concluded that there was a core of shared values throughout the world.")

Juergensmeyer also observes that the agreement on human rights documents among religious traditions often represents an agreement only of their more liberal constituents. He cautions that "we need to accept the fact that for many people in other traditions on the *fundamentalist* end of the spectrum the resources within those traditions are a better basis for the universality of ethics than are the proud proclamations of our own tradition of human rights" (ibid. 49 [italics mine]). Peter Awn agrees, reminding us of the emphasis placed on divinely revealed religious law by some communities in Islam, Judaism and Christianity. He notes that "such divinely revealed legal systems do on occasion run counter to some of the ideals articulated in the Global Ethic and in the Declaration of Human Rights" (Awn 1995, 69). This is an underlying critique of this study overall, that besides differences between East and West, there are major differences between more "fundamentalist" and more "liberal" adherents of these religious traditions.

And this is to say nothing of the fact that within each religious tradition there are often beliefs and practices which themselves seem antithetical to the concept of human rights. Some of these will be examined briefly within this chapter within particular Eastern and Western traditions. Yet a primary concern overall is that if modern human rights theory cannot be grounded in religion in some way, it may not be grounded in anything at all.

Carl F. H. Henry agrees that "the effort to exhibit rights only through an appeal to human nature, as necessary to the ideal community, or as essential to the concept of human justice, remains the vulnerable point" (Henry 1986, 34). He cites van Eikema Hommes who "finds evidence of a conceptual instability traceable to the loss of an objective transcendent anchorage for law," and John Warwick Montgomery who "emphasizes that none of the seven most influential contemporary philosophies of rights can ... uphold human dignity" (ibid. 35).

Thus, the need exists for religion *to be involved* in the discussion of human rights. I argue that human rights theory needs the transcendent ground and universal application that religion can offer.

At this point, perhaps a note on the term "religion" is in order. I would prefer to think of "religion" in a more general way, recognizing that some forms of Buddhism are non-theistic. Therefore, I will not equate religion strictly with theism.

Maguire defines religion as "the response to the sacred, to that which we experience as having ultimacy in value" (Maguire 1993, 9). Rudolf Otto spoke of religion involving the concepts of "the Holy," of a "numinous" experience, a sense of "awe" and "dread," of a "creature -feeling" of dependence. Otto also emphasized the moral aspect of religion, noting that in religion "the appreciation of moral obligation and duty … has been developed side by side with the religious feeling itself" (Otto 1923, 51).

Paul Tillich referred to faith as "the state of being ultimately concerned" (Tillich 1957, 4). Hans Küng speaks of an attitude of "trust" toward reality itself, explaining that "fundamental trust means that a person, in principle, says *Yes to the uncertain reality* of himself and the world, making himself open to reality." He explains that this attitude "implies an antinihilistic fundamental certainty in regard to all human experience and behavior, despite persistent, menacing uncertainty" (Küng 1978, 445 [italics Küng's]).

And, as Augustine observed, this response to the Wholly Other, this religious disposition, leaves one "both a-shudder and a-glow. A-shudder, in so far as I am unlike it, a-glow in so far as I am like it"[6] (*Confessions* cited in Otto, 28). All of these are characteristics which this study would like to include in its understanding of religion. Thus, it focuses heavily on *experience*, past and present, and in a fundamental *attitude toward and response to* reality, as well as a perceived "deepness" and "value" to reality and what lies beneath or grounds it. Therefore, religions are not merely static organizations, historical or sociological, but living realities based on people's lived experiences which gives them a general orientation toward reality. This working concept of "religion" functions for both Buddhism and Christianity, and in the interreligious global concerns of this study, and does not limit the concept of "religion" to dogma or ritual or structure alone. In this sense, it

6   "Et inhorresco et inardesco. *Inhorresco*, in quantum *dissimilis* ei sum. Inardesco, in quantum similis ei sum."

may be a more overarching view of religion than that to which more "fundmentalist" or "literalist" adherents of religions would adhere to. Given this, I next examine some of the possibilities which exist for the concept of human rights within religion in general.

B. POSSIBILITIES FOR THE CONCEPT OF HUMAN RIGHTS IN RELIGION

Upon drafting the United Nations' Universal Declaration of Human Rights, one member of the commission is reported to have said, "We are unanimous about these rights on condition that no one asks why" (Cited in Kasper 1990, 149). This "why" is the realm of religion, which emphasizes the role that religion can and must play within this discussion. It also exposes the weakness of human rights theories which do not involve religion.

Wilfred Cantwell Smith suggests that "no one has any reasonable grounds ... to talk about human rights who rejects metaphysics" (Cited in Traer 1991, 86). And Robert Bellah writes that "religion is the deepest apperception of truth that human beings are capable of, for it is an apperception of truth that transcends human beings" (Bellah 1978, 149). Religion takes human rights theory beyond the physical realm, to the transcendent. In addition, this transcendence is objective and is the source of morality. Corresponding to this morality is a sense of duty related to rights. All of these are elements that religion brings to the discussion of human rights.

Walter Kasper argues that the theological foundations of human rights were affirmed in the Second Vatican Council, which declared that "to acknowledge God is in no way to oppose human dignity, since such dignity is grounded and brought to perfection in God" (*Gaudium et Spes* cited in Kasper 1990, 156). It affirms that "the recognition of the transcendence of God is thus the foundation of the transcendence of the human person" (ibid. 157). (Note the difference in mindset from Prozesky, who sees human rights as giving humans a sovereignty which is logically opposed to God's sovereignty.)

Stanley Harakas agrees, arguing that "secular approaches to rights need to be seen as appeals to a sinful and distorted empirical reality which cannot sustain the claim to rights." He emphasizes that "only the appeal to our common origin in God's image and likeness transcends the limited view from below and surely grounds human rights in an unshakable, transcendent truth" (Harakas 1982, 19). J. Bryan Hehir goes even further, asserting that "the argument from transcendence does not erode the philosophical truth about the unique dignity of the person, but it provides this insight with a degree of conviction and content that *transforms the discussion from respect for the person to reverence for the person*" (Hehir 1980a, 6 [italics mine]).

Stackhouse and Healey suggest that, as we transcend the horizons of this world, we begin to conceive of the world as a unity, and "suspect that it is governed by a unified moral law" (Stackhouse and Healey 1996, 486). They concur that "the remarkable resurgence of the question of religion in relation to human rights over the past few years … has many causes." They observe that "the most profound cause is that societies and souls cannot flourish without a deep substratum of awareness about the moral basis of life, a substratum that generally does not occur without a religious orientation" (ibid. 491).

Both authors argue that, today, "human rights are a modern way of speaking about cross-cultural ethical concepts" (ibid. 494), contending that "human rights as a normative concept adds that there is one humanity with a rich variety of individual lives, traditions, communities, and religions that ought not be violated." They explain that this is "a theological hermeneutic that includes unity and difference" (ibid. 502).

Stackhouse and Healey observe that "all of the axial religions express metaphysical-moral visions that entail normativity, and their civilizational expansiveness verifies their sustainability" (ibid. 505). They assert that "the world religions are allies in identifying a fundamental need to transform reality as we now find it," noting that "every religion has something like universal moral laws" (ibid. 508). Therefore, these religions "offer constructive, forward-looking visions or teleologies, that is, guidance about how to discern good from evil consequences of our actions by considering them in reference to ultimate aims" (ibid. 511). Bellah agrees, noting that "social criticism, an insistence on justice and equality, can be found in the religions centuries and even millennia before the birth of modern ideology" (Bellah 1978, 163).

Jon Sobrino reminds us that religion is often the primary hope for the poor and marginalized. He contends that "in every religion there is an important seed of liberation," by liberation meaning "that which frees the poor from the proximity of death and encourages them to live" (Sobrino 1992, 114). He observes that "religion provides a framework in which to live and organize one's life; it proposes a way in which to move forward; it offers meaning and hope; and it gives a measure of dignity" (ibid.). Thus, he argues that, "in the present world, filled with massive injustice and with little prospect for change, religion is normally the only thing left for the poor to hold on to, to manage their lives" (ibid. 115).

Sobrino asserts that "religion contains the basic ethical affirmation that giving life is good, and that good is fundamentally defined as giving life" (ibid. 116). Thus, he concludes that "in religion in any of its forms, there is something good and positive that can unite human beings to work for peace and promote greater social justice and commitment to such things as liberation" (ibid. 125).

This universal moral sense is a key component in the discussion of religion and human rights. Mark Juergensmeyer observes that

> ✳ every single religious tradition affirms not only its peculiar version of truth but the universality of truth itself. There is not a single religious tradition that doesn't to some extent claim to have a window on a larger and global sense of virtue and well-being (Juergensmeyer 1995, 48).

Traer agrees, asserting that "human rights are at the center of a global moral language that is being justified, elaborated, and advocated by members of different religious traditions and cultures" (Traer 1991, 10).

Thus, despite the different systems of belief in the world's religions, and possibly different moral motivations in those systems, most would argue for at least a minimal moral common ground based on an examination of the scriptures and traditions of the religions. Cox and Sharma go so far as to state that "moral consciousness is more universal than theistic consciousness." They note that excluding the term "God" from the *Declaration Toward a Global Ethic of the Parliament of the World's Religions* was not only an accommodation to Buddhist objections, but that it affirmed this "profounder truth about human nature" and morality (Cox and Sharma 1994, 76 [see also Küng, *A Global Ethic*]).

Peter Donovan argues that, while methods and metaphysical systems may differ, "it is much more beneficial to try to implement in daily life the shared precepts for goodness taught by all religions rather than to argue about minor differences in approach." He observes that ✳ "the discovery of a number of shared moral precepts (e.g. versions of the Golden Rule) amongst different religions seems to offer *prima fa-cie* evidence, at least, for moral common ground as a reality" (Donovan 1986, 368).

An example of this can be seen in the saying of Mencius (372-289 B.C.E.), who argued for the belief in the basic goodness of all human beings and the experience of compassion. He observed:

> I say that every man has a heart that pities others, for the heart of every man is moved by fear and horror, tenderness and mercy, if he suddenly sees a child about to fall into a well. And this is not be-cause he wishes to make friends with the child's father and mother or to win praise from his countryfolk and friends, nor because the child's cries hurt him.
> This shows that no man is without a merciful, tender heart, no man is without a heart for shame and hatred, no man is without a heart to give way and yield, no man is without a heart for right and wrong (Cited in Hick 1992, 158). (Mencius was an orthodox Confucian philosopher who systematized Confucius' teachings. See Jonathan Z. Smith 1995, 699.)

Yet, while there may be a moral common ground, is the language of "human rights" common in the various traditions? Certainly it is not. Arlene Swidler writes that "neither the term nor the concept is tradi-tional in religious thought," yet "dealing as they do with our basic un-derstanding of what it means to be human, what we are doing on this earth, and how we ought to relate to one another, human rights are at the center of religious thought and practice" (A. Swidler 1982, vii). Cox and Sharma argue that "if one goes to the core ideas, central val-ues of human dignity and well-being, basic scriptures, most powerful images, exemplary persons, and key interpreters in these traditions, a wealth of constructive material can be found" (Cox and Sharma 1994, 62). In addition, they reflect that "differing cultures can arrive at a simi-lar conclusion about rights by rather different routes" (ibid. 77).

However, while it may be an oversimplification, one can observe that the Eastern emphasis in general is more on "duties," while it is the modern Western emphasis which is on "rights." Many argue that the language of "human rights" is another form of Western imperialism upon the East, forcing those religions to succumb to Western concepts (see Panikkar 1982). Cox and Sharma note that the preliminary ques-tion that must be asked is "whether religions of the East can be a positive resource in the context of human rights" (Cox and Sharma 1994, 66).

Their answer to this is a resounding "yes." Cox and Sharma observe that "duties have a logical priority over rights, in the sense that unless fulfilling a right is someone's duty, that right leads a vaporous existence." They conclude that "emphasis on the inalienable character of rights seems more desireable," observing that "in the various religious traditions this inalienable character is affirmed in terms of human dignity and worth" (ibid. 74).

One could argue that, until the modern period, the Judaeo-Christian tradition emphasized duties over rights as well. Henry emphasizes that modern Western theorists of human rights "continued to detach human rights from equivalent attention to duties, not to speak of the priority of duty and of God as its basic referent and specifier." After this separation, "the rights of humanity were the main concern; God and duty were marginal" (Henry 1986, 37). In regard to duties, R. Harrison observes that "if you really want to see what you have got when you are told that you have a right, see what duties are laid on other people" (Cited in Jack Mahoney, 329). Therefore, the disparity between rights and duties is not such a clear-cut contrast as is often assumed, but is rather a more fluid symbiotic relationship that is severed artificially by a Western, modern, secular approach.

Twiss argues that, "far from preempting or replacing the moral teachings of various cultural traditions, specific expressions of human-rights concerns have arisen from the mutual recognitions by adherents of these traditions that they have a shared interest in the protection of certain important substantive moral values" (Twiss 1996, 363). He reminds us that there are now three generations of human rights, ranging from individual to collective, and argues that "within this understanding, human rights in general are intended to be compatible in principle not only with cultural traditions and societies that emphasize the importance of individuals within community (a more apt characterization of Western liberalism) but also with cultural traditions and societies that may emphasize the primacy of community and the way that individuals contribute to it" (ibid. 366). Thus, modern human rights theory does address the importance of duty as corresponding to rights, and the importance of the community, hence softening the "East-West debate" over the language and concept of human rights.

Twiss offers the examples of the U.N. Draft Declaration of the Rights of Indigenous Peoples, which "speaks for the views of over 120 indigenous traditions that are largely communitarian and that clearly acknowledge all three generations of human rights." In addition, he notes Catholic social teachings, which "simultaneously reject radical individualism, advance a thoroughly social understanding of the person and the importance of the community as well as duties and virtues oriented to the common good, and yet accept human rights in their three generations" (ibid. 367).

W. Theodore DeBary argues that "nothing is gained by arguing for the distinctively Western character of human rights." He observes that "if you claim some special distinction for the West … you are probably defining human rights in such narrow terms as to render them unrecognizable or inoperable for others" (DeBary 1988, 184). DeBary continues that "if, however, you view *human rights* as an evolving conception, expressing imperfectly the aspirations of many peoples, East and West, … one can arrive at a deeper understanding of human rights problems in different cultural settings" (ibid.). This interpretation of the concept of "human rights" is key to this study.

For example, Kana Mitra observes that, in Hinduism, "suggested Sanskrit words do not have the precise connotation of 'right' as it is used in the Universal Declaration of Human Rights." Yet, Mitra suggests that

* in order to obviate these difficulties of terms and contexts it is useful to define words in terms of their intentionality and not simply literally and philologically. It can then be seen whether the same intentionality is present in other traditions, even if the same literal word is not used.

Mitra concludes that "following this suggestion will reveal that 'right' as it is used in the Declaration means a claim which is in accord with justice and propriety" (Mitra 1982, 78). This will be a conclusion of this study as well.

It is within this framework, then, which this study will proceed. "Human rights" language can operate as a framework for common concerns and political alliances. Cox and Sharma state that "virtually every religious tradition articulates in one way or another a basic conviction about the unity of the human family." In addition, they note that these same traditions "emphasize the unique value of each

⁂ person," and observe that "the fact that human life is seen within the larger context of a divine or cosmic order is a reminder of this conviction" (Cox and Sharma 1994, 71). While the answer to the question "Why is this flesh so precious?" (Maguire 1993, 227) remains metaphysically different in each of the world's religions, the answer is still an affirmative "yes" to the value of each human being. I will argue that all the major religions have a theory of justice, and therefore of human rights.

John Kelsay speculates that to say human rights are universal is to say that they are hoped to be, and that there is good reason for that hope (Kelsay, 1997). Traer argues that, while plurality exists, there is evidence for universality in that "persons are able to translate concepts from one language and culture to another, to communicate, to persuade, and to change not only their own way of thinking but that of others" (Traer 1991, 217). In addition, he observes that "despite differences of doctrine, men and women of various religious traditions are in fact working together with those who profess no religious conviction, to secure human rights for all peoples" (ibid. 208). He concludes that "faith in human rights is not merely international but interreligious" (ibid. 207).

Christopher Mooney reminds us that "morality ... is not a purely rational phenomenon; it is also a product of affectivity, mysticism, and faith" (Cited in ibid. 219). Peter Awn notes that "oftentimes it is the mystics who have challenged isolationist and rigid understandings of the place of law and institution within a religious structure," adding that "they have insisted that there is an experience of God that takes us beyond the limits of our own society" (Awn 1995, 68). At the very least, Jack Mahoney observes that "the steady and increasing human persuasion that people are not to be explained away ... in the pursuit of the general welfare of any society is saying something which is both real and important" (Jack Mahoney 1990, 331).

Thus religion, by its very nature, has much to offer to the current discussion on human rights. Religions emphasize the value and dignity of the individual person, although the nature of that person may be perceived differently from one tradition to the next. Religions emphasize the connection between the individual and the community, yet stress that one need not be restricted only to the concerns of the community or society. Thus, they push the individual to transcend themselves, and their community, to achieve a more universal perception of reality. Having examined some problems and possibilities for the concept of human rights in religion in general, I will now briefly examine concerns and resources for the concept of human rights within particular Eastern and Western religious traditions.

1.4 PROBLEMS AND POSSIBILITIES WITH THE CONCEPT OF HUMAN RIGHTS WITHIN EASTERN AND WESTERN RELIGIONS IN PARTICULAR

This section examines problems with and possibilities for the concept of human rights within particular Eastern and Western traditions. This includes resources for human rights within the Western religious traditions, here examining the Judaeo-Christian tradition and also Islam as a continuation of that worldview. I discuss Roman Catholicism briefly in the context of Christianity overall, thus setting the stage for its more thorough examination in Chapter Three and the remainder of the book. I also explore elements for human rights within the Eastern religious tradition of Hinduism. Since Buddhism develops out of this worldview historically, and will be examined in detail in Chapter Two and throughout the remainder of this book as well, this general outlook will pave the way to situate Buddhism within the context of the Eastern worldview and to contrast that worldview with the Western traditions.

A. HUMAN RIGHTS IN WESTERN RELIGIONS

This section looks at the concept of human rights from the perspective of the three Abrahamic, or Western, religions: Judaism, primarily as it influences Christianity in its development, Christianity itself, and Islam. The monotheistic worldview of these religions offers a similar ethic in regard to social justice concerns, and therefore human rights.

I. HUMAN RIGHTS AND THE JUDAEO-CHRISTIAN TRADITION

Throughout this book, I assume that the actual current term "human rights" is a modern Western concept and is therefore to a large extent a product of a Judaeo-Christian culture. Stackhouse and Healey assert that "the deep roots of human rights ideals are rooted nowhere else than in the biblical tradition, for it is here that we find the decisive unveiling of a perspective in which moral first principles demanding the respect for the neighbor are made known to humanity by a reality that is universal and absolute." They contend that this reality, which the Western traditions call 'God,' is neither a figment of human imagination, a projection of our personal needs or tribal consciousness, nor a product of human creativity. Nor is this God morally neutral. This is an ethical God (Stackhouse and Healey 1996, 492).

R. J. Henle concurs, observing that "when Yahweh revealed Himself to the Hebrew people and thus entered human history, He stood apart from all the multitudinous gods of the Middle East ... as the God of righteousness and justice." He continues that "the terrible condemnations of injustice in the Psalms and the Prophets, the absolute demand for justice-which transcended sacrifices and prayers-have echoed through the Christian tradition" (Henle 1980, 87). Henle observes that "the love of neighbor is seen as an intrinsic consequence of man's love for God and as a formal correlate to God's love for man" (ibid. 89).

While Walter Harrelson admits that "the Bible knows little or nothing about human rights in our sense of the term," he does contend that "it does know and say a great deal about the obligation of individuals and of the human community to the Lord and Giver of life and to fellow human beings." Therefore, he agrees that "in that sense, the Bible has much to say about human rights," concluding that "it is possible to see in the basic understanding of human rights, reflected in, for example, the United Nations' Universal Declaration of Human Rights, a large measure of the biblical understanding of human obligation under God" (Harrelson 1980, xv).

This understanding of human rights is rooted in the biblical understanding of human dignity which is exemplified in the Genesis creation accounts. In addition to the account of human beings made in the image of God, the story of the creation of Adam also contributes to the concept of human dignity and human rights. Daniel Polish notes that, in the Jewish interpretation of that scripture account, "the Rabbis, the classical commentators on Torah, were intrigued about why that account is couched in terms of a single individual rather than in terms of multitudes." He explains that "the story, they state, is cast in this way to teach the value of the worth of the individual," and observes, therefore, that "every individual person is equivalent to that first human created by God" (Polish 1982, 41).

The Mishnah from the second-third century C.E. reads:

It was for this reason Adam was created alone: to teach you that anyone who destroys a single life, it is to be accounted to him by Scripture as if he had destroyed the whole world, and whoever preserves a single life, it is accounted to him by Scripture as if he had preserved a whole world ... and also to teach you the greatness of God: for a person stamps many coins with one die, and they are all similar; but God has stamped every person with the die of Adam, yet no one is similar to his fellow. Therefore, everyone must say: "For my sake was the world created." (M. Sanhedrin 4.5, cited in Fishbane 1988, 19).

Polish concludes that "the core theological affirmations of the Jewish faith demand recognition of the sanctity of the individual and the equality of all individuals as children of God, subject equally to the laws, protection, and love of their Creator" (Polish 1982, 46). In addition, he emphasizes the role of the individual conscience in arguing that "Judaism affirms that the right of conscience cannot be abrogated by law." An example of this is seen in the fact that "Scripture asserts the responsibility of the prophets to deliver their message-their right to utter unpopular ideas" (ibid. 48).

Earlier in this chapter I dealt with some of the historical roots of the concept of human rights in the Judaeo-Christian tradition, and will not need to re-examine those again here. But the point worth reiterating is that this concept of human rights from Judaism does flow through Christianity as well, and Christians today do generally accept the concept. In regard to Christianity today, Traer observes that "liberal Protestants fundamentally agree with Roman Catholics and evangelical Protestants about human rights, despite quite different theological approaches" (Traer 1991, 10).

In 1980, the Consultation by the World Council of Churches with the Lutheran World Federation, the World Alliance of Reformed Churches, and the Pontifical Commission *Justitia et Pax* affirmed that "a common understanding does exist in the basic doctrine that all theological statements on human rights derive from the Christian anthropology of the human person created in the image of God" (Trutz Rendtorff cited in ibid. 88). The shift among many Catholic authors since *Pacem in Terris* from natural law to human dignity has helped in smoothing relations between Catholics and Protestants on this issue (Traer 1991, 89). In addition, Jack Mahoney notes that this shift in Catholicism from human "nature" to human "person," has surmounted some difficulties between Catholicism and modern philosophical and socio-political views on human rights (Jack Mahoney 1990, 327 [see also John Mahoney, 1989, 113-114]).

Thus, Traer concludes that while "neither the Bible nor traditional doctrines refer to human rights directly … , Christians derive human rights from both." He contends that human rights "are derived from faith and involve duties to God and one's neighbor" and "are relational" (Traer 1991, 90). Along this line, citing from the 1971 Synod of Bishops *Justice in the World*, Walter Kasper reminds us that "from the theological foundation of human rights it follows that the commitment to human dignity and to human rights intrinsically belongs to the witness of the gospel"(Kasper 1990, 159). He emphasizes that a specifically Christian interpretation of human rights "transcends the promotion of mere justice by the pursuit of compassion and love" (ibid. 163).

In this sense, human rights are not an abstract concept, but a recognition of human worth and dignity that leads to action with and for individual human persons. This is perhaps best exemplified in the Judaeo-Christian tradition in the stress on the dignity and value of the poor and marginalized. A brief examination of attitudes toward the poor and marginalized within the Judaeo-Christian tradition will help in giving a concrete example of the concept of human rights within that tradition, as well as in emphasizing the relational aspects of love and compassion within this concept of human rights. Indeed, as Trutz Rendtorff argues, it was "the 'weak' Christian concept of love for the poor and needy" that "had to be transformed into the 'strong' concept of rights and legal claims" (Rendtorff 1988, 44).

2. THE POOR IN THE JUDAEO-CHRISTIAN TRADITION

Judaism's view of Yahweh as a defender of the poor runs throughout Christianity, with the poor being given a favored status. Henle observes that

> although these biblical terms – 'righteousness' and 'justice' – do not exactly match modern usage, it is clear that justice included what we now call human rights. This is illustrated by the repeated emphasis on the protection of the widow, the orphan, the 'alien in your midst,' and the poor (Henle 1980, 87).

Daniel Maguire notes that "biblical justice (commonly called *sedaqah*) is the foundation of the reign of God" (Maguire 1993 126), and that "it is unequivocally partial to the poor and suspicious of the 'rich'" (ibid. 131). Norman Snaith observes that the biblical root for *sedaqah* "has from the first a bias towards the poor and needy," noting that the related Aramaic word *tsidqah* meant "showing mercy to the poor" (Cited in ibid.).

This view of the poor was unique to the Hebrew people and was not largely shared with or imported from surrounding ancient Near Eastern religions. For, while charity toward the poor is apparent in these other religions, the actual notion of justice towards the poor seems quite foreign. Friedrich Hauck explains that "the very idea that the poor are under special divine protection is quite alien to the Greek world," noting that "in social conflicts the poor could not even invoke the help of the gods" (Kittel and Friedrich 1968, 887).

Ernst Bammel writes that "Yahweh, unlike the Greek gods, is the protector of the poor" and that "the older prophets took up the cause of the poor in the name of Yahweh" (ibid. 890). Daniel Polish agrees that "the Torah is filled with injunctions not to oppress or exploit the poor." He explains that "God 'pleads the cause of the poor' (Ps. 146:7), rewarding those who champion the needy, and punishing those who do them wrong (Deut. 24:13)," and emphasizes that "the books of the prophets are replete with denunciations of those who do evil to the poor" (Polish 1982, 49 [see Amos 2:6-8, 4:1-3, and 5:8]).

In the New Testament, πτωχοὶ is the usual term for the poor, occurring 31-35 times, mostly in the Gospels and especially in the Synoptics (Mk 4-5 times, Mt 4-5, Lk 10) (Bammel cited in Kittel and Friedrich 1968, 902). In the Gospel of Luke, Jesus' reading of Isaiah in the synagogue is seen by many today as programmatic for his entire ministry: "The Spirit of the Lord is upon me, because he has anointed me to bring good news to the poor" (Lk 4:18, NRSV). In the Lucan beatitudes, Jesus says "Blessed are you who are poor, for yours is the kingdom of God" (Lk 6:20).

Walter Pilgrim observes that "we are again put on notice by Luke that the people to whom Jesus ministers are those living on the margin of society; socially, ethically, and religiously" (Pilgrim 1981, 73). Pilgrim states that "Jesus is powerfully portrayed as one who revives the prophetic voice on behalf of the poor and oppressed. The poor know through Jesus, that God is for them" (ibid. 161). In Acts, Pilgrim writes that Luke "offers his description of the early church's radical care for the poor and needy as an alternate vision of what the human community should be like, a vision strikingly different from the Graeco-Roman culture in which he lived" (ibid. 163). David Mealand emphasizes that

> it is certainly not true that either Jesus or his immediate disciples simply endorsed the existing order in general or the gulf between rich and poor in particular. Rather, they saw the sufferings of the poor as part of the evil of the present order which was in need of being transformed (Mealand 1980, 98).

Mealand observes that "both the Hebrew Bible and the New Testament are highly critical of any state of affairs in which some have plenty while others starve," and concludes that "the New Testament gives no comfort to those who think that religion or morality can turn a blind eye to oppression, injustice, or flagrant inequalities" (ibid.).

In summary, the Judaeo-Christian tradition has affirmed in theory the concept of human rights, as seen in the emphasis on the dignity and value of the individual, based on creation in God's image. In practicality, it has affirmed this in its attitude toward the poor and marginalized, as one example. Stanley Harakas correctly notes that historically "the Church's accent has been not on the claim of one's own rights or even the rights of the Church itself, but rather on the concern for the violation of the rights of others-in particular, the weak and the poor and the defenseless." He emphasizes that "it is here that 'rights' are most clearly identified" (Harakas 1982, 17).

It is within this context of human rights which I will proceed in this chapter, examining primarily the concept of human rights but also noting attitudes toward the poor and marginalized within these traditions, since here human rights are often the most violated. Jürgen Moltmann rightly contends that Christians should "press for the *restoration of those particular human rights* which through one-sided progress and established priorities have become neglected, weakened, or repressed" (Moltmann 1984, 35).

3. HUMAN RIGHTS IN ISLAM

Partially influenced by these Judaeo-Christian foundations, Islam's approach to the issue of human rights is more akin to its Western predecessors than the religions of the East. Roger Garaudy reminds us that "Islam is not a new religion, born with the preaching of the prophet Muhammad. The Qur'an includes him expressly in the line of Abraham" (Garaudy 1990, 46). He continues that "according to the Qur'an, Islam began with the first man, with Adam," and concludes that "the basis of human rights in Islam is the same as that of all revealed religions: the transcendent dimension of human beings" (ibid.).

Peter Awn agrees, observing that Islam's "consistent reverence for human beings is clearly embedded in the Koran itself, which tells us that God created all humans by breathing into them his very own spirit." He continues that "that is what distinguishes us from all other aspects of creation: to literally possess within ourselves the spirit of God" (Awn 1995, 68).

Riffat Hassan explains that "when Muslims speak of human rights, they generally speak of a multitude of rights, some of which are derived from a reading of the Qur'an, the Hadith, and the Sunnah, and the rest largely from a study of Islamic history and Islamic law" (Hassan 1982, 52). She continues that "as human beings who have a covenantal relationship with God, we must strive under all circumstances to secure and to guard those rights which we believe have been given to us by God and which, therefore, no one else has the right to take away" (ibid. 55).

The Qur'an states "Towards God is thy limit" (Sura 53:43), pointing to the value and potential of each human being. Yet, while all human beings are to be respected, "the Qur'an maintains that the recognition of individual 'merit' is also a fundamental human right. The Qur'an teaches that merit is not determined by lineage or sex or wealth or worldly success *or religion* – but by 'righteousness,'" she explains (ibid. 56 [italics mine]).

In addition, Hassan writes that "the ideal 'ummah' [community] cares about all of its members as an ideal mother cares about all of her children, knowing that all are not equal and that each has different needs" (ibid. 57). Awn concurs, emphasizing that "in the Koran, there is a constantly reiterated concern for those most vulnerable within society—for the poor, for widows, for orphans, for those who normally fall through the cracks," noting that "the responsibility for those human beings falls upon the community itself" (Awn 1995, 68).

In this respect, Hassan sees many of the Islamic restrictions on women to have originally been concerned with their protection rather than discrimination. She argues that "it is a clear teaching of the

Qur'an that man and woman are equal in the sight of God" (Sura 3:195; 4:124; 9:71-72; 16:97; 33:35; 40:40). Finally, she observes that the Qur'an "protects the right of a human being to be treated with sensitivity and compassion," noting that in its teachings "justice is a prerequisite for peace" (Hassan 1982, 62).

Abdullahi Ahmed An-Na'im agrees, noting that "general principles of justice, equality and freedom, etc., without discrimination on grounds of race, colour, gender or religion, can be found in the Qur'an, especially at the earlier stage of revelation in Mecca" (An-Na'im 1990, 62). However, he also points out that "specific rules established by the Qur'an itself during the subsequent Medina stage of 622 to 632 C.E. clearly discriminate against women and non-Muslims." He argues that "any discussion of human rights in Islam should not be confined to the bare text of the Qur'an" (ibid.), but also to the way the Qur'an has been interpreted and to the Sunnah and Sharia. That Sharia, developed primarily in the seventh through ninth centuries C.E., would today "violate many of the fundamental human rights of women and non-Muslims" (ibid. 63).

Yet, An-Na'im observes that "the early Muslims have exercised their right and responsibility to interpret the divine sources of Islam in the light of their own historical context in order to produce a coherent and practicable system which achieved significant human rights improvements on its predecessors and contemporaries." Thus, he concludes that "it is the right and responsibility of contemporary Muslims to do the same in order to produce modern Islamic Sharia for the present radically transformed context" (ibid. 68).

However, another factor involved is that a segment of this modern reinterpretation of Islam has veered toward militant fundamentalism. Mansour Farhang suggests that this emergence of Islamic fundamentalism must be seen in the context of "the failure of the secularists and religious modernists to reach a functioning synthesis between Islam and modernization," and in light of the desperate living conditions of the urban poor within those societies (Farhang 1988, 66). (Unfortunately, this became apparent to most Americans only after the terrorist attacks of September 11th.) Farhang also notes that "there is no unified Islamic legal system," offering the example that "Saudi Arabia, Libya, Pakistan, and Iran all consider themselves as Islamic states but none of them is recognized by the others as authentic" (ibid.

65), further exemplifying the tension between various interpretations of Islam today. Farhang explains that "freedom in Islam is not an inherent right," continuing that "individual freedom is perceived as personal surrender to God" (ibid. 64). However, Lafif Lakhdar points out that "the best Arab poets and thinkers of the early centuries of Islam would not be able to exist in the present-day Arab world" (Cited in Mayer 1988, 98). Thus, modern fundamentalist views on human rights in Islam may not be consistent with that tradition historically. In this sense, David Little emphasizes that Islam does share some common elements with the West on ideas such as freedom of conscience, and that "current human rights formulations, along with the important notions that underlie them, are by no means necessarily irrelevant to cultures outside the West" such as Islam (Little 1988, 31).

4. THE POOR IN ISLAM

A concern for the poor and marginalized is carried over into Islam as well, as seen by *zakat* (the obligatory alms paid by self-sufficient adult Muslims to aid the Islamic community) being one of the Five Pillars of Islam (J. Smith 1995, 1148). Garaudy explains that "all the dictates of the Qur'an, notably the *zakat*, ... and the banning of the *riba*, namely of any increase in wealth unaccompanied by work in the service of Allah, tend to prevent the accumulation of wealth at one pole of society and poverty at the other" (Garaudy 1990, 48).

Hassan notes that

> righteousness consists not only of 'just belief' (*iman*) but also of 'just action' (*amal*) as pointed out with clarity in Sura 2:177: 'To spend of your substance,/ Out of love for Him,/ for your kin,/ For orphans,/ For the needy,/ For the wayfarer,/ For those who ask,/ and for the ransoms of slaves'(Hassan 1982, 57).

She explains that the concept of *ihsan* means literally "restoring the balance by making up a loss or deficiency," and that the concept "shows the Qur'an's sympathy for the downtrodden, oppressed, or weak classes of human beings (such as women, slaves, orphans, the poor and infirm, and minorities)" (ibid.).

The Qur'an states that "Anyone who is stingy, is stingy only with his own soul. God is Wealthy while you are poor" (Sura 47:38, cited in Wilson 1995, 664). Another Sura adds that "They feed with food the needy wretch, the orphan, the prisoner, for love of Him, saying, 'We wish for no reward nor thanks from you'"(Sura 76:8-9, cited in ibid. 697).

The Hadiths also speak of action toward the poor. The *Hadith of Bukhari* states that "a man once asked the Prophet what was the best thing in Islam, and the latter replied, 'It is to feed the hungry and to give the greeting of peace both to those one knows and to those one does not know'" (ibid. 686). In the *Forty Hadith of an-Nawawi*, we find that "Whosoever alleviates the lot of a needy person, Allah will alleviate his lot in this world and the next ... . Allah will aid a servant of His so long as the servant aids his brother" (ibid. 699).

Thus, Islam is in keeping with the other monotheistic Western religions of Judaism and Christianity in the "substance" of its fundamental concept of human rights, although the "term" itself may not exist traditionally. In regard to the poor and marginalized, it emphasizes the action of *charity* but cautions that that is not enough. There is also a strong realization that *justice* must ultimately be enacted to bring about changes in unjust social systems. This view of human rights is rooted in the transcendent dimension of the human being as created by God and ultimately destined to return to God. It emphasizes the preciousness and uniqueness of each individual, and the need for protection of the rights of that individual, while recognizing the ultimate sovereignty of God.

This general worldview will differ from that shared by Eastern religions. I will now examine Hinduism in itself and as a general worldview out of which Buddhism develops.

B. HUMAN RIGHTS IN EASTERN RELIGIONS

I. HUMAN RIGHTS IN HINDUISM

For Westerners, perhaps no religion seems more antithetical to the concept of human rights than Hinduism, with its emphasis on duty supported by its traditional structure of the caste system. Yet it is also a primary example of an evolving religion, adapting itself in response to current world situations. John B. Carmen cites the Indian Constitution of 1949 as "signaling a participation of the political leaders of modern India in this shift from the language of duties to the language of rights" (Carman 1988, 118). Yet, he observes that "our Western notion of rights goes back much further than the affirmation of *equal rights.*" He continues that "what is one's right is what is one's due, whether because of who one is by birth or because of what one has accomplished. It is one's fair share even if it is not an equal share." Thus, Carman explains that "that notion of right is certainly deeply imbedded in the Hindu social system" (ibid. 121).

Carman observes that most educated modern Hindus believe that "all people have ... a common *dharma* of fundamental duties, of which the most important are truth telling (*satya*) and not harming living be-✗ ings (*ahimsa*)" (ibid. 126). He states that most "would agree theoretically with this emphasis on the common dharma, not only of Hindus, but of all human beings" (ibid. 127). In addition, in regard to India's Constitution, he states that most educated Hindus "not only accepted these fundamental rights but insisted that they expressed age-old Hindu principles" (ibid.).

Kana Mitra examines the issue of human rights in Hinduism by looking at a document which seems most opposed to it: Manu's Code which is called *Manava Dharma Sutra* (*The Treatise on Human Duties*), ca. 200 B.C.E–200 C.E. (Jonathan Smith 1995, 682). This document has traditionally been a primary source for arguments in favor of the caste system. Yet, Mitra states that while most tradition-oriented Hindus believe that Manu's Code "is not acceptable in its entirety to contemporary Hindu society, it can yet contribute to the establishing of a just society" (Mitra 1982, 77).

Mitra explains that in Manu's Code, "people's duties and rights are specified not in terms of their humanity but in terms of specific caste, age and sex" (ibid.). Thus, differences are acknowledged, but the varying rights and duties are often seen as a source of protection rather than discrimination (ibid. 81). Yet, despite these differences, there is a recognition of equality or essence that goes beyond differences. Carman observes that "there is a human equality before God, both in the acknowledgement of a vast gulf between human and divine and in the secret knowledge of a profound kinship or an intimate relation between God and the devotee" (Carman 1988, 122).

Historically, under the umbrella of rituals and beliefs which is labelled "Hinduism," various traditions have developed which deal with this problem of unity and diversity. Mitra explains that, in the Bhakti groups[7], "all humans are equal as God's creation but are not the same; therefore all should give and receive according to their own nature.

7   Bhakti is defined as loving devotion to a particular god.

These groups uphold the idea of following one's own nature (*svad-harma*) as advocated in the *Bhagavad-Gita.*" Mitra states that most of these Hindu devotional schools believe that following one's own nature is a means to eternal truth (*sanatana dharma*) (Mitra 1982, 80). On the other hand, Mitra notes that the various Vedanta groups "uphold human rights on the basis of all human beings having the same essence. *Advaita Vedanta* advocates the nonduality of the essence of humans and the divine" (ibid. 81). Therefore, theories of equality exist even though differences are recognized.

Mahatma Gandhi stands as an example of a modern Hindu reformer who considered himself an orthodox Hindu. He stated that

> ✳ Men are equal. For, though they are not of the same age, same height, the same skin and the same intellect, these inequalities are temporary and superficial. The soul that is hidden beneath this earthly crust is one and the same for all men and women, belonging to all climes (Cited in Mitra 1982, 82).

Mitra observes that Gandhi believed that "no form of Hindu theology justified an inequality of humans. Theistic Hinduism upholds human equality on the basis that all are God's creatures. Nontheistic Hinduism emphasizes the identity of the essence of all humans" (Mitra 1982, 82). Margaret Chatterjee agrees, stating that "Hindus will say, and Gandhi speaks for them, that we all share a common humanity and as such share a divinity which is yet to be 'realized' or brought to full consciousness" (Chatterjee 1983, 44).

Chatterjee also observes that "in the strict sense there is no word for 'religion' in Indian languages." She explains that "the word *dharma* serves where in other languages the word religion would be used. It is basically an ethico-religious concept, ... one can liken it to the Judaic idea of righteousness" (ibid. 18). She continues that "the defense of *dharma* involved the righting of injustices, the restoring of balance which men in their ignorance or out of selfish passions had disturbed" (ibid. 19). In regard to Gandhi, Chatterjee states that "as was laid down in the *Gita*, he linked the dharma of the individual with *lokasamgraha*, the welfare of all. Dharma then, could be appealed to in the cause of transforming society" (ibid. 20).

Even Panikkar, who argues against human rights as a universal term, concurs that "dharma (dhamma) is perhaps the most fundamental word in the Indian tradition which could lead us to the discovery of

a possible homeomorphic symbol corresponding to the Western notion of 'Human Rights,'" and that "a reflection at the level of dharma
may help us find our footing on a common ground" (Panikkar 1982,
95). He explains that "dharma is that which maintains, gives cohesion
and thus strength to any given thing, to reality" and that "dharma is
primordial" (ibid. 96). (He observes that the root is *dhr*: to hold, to
maintain, keep together. Cf. Latin *tenere* and English *tenet*.) Therefore,
in contrast to the West, he argues that "a world in which the notion
of dharma is central and nearly all pervasive is not concerned with
finding the 'right' of one individual against another or of the individual
vis-a-vis society." Rather, the Eastern view is concerned "with assaying
the *dharmic* (*right, true,* consistent . . .) or *adharmic* character of a thing
or an action within the entire theanthropocosmic complex of reality"
(ibid.).

Panikkar also observes that "there is no universal dharma above and
independent of the svadharma," which he describes as "the dharma
which is inherent in every being" (ibid.). Therefore, he agrees that "the
homeomorphic equivalent [to human rights] is svadharma." He concludes that "in order to have a just society, the modern West stresses
the notion of Human Rights. In order to have a dharmic order, classical India stresses the notion of *svadharma*" (ibid. 97).

Thus, while the term human rights is not traditionally within
Hinduism, and while some would argue that there can be no true universal concepts that operate among religions, I contend that the concept of human rights can function in Eastern traditions, and its intent
is expressed in various other terms such as in the concept of dharma.
Yet, in contrast to the West, the Eastern worldview does not traditionally highlight the advocacy for the human rights of certain groups
or individuals, such as the poor and marginalized. While advocating
charity for the poor, the emphasis on overcoming injustices on their
behalf is more elusive traditionally in the East.

2. HINDUISM AND THE POOR

Mark Juergensmeyer writes that "if by 'human rights' one means minority rights, then Hindu society can be said to have a human rights
tradition, for it has always had a way of incorporating the poor and
socially ostracized into the social whole" (Cited in Traer 1991, 129).
While they may have been incorporated, however, their overall status
as poor does not traditionally seem to be challenged or overturned. On

the one hand, the Hindu notions of karma and reincarnation reflect a view of a just universe, where those who were true to their dharma and built up good karma in one life were reborn into a higher life form or caste in the next. Thus, the poor and outcast were largely seen as meriting their station in life, and by their own efforts they could overcome it in future lives. On the other hand, compassion, charity and ahimsa are a part of the tradition, as well as the association of the individual soul with the divinity itself.

The concept of ahimsa was adopted from the Jains. The *Tattvarthasutra* of Jainism states that one should "have benevolence toward all living beings, joy at the sight of the virtuous, compassion and sympathy for the afflicted, and tolerance towards the indolent and ill-behaved" (*Tattvarthasutra* 7.11, cited in Wilson 1995, 684). This emphasis is also contained within Hinduism.

In the *Bhagavad Gita*, Krishna explains to Arjuna that

> Every selfless act, Arjuna, is born from the eternal, infinite Godhead. God is present in every act of service. All life turns on this law, O Arjuna. Whoever violates it, indulging his senses for his own pleasure and ignoring the needs of others, has wasted his life. But those who realize the God within are always satisfied.

This passage continues that "the ignorant work for their own profit, Arjuna; the wise work for the welfare of the world, without thought to themselves … . Perform all work carefully, guided by compassion" (*Bhagavad Gita* 3.10-26, cited in ibid. 689). The earlier *Rig Veda* states that "He who gives liberally goes straight to the gods; on the high ridge of heaven he stands exalted" (*Rig Veda* 1.125.5, cited in ibid. 694).

Yet it was Gandhi who most profoundly took modern Hinduism from charity toward the poor to political action on behalf of the poor, stating that "those who say that religion has nothing to do with politics do not know what religion means" (Gandhi 1995, 53). His association with the poorest of the poor, the Untouchables who he renamed Harijans, led to the legal abolishment of untouchability, although it still exists socially. He admonished that "You Hindus, are believers in *abheda* [i.e., absence of essential difference between one creature and another]. How can you regard a human being an untouchable? Are you not ashamed of this ostracism?" (Cited in Chatterjee 1983, 31 [brackets Chatterjee's]).

Gandhi is noteworthy for his reinterpretation of traditional Hindu concepts in light of the human rights of the poor. Thus, he serves as an example of one who could take traditional concepts within an Eastern religion, and reconcile their intent with the modern Western language of human rights. Chatterjee observes that, for Gandhi, "the karma theory and serving the lowly are perfectly compatible" (Chatterjee 1983, 24). She explains that Gandhi "thought of action not as a way of undoing past *karma*, of accumulating merit, … but as a matter of pressing concern in *this* life, a life in which our main duty was to alleviate the miseries of others so that they could fulfill their own destiny" (ibid. 27). In addition, she states that Gandhi frequently quoted the writings of the saints, including "a line from Surdas, the blind mediaeval saint-bard, saying that 'the essence of our religious books can be boiled down into the simple adage: 'Nibala ka bala Ram, (God is the strength of the helpless and weak)'" (ibid.).

Chatterjee explains that in Gandhi's idea of service "there is an echo here … of Swami Vivekananda's concept of *Daridranarayan*, or 'My God the Poor'" (ibid.) Gandhi also reminded others of the *Ksatriya* (warrior caste) virtue of protection of women and the poor (ibid. 38). Chatterjee states that, for Gandhi, "*bhakti* speaks of the law of love which enables us to respond to those in need, [and] *karma* is the path not just of action but of *service*," which is "not for the maintenance of the stability of society as it is, … but in order to *transform* it in accordance with the vision of a new society" (ibid. 39). In addition, she points to "his own conviction that if all living creatures are bound together in one great chain of existence the liberation of each is tied up with the liberation of all" (ibid. 34).

A. Pushparajan observes that "if the individual soul (the *atman*) of a caste Hindu is the same as the cosmic soul (the *brahman*) as the advaitin would have it, so is the *atman* of the outcaste too" (Pushparajan 1983, 395). Pushparajan sees the oppression of the Harijans as a moral problem rooted in a "non-recognition of human dignity" (ibid. 394). He argues that "caste Hindus have failed to recognize and refused to give to Harijans the dignity a human being deserves," and that "the 'outcaste' himself did not recognize his own dignity as a person" (ibid.).

In Gandhi's advocacy for the Harijans, Hinduism's concern for human dignity and for the poor are brought to its fullest modern fruition. In addition, it must be noted that while Gandhi's promotion of human rights did draw from Western concepts, including Christianity, it also drew most passionately for him from within Hinduism itself. Thus, *from a practical standpoint, Gandhi's views offer an example of modern Hinduism, and an Eastern worldview, being compatible with the modern concept of human rights.*

1.5: CONCLUSION

I have pointed out in this chapter that the language of human rights poses problems for religion in general and religions in particular. The language itself is modern, and is not traditionally contained within specific traditions. Yet, this problem can be overcome by realizing that the language of human rights can express the intent of many religions, which in different ways value the individual and argue against their mistreatment and abuse. In addition, they speak of human fulfillment and of the importance of community, which ties rights to the language of duties.

This chapter has offered a brief historical sketch of the development of the concept of human rights, and has articulated its current use politically. It has also addressed the major general issues in the discussion of human rights and religions. This includes some fundamental differences between Eastern and Western traditions. However, it has also noted similar concerns and values in particular religions, East as well as West. This is evidenced in specific social justice issues such as a concern for "the poor" and marginalized, and in general issues such as the value of the individual and the importance of the community. Therefore, I assert that the concept of "human rights," and a general concern for social justice, are apparent in the major world religions, East as well as West.

In the next chapter, the issue of human rights within Buddhism will be examined in detail. As with Hinduism, on the surface there appear to be many problematic concepts within Buddhism for the concept of human rights. These include the concepts of *anatta* (nonself) and *paticca samuppada* (dependent co-arising). Yet, much like Gandhi in Hinduism, many Buddhist reformers are advocating that these concepts can actually *contribute to* the discussion of human rights, rather than detracting from it. Having examined the concept of human rights in religion in general, and stressing the importance of religion to the dialogue on human rights, I now focus on the concept of human rights within Buddhism and Roman Catholicism.

CHAPTER 2

HUMAN RIGHTS AND THE INDIVIDUAL
IN CURRENT BUDDHIST THOUGHT

2.1: INTRODUCTION

This chapter brings us to the specific examination of Buddhism, and whether the concept of human rights can be said to apply or hold any validity within that system. With its unique concepts of God, the human being, and reality itself, Buddhism often appears to be radically opposed to basic religious assumptions and beliefs within other traditions. Hence, this is part of the value I see in comparing it with previous traditions in Chapter One and with Roman Catholicism in the remainder of this study, all of which are more "theistic" in their approach than Buddhism. Because of its beliefs and history, there is considerable debate whether the term "human rights" applies within the Buddhist tradition. However, if it does apply within this system, it gives considerable credence to the thesis which I am putting forward that the term "human rights" can be seen as a universal term which can apply toward a global ethic.

But first, a few parameters must be set. Although I address "Buddhism," I do not assume that Buddhism is a monolithic tradition. The religion itself contains different major traditions. These traditions include Theravada ("the tradition of the elders"), the oldest form of Buddhism which is found primarily in Sri Lanka and Southeast Asia. A less complimentary term for this tradition is Hinayana ("the Lesser Vehicle"). Mahayana ("the Greater Vehicle") is found primarily in Northeast Asia, and incorporates more traditional religious practices than Theravada. However, it also incorporates Zen, a reform movement within that tradition which rejects most of those practices. Finally, Vajrayana is the unique form of Buddhism found in Tibet. Each of these traditions contain various schools within themselves.

While this book does acknowledge as well that "there are at least as many conceptual difficulties in the definition 'Buddhism' as there are

in the definition of 'religion'" (J. Smith 1995, 149), it does also recognize that for many centuries "Buddhist philosophers have spoken
of the 'essence' or 'heart' of the tradition (often identified as the doctrine of no-self or emptiness)" (ibid. 150). James S. Dalton observes
that "most scholars would argue that they are expressions of a single
tradition that shares the fundamental starting points of the Buddha:
the *Dharma* (the teachings of the Buddha and its sacred, saving reality) and the *Sangha* (the Buddhist community, especially the monastic
community)" (Dalton 1999, 35).

Hans Wolfgang Schumann, a German scholar and diplomat to
India, articulates more specifically the common elements within the
teachings themselves. He argues that "the characteristic features of all
Buddhist schools are 1) the evaluation of individual existence as sorrowful and consequently requiring deliverance, 2) the belief in rebirth,
3) the assumption of a moral natural law which rules the process of
karma and rebirth and was neither created by a deity nor is supervised
by him, and 4) the view that the phenomenal world is without substance and in a constant flux." He continues that "analogous to this 5)
the empirical person is considered as without Self and as a complex of
soulless factors, with which 6) the goal of extinction of the sorrowful
personality is logically connected." He adds that "further characteristics are 7) the conviction that liberation is only achievable through the
extirpation of greed, hatred and delusion and by gaining enlightenment (= wisdom) and lastly 8) faithful confidence in the Buddhas, be
they regarded as human teachers, supermen or transcendent beings."
Schumann concludes that "any doctrine which possesses *all* these features must be called Buddhistic" (Schumann 1974, 94).

I, then, focus on common elements within Buddhism, and primarily use the term "Buddhism." Specific traditions and teachings within
those traditions are noted where applicable. Since this study addresses
current Buddhist thought on the issue of human rights, this gener-
alization of "Buddhism" is further legitimized by the fact that most
current writings on the subject of human rights and Buddhism do not
delineate between different schools or traditions of Buddhism. Hence,
most of the research itself is addressed to the issue of human rights in
Buddhism in general.

Damien Keown explains that the justification for this "lies in the
belief that whatever concept of human rights we regard Buddhism
as holding must be one which is universal in form." He observes that

"it would be as strange to have distinct 'Theravada,' 'Tibetan' and 'Zen' doctrines of human rights as it would be to have 'Catholic,' 'Protestant' and 'Eastern Orthodox' ones." Keown argues that "to insist on the priority of cultural and historical circumstances would be tantamount to denying the validity of human rights as a concept" (Keown 1998, 17).

In the next section, I focus on the concept of *anatta* (nonself), a concept which is key in trying to understand the Buddhist perception of the "individual" or "self." This will occupy a major portion of the chapter. A related concept which I address is the Buddhist concept of interconnectedness of all reality: *paticca-samuppada* or dependent co-arising. (This concept will also be examined in Chapter Four with respect to its implications for Buddhism and ecology.) These two concepts form the distinct and radical Buddhist view of the self and reality in general, and are those which are primarily drawn upon to refute the compatibility of the concept of human rights with Buddhism. Hence, they will occupy a considerable amount of this chapter.

Section 2.3 examines the Mahayana doctrine of Buddha Nature and its complementary concept of Emptiness, or *Sunyata*. Both of these are further developments of and offer elaboration and insight into the original concepts of *anatta* and *paticca-samuppada*. Section 2.4 notes dissent with as well as support for the concept of human rights within Buddhism, based primarily on the above concepts. It also ties in elements from within Buddhist ethics which contribute to thoughts on human rights. Section 2.5 examines the issue of human rights within Buddhism from the perspective of social justice, looking at Buddhism's perception of the poor but also at current socially engaged Buddhists and their struggle for Buddhist social activism on the issue of human rights. Finally, I offer some concluding remarks on the concept of human rights within Buddhism and suggest connections between socially engaged Buddhism and Catholic liberation theology.

In early Buddhism, the rejection of the caste system and of the need for countless rebirths freed one from the hierarchical concepts of duties which were more pronounced throughout the Hindu tradition. While retaining the concept of *dharma* as duty, the concept in Buddhism was expanded to include the Buddha's teachings themselves and the Buddhist way of life in general. Robert Traer observes that the "Buddha transformed attitudes of respect and obedience contained in the ethnic Hindu notion of *dharma* into a universal morality." He continues that "by admitting members of lower castes and women into the

Bhikshu Sangha, the Buddha took 'concrete steps to destroy the gospel of inequality'" (Traer 1991,134 [End quote from B.R. Ambedkar in Traer]). (It must be noted, however, that Buddhism held misogynist views in its history as other religions have. The Buddha, for example, only sanctioned an order of nuns after much pleading from others, and regretted that now the demise of Buddhism would occur within 500 years rather than 1,000! [see Cabezon 1992 and Paul 1985]).

Yet, Masao Abe notes that "the exact equivalent of the phrase 'human rights' in the Western sense cannot be found anywhere in Buddhist literature" (Abe cited in Traer 1991, 134). And Winston King argues that even the more general concept of a social ethic is nowhere to be found in Buddhism (W. King 1964, 176). These are some of the concerns which I will address. And while these critiques may be true to some degree in a literal sense, an assessment of the possibility of a Buddhist notion of human rights must take into account unique concepts within Buddhism which affect its view of the self, society, and the world in general. These are the concepts of *anatta* (non-self) and *paticca-samuppada* (dependent co-arising).

In addition, the emphasis on the Buddha *dharma* as a way of viewing reality (right understanding) and as a way of life highlights the strong ties between one's inner frame of mind, spirituality, and intention, on one hand, and one's outer ethical conduct, on the other hand. Both aspects are fundamental to the Buddhist way of life, and highlight the practical aspect of Buddhism and Buddhist ethics.

The Harper Collins Dictionary of Religion explains that "the practical dimension of Buddhist philosophy is illustrated by a story about an encounter between the Buddha and a disciple named Malunkyaputta." This is the famous poison arrow parable, where Malunkyaputta argues that he will not take up the religious life until the Buddha answers the following metaphysical questions: "Is the universe eternal? Is the universe finite? Is the soul identical to the body? Does the Buddha exist after death?" The Buddha responds:

> Suppose that a man is shot by a poisoned arrow. When his friends bring him to a surgeon, he refuses to let the surgeon pull out the arrow until he knows who shot the arrow, what kind of bow was used to shoot it, and what the arrow was made of. That man would die before he could know any of those things. The same is true of someone who refuses to live the religious life until he knows the answers to your questions.

The parable shows the Buddha's apparent lack of concern for metaphysical, ontological questions and his concern for practical and ethical ones. It also focuses on the basic Buddhist view of reality as suffering and the basic Buddhist purpose of overcoming suffering. The parable "is taken to mean that philosophy should be pursued with a practical intent: to remove the illusions that generate suffering." And, in this regard, "the greatest of these illusions is the conviction that there is a permanent self (atman)" (J. Smith 1995, 163 [see also Burtt 1982, 32-36]). It is this Buddhist concept of self which I address next.

2.2: THE INDIVIDUAL AND THE CONCEPT OF ANATTA (NONSELF)

A. ANATTA

Frank Reynolds and Robert Campany observe that "one way of characterizing the Buddhist ethical tradition is to note the close association between the central Buddhist insight into reality as 'selfless' (anatman) or 'empty' (sunya) on the one hand, and authentic moral activity on the other." They explain that "in most Buddhist traditions the two are considered to be complementary and reciprocal. Insight into selflessness or emptiness informs moral activity, while moral activity supports the cultivation of insight" (Eliade 1987, 498). In addition, Masao Abe emphasizes that "in any religion, particularly in Buddhism, human rights and human freedom cannot be legitimately grasped without a proper understanding of the problem of self" (Abe 1995, 145). Hence, the need arises to address the Buddhist concept of self (as 'nonself') as a component of the overall Buddhist view of reality.

In Hinduism, out of which Buddhism grew, the atman was the concept of "soul" or "self" which was reincarnated, and which in actuality was of the same essence as the ultimate reality, Brahman. P. H. Ashby explains that "atman (Self) had come to be used in reference to Brahman, and it was also in common usage a reference to the intrinsic human self." Thus, the classical formulation that "atman equals Brahman, Brahman equals atman, 'That art thou' (tat tvam asi)." Ashby points out that, although "later Hindu thinkers were to give various interpretations to the nature of this human self (atman) and its relationship to the ultimate Self (Brahman)," these interpretations generally acknowledged that if there was not an absolute identity between the two, there was at least a close relationship (Crim 1981, 309).

The Buddha, however, took this formulation one step further, arguing that if the self is truly Brahman, then there is really no self at all. K. K. S. Chen reminds us that the Hindu "Upanishads taught that the true self of man is the universal self, and that as soon as one realizes this unity, one becomes emancipated." In contrast to this, "such a belief in the permanence of a self was held by the Buddha to be a pernicious error, as it gives rise to attachment, ... and this binds the individual to further rebirth and suffering" (ibid. 127).

The historical Buddha's search for enlightenment began with the shock of seeing suffering for the first time, in the form of sickness, old age and death. Thus, in Buddhism, "to take the right view of things is to hold to the truths that all existence is suffering (*Dukkha*), all existence is impermanent (*Anicca*), and there is no permanent self or soul (*Anatta*)" (ibid.). This is fundamental to the Buddhist view of reality. Schumann explains further that this definition "which came into existence after the Buddha's death classifies threefold: Suffering resulting from pain (*dukkha-dukkha*), suffering from change or impermanence (*viparinama-dukkha*), and suffering arising out of the personality-components (*sankhara-dukkha*)" (Schumann 1974, 41).

Schumann points out that "*dukkha* in Buddhism is a philosophical term. Whatever is subject to the cycle (*samsara*) of becoming and passing, is suffering" (ibid.). Sue Hamilton contends that a better understanding of *dukkha* is "unsatisfactoriness." She asserts that "it is much more of a profound term than just suffering, and applies to every aspect of human existence, not just the parts of it that are overtly unpleasant." She explains that "it means that nothing within the human condition, the cycle of rebirth, is *ultimately* satisfactory, nothing can be seen as offering a permanent satisfactory answer to our needs" (Hamilton 1995, 48). This is seen in the formulation of the Four Noble Truths, which begin with 1) All life is suffering, and continue that 2) Suffering results from desire or greed, 3) Suffering ceases when desire ceases, 4) the cure lies in following the Eightfold Path. This perception of the Buddha is seen as not being pessimistic, but rather realistic and practical, as in the above mentioned parable of the poisoned arrow.

Hammalawa Saddhatissa observes that "the *anatta* doctrine is counted among the three characteristics of existence as put forward in the Buddha's teaching," and that these three "are essentially present in all teachings claiming to be Buddhist" (Saddhatissa 1997, 23). He notes that, according to the *Dhammapada*:

'All mental and physical phenomena are impermanent.' Whenever through wisdom one perceives this, then one becomes dispassionate towards suffering. This is the road to purity. 'All mental and physical phenomena are painful.' Whenever through wisdom one perceives this, then one becomes dispassionate towards suffering. This is the road to purity. 'All things are without self.' Whenever through wisdom one perceives this, then one becomes dispassionate towards suffering. This is the road to purity (*Dhammapada*, vv. 277, 278, 279, cited in ibid.).

Anatman is the Sanskrit term in Hinduism and Buddhism for the negation of the *atman* or soul, hence *an-atman*. The vernacular Pali term in Buddhism is *anatta*. Anthony Fernando and Leonard Swidler explain that "it is composed of the negating prefix *a* and the term *atta*." They point out that the term *atta* has two different meanings and usages. In Pali, the most common usage would be a reflexive pronoun with a distributive connotation, such as "one," "oneself," or "each one," or adjectivally such as "of one's own" (Fernando and Swidler 1985, 58). The second usage, they explain, "is restricted to the language of philosophy, principally metaphysics" and in that sense "it commonly refers to the 'soul'" or can also be translated as "self" or "individuality" (ibid. 59).

What, then, is the self, the human person? Schumann points out that "in Buddhism the question of what man is is always answered by the enumeration of the Five Groups of Grasping (*upadana-Kkhanda*)" (Schumann 1974, 42). Given the Buddhist concepts of nonself and impermanence, the person is perceived as being a collection of elements, always changing, with no fixed, true or eternal "self."

The *Majjhimanikaya* reads:

And which, monks, are in brief the Five Groups of Grasping which are sorrowful?:
The Group of Grasping 'body' (*rupa*),
the Group of Grasping 'sensation' (*vedana*),
the Group of Grasping 'perception' (*sanna*),
the Group of Grasping 'mental phenomena' (*sankhara*),
the Group of Grasping 'consciousness' (*vinnana*) (*Majjhimanikaya* 141 III p. 250, cited in ibid.).

Schumann explains that "'Body' (literally 'form') means the physical frame of man" and that "the remaining four non-physical groups or components of the person are collectively called 'name' (*nama*)."

He elaborates further that "'sensations' are the sense-impressions, the contacts of the sense-organs with objects of the external world. When these have been picked up by the brain and become reflections in the head of the observer, they are called 'perceptions.'" He continues that "they produce in man reactions which the Buddha collectively labels 'mental phenomena': notions, ideals, longings, moods, etc." (Schumann 1974, 42). Finally, 'consciousness' is "the accumulative element which collects the mental phenomena" and "is repeatedly interpreted as sense-consciousness" which earlier texts identified as "mind" or "thought" (ibid. 43).

Schumann explains that while the Pali texts do not specifically pose the question whether there is "something belonging to personality beyond the groups," nevertheless he emphasizes that "in Buddhism, man is always analysed into the Five Groups and only into these" (ibid.). Schumann notes that "they are called Groups of 'Grasping' (upadana) because every undelivered being grasps, that is appropriates, them at the moment of rebirth as his new personality" (ibid. 42).

The Buddha replied that:

> There is, monk, no body whatsoever which is permanent, fixed, lasting, not subject to the law of decay (and) forever remaining the same.
> There is, monk, no sensation whatsoever ... , no perception whatsoever ... , no mental phenomenon whatsoever..., no consciousness whatsoever which is permanent, fixed, lasting, not subject to the law of decay (and) forever the same (Samyuttanikaya 22, 97, 9-13 III p.147, cited in ibid.).

Schumann asserts that "the impermanence of the Five Groups, that is of the personality, as well as the temporariness of all things, forms a central theme in Buddhist literature" (Schumann 1974, 43). In the Majjhimanikaya, the Buddha asks:

> Is it right then to regard that which is impermanent, sorrowful, subject to the law of decay, as 'This is mine,' this am I, this is my Self'?

to which the monks reply "Surely not, Sir" (Majjhimanikaya 22 I p.138). (Cited in ibid. 44).

Fernando and Swidler emphasize that "for Gautama there was nothing so detrimental and so harmful to a human being's achievement of true nobility as the blind adherence to the 'self' that he termed the 'Five Aggregates.'" They assert that "he spoke against it so vehemently and so incessantly that without any hesitation we have to say that his religious philosophy was basically one of 'no-self' or 'anti-self'" (Fernando and Swidler 1985, 67).

How then should one view the individual human being, the "person"? One famous analogy was that of the chariot in *The Questions of King Milinda (Milindapanha)*. In contrast to the analogy which viewed the person as a chariot (the body) controlled by a charioteer (the soul or true self), the Buddhist analogy viewed the person as the chariot itself, as a collection of various parts which one labels "chariot." Winston King observes that "at the end of a long discussion, the monk Nagasena and King Milinda come to the conclusion that just as the term 'chariot' is only a way of naming a collection of particular items, so too is the term for 'human being.'" He continues that "human being signifies only a loosely joined set of physical body-parts; or more inclusively, five temporarily connected 'heaps' (*Skandhas*)" (Crim 1981, 30).

Schumann offers another analogy. He suggests that "man is comparable to a melody. No single sound or chord possesses duration and emotional value, but the continuous succession of sounds produces the phenomenon of a melody" (Schumann 1974, 122). Just as a melody is a unique collection of sound at a moment in time and space, so too is the human being an impermanent collection at a point in time and space, and always changing.

What, then, becomes reincarnated? Chen explains that "the Buddha taught that at death the five aggregates which constitute the living being disintegrate." However, he continues that "the karma which that living being had accumulated in the past does not perish but must bear fruit in the rebirth of a new living being which is not the same as the former living being but which is not different either," since "the new living being has inherited the karma of the previous one" (Crim 1981, 127). The Buddha gave the example of a flame passing from one candle to another, or the example of a river, "which appears to maintain one constant form, though the water of the river at any one point is always changing (ibid.). Schumann offers the analogy of a series of billiard balls, where energy passes from one ball to another to another but the original ball hit is not the final ball which ends up in the pocket (Schumann 1974, 58).

But, in the end, is this nihilism? Saddhatissa poses the question that "if for Buddhism there was to be no Brahman, no god, no inherent

self, did the whole spell complete annihilation?" He argues that "this
the Buddha repudiated entirely," arguing instead that "the goal is completely unconditioned, and to attempt to describe it in terms of the
conditioned state that we know at present is ... futile" (Saddhatissa
1997, 13).

Saddhatissa explains that "the Buddha compared this state of affairs
to that of a man who declared himself in love with a beautiful woman
whom he had never seen and whose appearance and lineage he knew
nothing whatever about." Hence, Saddhatissa concludes that "if then
we have no details of the state of happiness, other than that it is happy,
it remains only to consider what things give rise to unhappiness and
to avoid them" (ibid. 14). This again points to the practical aspect of
Buddhist ethical thought, as well as to the common use of negative
language in its terms.

This final unconditioned state refers to Nirvana, which lies beyond
the scope of this study. However, the issue of language is briefly addressed in the section on current perceptions of the concept of anatta.
I raise it here to show that the doctrine of anatta did not lead to a
nihilistic view of reality. While reality was not seen as being created
or controlled by a good God, there was perceived to be that which
is good ("the lovely") as well as a purpose and meaning to life itself,
which supported an ethical way of life. Richard Henry Drummond
emphasizes that "the word anatman (Pali: anatta), which appears in
the early texts and means 'not-self' or 'non-self,' is, as commonly found
in early Buddhism, a negative term employed to teach positive truth"
(Drummond 1995, 51).

But this is entering into the realm of interpretation of the anatta
concept, which I will take up shortly, along with perceptions of the
anatta doctrine in light of the concept of human rights. But first, I
would like to take a very brief look at a related doctrine, that of paticca-
samuppada, or dependent co-arising. (I am using the Pali term paticca-
samuppada, rather than the Sanskrit pratitya-samutpada, because it is
the more prevalent term used in current Buddhist scholarly literature
on the issues of human rights and ecology. I also focus more on the
Pali, and hence Theravada, interpretations of anatta.) Along with
anatta, this concept forms the unique Buddhist worldview, and any
discussion of anatta would be incomplete without understanding how
the concept of paticca-samuppada interacts with it.

Japanese Zen Master Dogen Zenji (1200-1253 C.E.), founder of the Japanese Soto school of Zen, wrote that:

> To study the Buddha way is to study the self.
> To study the self is to forget the self.
> To forget the self is to be actualized by myriad things (Cited in Kaza 1993, 54).

Having briefly defined the Buddhist concept of self, I would now like to turn to how it relates to, and interacts with, these other "myriad things," the rest of reality.

B. PATICCA-SAMUPPADA (DEPENDENT CO-ARISING)

For the Buddha, refusal to speculate on metaphysical beings, existence and the observation of reality itself led him to refrain from speculating on a First Cause of all beings, as Thomas Aquinas did in medieval Catholic thought. Gautama simply observed that all things are the product of a myriad variety of causes, thus forming a chain or web of causation. This concept ties in with the Buddhist concept of the individual human being, or *anatta*.

Chen observes that "right view" in Buddhism included not only the truths of suffering, impermanence and anatta, "but also a correct understanding of the chain of causation (*Paticca samuppada*), or the formula of dependent origination." He explains that "the Buddha enunciated this formula to emphasize the truth that events follow one another in regular sequence and not just by chance or by the arbitrary will of a divine agent" (Crim 1981, 128).

The scripture reads:

> I will teach you the doctrine, when this exists, that exists;
> with the arising of that, this arises;
> when this does not exist, that does not exist,
> with the cessation of that, this ceases (*Majjhima Nikaya* 3.63, cited in ibid.).

Chen explains that "the formula conveys the idea that no phenomenon in the universe is isolated and without cause but is linked with every other phenomenon" (ibid.).

This doctrine, referred to as dependent co-arising or the Nexus of Conditioned Origination or dependent origination, is *paticca samuppada* in Pali and *pratitya samutpada* in Sanskrit (Fernando and Swidler 1985, 33). Kaza explains that "*paticca* means 'grounded on or on account of,' *sam* is 'together,' and *uppada* means 'arising.' Thus the whole phrase can be translated 'the being-on-account-of-arising-to-gether.'" She comments that, in this view, "all events and beings are interdependent and interrelated. The universe is described as a mutually causal web of relationships, each action and individual contributing to the nature of many others" (Kaza 1993, 57).

This concept, then, has profound ramifications for the Buddhist concept of "person" or anatta. Schumann observes that, *in Buddhism, "existence is a process of fluctuation, not being"* (Schumann 1974, 64 [italics mine]). I will return to this point in the next section on current perceptions of the anatta concept. The point here is that the Buddha is not concerned with speculation on the nature of things, with Being itself (as in Thomas Aquinas, for example), but with practical steps to take to overcome suffering. Therefore, the concept of a chain or web of causes is integral to understanding the Buddhist concept of anatta. Schumann strongly asserts that *"Nexus of Conditioned Origination= empirical person= suffering – this is the formula which underlies the Buddhist conception of man"* (ibid. [italics mine]). He continues that the truth of human existence, therefore, "lies in between identity and isolation: In conditional dependence" (ibid. 65). This is typical of the Buddhist tendency to adhere to a "Middle Path" between two extremes or polar opposites.

Joanna Rogers Macy points out that "the doctrine of *paticca samuppada* or dependent co-arising is fundamental to Buddhist ethics." She explains that, "in this vision of radical relativity, reality appears as an interdependent process wherein change and choice, doer and deed, person and community are mutually causative." She emphasizes that "morality is grounded in this interdependence, as in the corollary Buddhist views of *anatta* and *karma*." In addition, she suggests that "it reveals a reciprocal dynamic between personal and social transformation" (Macy 1979, 38). This final point is important and will be emphasized later in the section on Buddhism and social justice.

This view of interconnectedness also seeks to avoid the duality between spirit and matter, between "soul" or "mind," and "body," in seeking to describe the person. Macy admits that "this refusal to lift consciousness onto another ontological level must have been a tough point for some of his followers to swallow, for the Buddha repeatedly and often with some asperity corrects their tendency to see consciousness as aloof from materiality" (ibid. 46 [She cites as examples the *Majjhima Nikaya* I, 258 and the *Digha Nikaya* II, 83]).

Finally, Macy summarizes that in this vision of dependent co-arising, "reality appears as an interdependent process. All factors, psychic and physical, subsist in a web of mutual causal interaction, with no element or essence held to be immutable or autonomous." She reflects that "our suffering is caused by the interplay of these factors, and particularly by the delusion, aversion and craving that arise from our misapprehension of them" (ibid. 39).

Thus, the doctrine of *paticca-samuppada*, along with the concept of karma and the process of reincarnation, function as somewhat of a check on the *anatta* doctrine becoming an isolationist and nihilistic concept. In effect, it contributes a relational element to the anatta concept. I will return in more detail to the concept of *paticca-samuppada* in the later chapter on Buddhism and ecology, where it has profound ramifications. Having briefly defined the key concepts of *anatta* and *paticca-samuppada*, I would next like to examine current interpretations of the anatta concept.

C. CURRENT INTERPRETATIONS OF THE CONCEPT OF ANATTA

The doctrine of anatta is the one that is used most frequently by those rejecting the compatibility of the concept of human rights with Buddhism. Yet, others cite it as offering greater insight into the concept of human rights, particularly on the communal level. It is a concept which is interpreted in a variety of ways within Buddhism, often conflicting ones. Outside of Buddhism, interpretations seem to vary onto an even wider range, as scholars interpret the doctrine in light of their own religious traditions. While reviewing various interpretations of the doctrine by Buddhists and non-Buddhists, it is important to keep in mind that it is a Buddhist doctrine, and one must be cautious of straying too far from its general interpretation throughout that tradition.

Because the doctrine is so radical, and seems to run so much against our natural inclination toward self-hood and wanting to live forever, the general tendency seems to be to water it down to make it less radical. One could hardly make it more radical unless one resorted to a nihilistic approach to reality, which the Buddha rejected. Therefore, the tendency by some non-Buddhists seems to be to attempt to appropriate a concept of "self" into it. This is even done within Buddhism itself.

The concept of "Buddha-nature" in Mahayana Buddhism appears to be an attempt to apply a more positive term and outlook onto the nihilistic sounding anatta concept. I will examine this briefly later in this chapter.

Christian scholars in particular seem prone to identify the anatta concept with the attitude of selflessness within Christianity. Some argue that anatta is more of an attitude toward self, rather than a denial of self. For example, Drummond argues that "the negative perception that nothing among all the elements of phenomenal existence, either person or things, is ultimately real or worthy of ultimate aspiration is for the sake of a positive reorientation of self" (Drummond 1995, 45). He continues his discussion of anatta and concludes that "this is to say that the human self in its true condition is not describable by the language normally used to describe the empirical human self, but it is by no means to be denied" (ibid. 54). This raises the issue of whether the self is actually denied, or whether the negative language is used to describe something which is beyond empirical description.

While it is not within the scope of this study to examine the issue of language in describing religious concepts, it is one line of reasoning on the concept of anatta and we will see it reflected in some conclusions concerning it. However, it is important to note that throughout Buddhist history, schools which actually attempted to affirm the reality of "self" were considered "heretics" in the Buddhist sense of that term.

For example, "one of the most important of the early doctrinal controversies had to do with the existence of a 'person'(pudgala)." It is noteworthy that "in the third century B.C., about two hundred years after the death of the Buddha, a school known as the Vatsiputriyas claimed that, while there is no 'self' (atman), there is something called the 'person' that continues from one life to the next." The other schools felt that the Vatsiputriyas "were attempting to smuggle the doctrine of the 'self' back into Buddhist teaching," and "the doctrine of the 'person' was eventually rejected by the vast majority of Buddhist schools," although this was "not without considerable controversy" (J. Smith 1995, 164).

T. O. Ling points out that, while there is really no equivalent of the term "heresy" in Buddhism, the "nearest approximation is ditthi (Pali), drsti (Sanskrit), literally a view, usually a 'wrong' view, that is due not to reason but to craving or desire (tanha)." He emphasizes that "the most serious form of *ditthi* is to assert the reality and permanence of the individual human ego, i.e., the assertion of atman." He continues that this view "was maintained by certain Buddhists known as Pudgala-Vadins," and that these monks maintained their existence until the 7th century C.E., when they amounted to about a quarter of the Buddhist monks in India. He observes that "they were regarded by all other Buddhist schools of thought as weaker brethren, and in error," and that the general attitude toward them was that "more prolonged meditation would eventually cause them to see error involved in this view, and its abandonment" (Ling cited in Abe 1986b, 198). Thus, it appears that strong affirmation of the reality of "self" was seen as incongruent with the Buddha's original teachings.

Although terms such as "I," "mine," and "one's-self" are used in the scriptures, Steven Collins notes that this is explained by the differentiation between "conventional" or "worldly" talk and that of ultimate truth. Collins points out that this differentiation was used "to explain how the Buddha and other enlightened men could see the truth of not-self but nevertheless continue to use ordinary language with its personal pronouns, adjectives, and so on" (Collins 1982, 265).[1] He maintains, however, that "whenever there is any explicit question of the 'ultimate truth,' it is always and unambiguously denied that any self ultimately or really exists" (ibid. 253).

Mahathera Walpola Rahula argues from within the Theravada tradition that it is "curious that recently there should have been a vain attempt by a few scholars to smuggle the idea of a self into the teaching of the Buddha, quite contrary to the spirit of Buddhism." He asserts that, "as far as we can see from the extant original texts," the Buddha never accepted the idea, and that if he had believed in God and a Soul, "he certainly would have declared them publicly" (Rahula cited in ibid. 255). Tenzin Gyatso, the fourteenth Dali Lama, argues that "the assumed independent existence of the atman after one has searched for

---

1   This article is a review of J. Perez-Remon's book, *Self and Non-Self in Early Buddhism*, Religion and Reason Series 22, (The Hague: Mouton, 1981). Collins is extremely critical of Perez-Remon's approach, which he feels is too accommodating to establish the reality of a self, and not in line with the general Buddhist tradition. Sallie B. King, in her text on Buddha Nature, bases some of her approach on Perez-Ramon, perhaps showing the Mahayana tendency to see anatta in a more positive light (see S. King, 1991, 139).

it both within and without the five heaps [the skandhas...] must be seen to be non-existent." He contends that "belief in an independent atman (soul) is actually the result of mental activity" and therefore is "proved logically invalid" (Gyatso cited in ibid. [brackets Collin's]).

Winston King offers an interesting description showing the contrast between the "personal" view of reality of Christianity and the Buddhist view of the "person" as illusion. King reflects that, "to the Buddhist, the Christian seems ineradicably trapped in Christianity itself by an all pervasive, totally defeating illusion of a narrowly conceived and largely static self or soul." He continues that "to compound his hopeless, helpless situation he projects personhood onto his ultimate reality, God, and views his salvation as the eternal perpetuation of his selfhood in heaven!" (W. King 1986, 160).

Cyril G. Williams argues that "the Christian is called not to a philosophical refutation of the concept of self but to selflessness in attitude and action." He recalls that "the object of his service are other selves as real as he is, and in his inter-relation-ship with these others, whether deserving or undeserving, he fulfils and finds himself" (Williams 1971, 166). He concludes that, in Buddhism as well as Hinduism, "'selflessness' has metaphysical implications as its primary connotation," while in Christianity "such expressions as 'losing oneself' or 'denying oneself' have a primary moral connotation" (ibid. 167).

These examples have been offered to point out that the Buddha did not affirm the reality of the self, and to caution that we should not rush to do so in our own comparative studies. However, given that, an issue which may also be raised is that questions such as "what happens to a 'person' after death" or "what is it that gets reincarnated or saved" are metaphysical questions, questions which the Buddha generally did not answer. Therefore, we may be asking the wrong questions, and our questions may imply an ontological answer on which the Buddha may not have intended to speculate.

Sue Hamilton offers a nice insight into this issue. She observes that the Buddha does not answer any metaphysical question, noting that "all of these questions are to do with being, questions of existence, ontological questions. The Buddha refuses to answer any of them" (Hamilton 1995, 55). She argues that, when we view the anatta doctrine as an ontological concept, "it is very odd that on the one hand all the main doctrinal teachings other than this one are concerned with *how* things are, and this one alone is concerned with *what* one is." She adds that "all the main doctrinal teachings other than this one are concerned in one way or another with understanding the human condition, not in establishing that the human being doesn't exist," noting that "there is never any suggestion that the experience of *dukkha*, suffering, is unreal" (ibid. 54).

Hamilton contends that "the formula of dependent origination explains how a human being comes to be born, and the *khandha* analysis explains how that human being, having been born, functions." Therefore, she emphasizes that "the constituents are not so much actual parts, but *faculties* or *functions* or *processes*" (ibid. 55 [italics in original]). She concludes that we should be aware that the doctrine of anatta "is most unlikely to have an ontological meaning" (ibid. 57), and that placing this sort of emphasis on it "draws attention away from the fact that the Buddha's central concern is with the reality of the human condition" (ibid. 56).

Schumann agrees, noting that "to the Buddha the question of a Self was insignificant. His thinking did not operate in terms of being and substance but in those of processes of becoming and conditional dependencies" (Schumann 1974, 47). Fernando and Swidler concur that this Indian theory "is not an attempt to explain the composition of the human being ontologically, as the Greek theory is." Rather, "it is an attempt to explain the appetitive or emotional nature of the human being in its sensations and sense perceptions." They continue that "it tries to show how a human being in its act of knowledge invariably becomes a victim of *maya* or illusion" (Fernando and Swidler 1985, 61). They explain that "the doctrine of the Five Aggregates ... , is not an invention of Gautama," and that "he used it exactly as it was commonly understood in the Indian society of his day." It referred to the behavior of human beings on the level of samsara, the cycle of death and rebirth. In India, "it did not undertake to analyze the physical structure of the human being, as did ... the Greek matter-form or body-soul theory" (ibid. 64).

Therefore, they contend that the concept of anatta "refers more to a fashion of life than to the fact of life" (ibid. 57), noting that "what Gautama is underlining here by the use of the term *anatta* is the autonomy-less-ness of an emotion-dominated life" (ibid. 65). In effect, from the original sense of the word *anatta* as "not one's own," Gautama "attached a very insightful nuance to it: 'not one's own because not under one's control'" (ibid. 66).

This "method" approach to anatta, as opposed to an "ontological" approach, is important, and consistent, I feel, with Buddhist teachings in general. While not solving the question of "being" or "nature," it does allow for an ethical and purposeful response to reality, and a practical way to overcome suffering within this life. A few further reflections on the concept of anatta are in order.

Abe reflects on the issue of why we appear, and feel we are, unique individuals on one level, yet why these differentiations eventually break down on an absolute level. He observes that "although we have self-identity in a relative sense, we do not have it in the absolute sense." He elaborates that "on the relative level, all of us have our distinct selfhood; yet, on the absolute level, we have no fixed, substantial selfhood but, rather, equality and solidarity in terms of the realization of non-self" (Abe 1995, 146). He emphasizes that "I am I and not you; you are you and not me. Hence, there is a clear distinction between self and other and, thereby, a clear realization of self identity or selfhood." He admits, though, that the question "is whether this self-identity or selfhood is *absolutely* independent, enduring, and substantial." To this, he concludes that "the answer must be 'no.' For there is no 'I' apart from 'you,' just as there is no 'you' apart from 'I'" (Abe 1986b, 204).

Drummond further emphasizes that "the cessation of craving for things or persons of this world does not mean the cessation of right relationships with persons or of right use of things." Rather, he notes that "the goal is such relationship and use that we are no longer 'hooked' (a term actually used in the texts), infatuated or carried away by them." He concludes that "only then are we free to be unselfishly benevolent and kindly toward other persons and discretely wise with reference to use of things" (Drummond 1995, 46).

In addition, given the Buddhist doctrine of impermanence, Abe reminds us that "in Buddhism, human beings are grasped as a part of all sentient beings or even as a part of all beings, … because both human and nonhuman beings are equally subject to transciency or impermanency" (Abe in Traer 1991, 134). This is where we can see the strong interconnection between the concepts of anatta and paticca-samuppada.

Kenneth Inada suggests that "what the Buddha has done is to point out that the ordinary self which we accept is really a limiting concept which closes the doors for the realization of an open existential nature." He maintains that "to be a self, in short, means to extend beyond itself" (Inada 1982, 72). Philip Eden reflects on the fact that one needs to "begin to consider carefully and systematically all that was necessary for you to be alive in this particular life at this particular time" (Eden, 1996, 269). Once we do that, we can realize that "we are one way in which the universe experiences itself," and that that realization "may help us to dissolve the delusion of self and other" (ibid. 270).

In this section, I have sought to define the key concepts of *anatta* and *paticca-samuppada*, and to show the connection between the two. I have also presented some interpretations of the anatta concept, which will be key in examining it in relation to the concept of human rights. But before looking specifically at the issue of human rights, one additional concept needs brief mention. That is the concept of Buddha-nature, present in the Mahayana tradition, and a refinement on the doctrine of anatta.

2.3: THE INDIVIDUAL AND THE CONCEPT OF BUDDHA-NATURE

A. BUDDHA-NATURE AND EMPTINESS

While the concept of anatta is the one used most frequently in discussions of human rights within Buddhism, another term which enters the discussion is that of "Buddha-nature." The concepts of "Buddha-nature" and "Emptiness (*Sunyata*)" can best be seen as Mahayana refinements or re-interpretations of the concepts of anatta and paticca-samuppada. Thus, references to the term "Buddha-nature" are intertwined with the term "Emptiness." In addition, the term "Buddha-nature" can be seen as an attempt to use more positive terms in interpreting the concept of anatta. This is especially so when "Emptiness (*Sunyata*)" is described as "suchness (*Tathata*)."

Winston King argues that "Mahayana Buddhism to some extent re-established selfhood" in its doctrine "of the Buddha nature as a kind of *true* selfhood found in every man" (Crim 1981, 30). Chen emphasizes as well that in Mahayana Buddhism, "one of the most important doctrines is that every sentient being possesses the Buddha nature and is therefore capable of becoming a Buddha" (ibid. 129).

In Zen (*Ch'an*) Buddhism, the Zen masters "argued that the essence of Buddhism was the inner experience of realizing the Buddha nature within us," and that this was done through meditation (ibid. 130). The Japanese term is *Bussho*, literally "buddha-nature," and "according to the

Zen teaching, every person (like every other sentient being or thing) has, or better, *is* buddha-nature" (Schuhmacher and Woerner 1994, 56). Phillip Kapleau contends that "buddha-nature (also dharma-nature, *hossho*) is identical with that which is called emptiness (Japanese, *ku*; Sanskrit, *shunyata*)." He argues that "the true substance of things, that is, their Buddha – or Dharma-nature, is inconceivable and inscrutable." However, "while Buddha-nature is beyond all conception and imagination, because we ourselves are intrinsically Buddha-nature, it is possible for us to awaken to it" (Kapleau cited in ibid.).

One way to view a distinction between the Mahayana concept of Buddha-nature and the Theravada concept of anatta is to see the concept of anatta as primarily relating to the concept of impermanence, whereas the concept of Buddha-nature is relating to the concept of emptiness (McKeon 1999), especially when it is described as "suchness" (*Tathata* or as-it-is-ness) (Abe 1986b, 195). Although there is no real "school" of Buddha-nature, and it is not fully developed as an Indian concept, it makes its way into Buddhism from China, where the concept of emptiness was also influenced by the Taoist understanding of Tao as nonbeing (J. Smith 1995, 338). In general, though, the Mahayana Buddhists were concerned that the anatta concept sounded too nihilistic.

Closely related to the concept of Buddha-nature is the concept of emptiness. Chen explains how the Mahayana concept of emptiness is derived from the concept of *paticca-samuppada* in the Theravada tradition. He reminds us that, "according to the Theravada teaching of dependent origination, all phenomena are conditioned; that is, they come into existence as a result of causes and conditions." He explains that "according to the theory of momentary existence, each element comes into existence for a brief moment and then disappears." Therefore, "the Hinayana claims these elements are real in that they exist, even though for the briefest moment" (Crim 1981, 129).

On the other hand, the earliest Mahayana sutras (known as the Wisdom Sutras, which probably date back to the First Century C.E.) "attacked this viewpoint that the *dharmas* are real and exist for a moment" (ibid.). Rather, they insisted that "the *dharmas* are empty and void, because they have to depend on causes and conditions for their existence." In other words, "take away the causes and conditions and the *dharmas* do not exist." Therefore, Chen explains that "they do not possess their own self-nature, they are empty of their own being, hence they are said to be empty or void (*sunya*)," and that "*Sunyata*, emptiness, is the mark of all the *dharmas*" (ibid.).

Chen observes that "the doctrine of emptiness stressed in the Wisdom Sutras was picked up and elaborated in greater details by Nagarjuna, the famous Mahayana philosopher who lived during the second century A.D. and who founded the Madhyamika School, or the School of the Middle Path" (ibid. 130). For Nagarjuna, emptiness could be understood through a doctrine of two truths, whereby "when reality is viewed from the ultimate perspective, by asking whether anything has an identity (*svabhava*) of its own, everything is seen as empty," but "when reality is viewed from the conventional perspective, … things can serve a useful function" (J. Smith 1995, 337).

In general, though, in the Mahayana scriptures, the concept of emptiness is approached in two different ways. On the one hand, "some Mahayana scriptures approach the doctrine of emptiness in a negative way and portray it simply as the denial of any real distinction between two things," while, on the other hand, "other Mahayana scriptures use a positive approach and focus not simply on the denial of duality but on the reality that is left behind" (ibid.).

An illustration that may be helpful in seeing the connection between Buddha-nature and emptiness is Fa-tsang's hall of mirrors. To explain the relationship of the self and the world to each other to a visiting empress, Fa-tsang had a room where huge mirrors covered the ceiling, the floor, all of the walls, and even the four corners of the room, and all faced each other. Then he placed a Buddha image in the center. He explained that "in each and every reflection of any [one] mirror you will find all the reflections of all the other mirrors, together with the specific Buddha image in each, without omission or misplacement" (Cited in W. King 1986, 158 [brackets King's]).

Winston King reflects that "thus the totality of mirrors and the Buddha image (the totality of all existents in the universe) is to be found entire and without distortion in each and every mirror." He observes that "no self or entity has any self-inclosed, independent reality of its own. It is, so to speak, but a crossroads, a convergence point wherein all the universe comes together." King points out that "it is a nexus of connections; no separate individual or self is to be found there" (ibid.)

Thus, despite the positive language of the "Buddha-nature" concept, we are still not talking about "essence" or "being." Joseph McKeon recalls that Zen master Dogen "expressly warns against viewing the Buddha-nature as a substantial core in all things." He explains that Dogen "rejects any identification of Buddha nature with an eternal, substantial self" (McKeon 1999, 10). What, then, is one to make of the concept?

Sallie B. King offers an interesting interpretation. King observes as well that "Buddhism embraces both the teaching that there is no self and the teaching that the goal of life is to discover the true self" (S. King 1984, 255). Thus, she attempts to come to terms with the seemingly conflicting concepts of anatta and Buddha-nature. To do this, she examines a primary text called the *Buddha Nature Treatise (Fo Hsing Lun)*, one of a number of texts written between 200-500 C.E. She explains that the idea of Buddha-nature originated in these texts, some of which were originally Indian and some of which were originally Chinese, yet all of which were important in the development of Chinese Buddhist thought.

She points out that "Buddha-nature thought may be summed up in the phrase, 'all sentient beings possess the Buddha nature,'" which means "that everyone has the potential to achieve Buddhahood or full enlightenment" (ibid. 257 [Citation from *Buddha Nature Treatise*, 788]). The author of the *Buddha Nature Treatise* writes that:

> with the wisdom of Thusness (*chen ju chih*), all Buddhas and bod-hisattvas realize the perfection of not-self (*anatman paramita*) of all things. Since this perfection of not-self and that which is seen as the mark of not-self are not different, the Tathagata says that this mark of the eternal not-self is the true, essential nature (*chen t'i hsing*) of all things. Therefore it is said that the perfection of not-self is self (*Buddha Nature Treatise*, 798, cited in ibid. 259).

King argues that "it is the true, essential, eternal nature of things to lack a self. Therefore this lack of self is real; it *is* the real nature of things. Therefore it may be called 'self.'" She continues that, therefore, the perfection of self "is not in conflict with the old *anatman* teaching, but is said to be the fulfillment of it" (ibid. 260). She suggests that the author of the *Buddha Nature Treatise* used the language of Buddha-nature "to give a more positive account of Buddhist practice," and also because the negative language psychologically "might be poor motivation" (ibid. 261). However, that author "consistently avoids speaking of the Buddha-nature in terms of what it 'is,' or in terms of essences" (ibid. 262), but rather speaks of it in terms of "action."

She concludes that "the mind or Buddha-nature is not a thing which perceives, but the act of perceiving itself." She emphasizes that "it is the *act* of turning within, the *act* of realizing that there is no self, which constitutes the true self." Therefore, the Buddha-nature concept, as presented in the *Buddha Nature Treatise*, "represents a crucial moment of transformation in the development of Buddhism from an emphasis on the non-existence of self in early Buddhism to insistence on realization of the true self in Zen." She maintains that "it is able to link these two teachings because … the non-existence of self is identical with the perfection of self" (ibid. 266). In this sense, then, "it is in the active … realizing of the emptiness of self that is found the perfection of self or Buddha-nature" (ibid. 267).

King offers an interesting and useful analysis of the Buddha-nature concept in light of the doctrine of anatta. It affirms the positive language of the concept but avoids going too far in taking that language as implying "essence" or "being" for the Buddha-nature concept. All in all, the general Buddhist reality of non-self, and the perception of self as non-self, remain. Therefore, we have avoided arguing for a "self," which the Buddha never affirmed, but have argued from the "perception" or "action" of non-self or Buddha-nature. A few final interpretations of Buddha-nature are in order before specifically examining how these Buddhist concepts of "self" relate to the issue of human rights.

Reynolds and Campany point out that the East Asian Mahayanists modified the classic Indian Mahayana renunciatory tone and "interpreted the doctrine so as to emphasize the positive presence of the void or the Buddha nature in every phenomenal entity." By doing this, they "placed an affirmative religious and ethical value on the natural world and on ordinary human activities" (Eliade 1987, 502).

This had a profound effect on Mahayana Buddhist ethics. Reynolds and Campany note that, "grounded in the realization of emptiness, suchness, or the primordial Buddha nature of reality, one continued to exhibit compassion," a compassion which "consisted in realizing the ultimate nondifferentiation of oneself and others, and hence in mentally substituting others for oneself." Thus, "right conduct became no longer a matter of discipline but instead the spontaneous expression of [one's] awareness" of Buddha nature (ibid. 501). This tied in with the Mahayana idea of the bodhisattva, held up as the ideal of a compassionate being.

Luis O. Gomez observes that, on first impression, "there seems to be a radical contradiction between the doctrine of nonself, or, even more, that of emptiness, and any possible moral obligation" (Gomez 1973, 362). However, that is not the case, philosophically or historically, within the Buddhist tradition. He points out that the difference between the Mahayana and the Theravada view of compassion is that "the latter conceives of it as a mere preliminary, whereas the Mahayana accepts it as a necessary counterpart of wisdom," noting that "once selflessness is attained, good conduct follows spontaneously" (ibid. 363). Gomez explains that, "there being no self, replies the Buddhist, there is no reason why we should avoid our sorrow and not that of others" (ibid. 365). He emphasizes that the view of emptiness or nonself does imply ethical values because "it destroys the only real obstacle to the exercise of goodness: self-conceit" (ibid. 373).

Winston King asserts that the concept of emptiness "is not mere nullity," but a "via negativa term, whose negative character is a witness to the indescribable fullness of sunyata" (W. King 1986, 171). He also uses the terminology of Rudolf Otto in maintaining that "Sunyata is conceptually nil (infinite emptiness) but mystically positive (Absolute Reality)" (W. King 1970, 98). He suggests that "the Buddhist 'impersonal' terms ... all express and describe a liberating, enlarging experience of a greater-than-ordinary-individual wholeness" (ibid. 173 [see also Abe 1982a]).

In this section, I have attempted to come to terms with the negative sounding concept of "emptiness (sunyata)," on one hand, and the more positive sounding "Buddha-nature" on the other. Yet, both are interrelated. And, both follow from the basic Buddhist concepts of anatta and paticca-samuppada. While the concept of Buddha-nature seems to imply a "true-self," it does not do so in the strong sense that the monotheistic Western religions do. Therefore, it still is in line with, and adds to, the unique Buddhist concept of a "self." Given this Buddhist view of self and worldview, I next address how the concept of human rights fits within this worldview.

2.4: ARGUMENTS ON THE CONCEPT OF
HUMAN RIGHTS WITHIN BUDDHISM

The concepts of *anatta* and *paticca-samuppada*, and *Buddha-nature* and *emptiness*, are integral to the Buddhist view of self. Hence, some or all of these terms are commonly involved in most discussions on Buddhism and human rights. In fact, they are the concepts most often referred to in dissenting *from* the use of the term human rights within Buddhism, as well as the concepts which are said *to* offer unique Buddhist contributions to the concept of human rights. Having examined these Buddhist concepts, I now turn to their specific application within the human rights debate.

Dissent against using the concept of human rights to apply to Buddhism falls into two categories. The more general argument falls within the East/West debate, arguing that Western philosophical, political and/or theological terms and concepts cannot apply, or be forced into, an Eastern view of person, society and reality. This argument was addressed in Chapter One and will not be specifically addressed here. However, it does form a general argument that underlies many of the dissenting views on the compatibility of human rights with the Buddhist tradition. Besides that general argument, though, there are specific arguments based primarily on concepts within Buddhism itself. In this section, I examine these arguments for, and against, the use of the concept of human rights within Buddhism.

A. DISSENT WITH THE CONCEPT OF
HUMAN RIGHTS WITHIN BUDDHISM

Although this section is not exhaustive, it raises some of the key objections to the use of the term human rights within Buddhism. While not arguing against Buddhist involvement with human rights issues, those raising these objections do argue that the concept is incompatible with key Buddhist concepts. The primary problem, of course, is the Buddhist concept of non-self as seen in the doctrine of anatta. If there is no self, or "person," who has rights? Following from this lack of person or self is the apparent lack of grounding for the concept of human dignity, a key component in the discussion of human rights. The transcendent basis for *why* a person *has* or *should have* rights appears to be lacking in Buddhism.

Damien Keown acknowledges that "one looks in vain to the Four Noble Truths for any explicit reference to human dignity, and doctrines such as no-self and impermanence may even be thought to undermine it." He observes that "if human dignity is the basis of human rights Buddhism would seem to be in some difficulty when it comes to providing a justification for them" (Keown 1998, 25). Keown admits as well that "because the transcendent dimension of human good is left obscure in Buddhist teachings, ... the transcendent ground for human rights is also obscure" (ibid. 34).[2]

Michel Clasquin argues that the concept of human rights is not logically permissible within the Buddhist tradition. He points out that, "considering the anatta theory ... there is no 'owner,'" emphasizing that "the person to whom these rights are intrinsically allotted by human rights theory has been dissolved by Buddhist philosophy into an ever changing flow of factors, none of them enduring or unchangeable or capable of possessing or being possessed" (Clasquin 1993, 95).[3]

He asserts that "the idea of the person as an independent, fully autonomous entity unaffected by circumstances is anathema to the Buddhist tradition" (ibid. 96). (Although, one could also admit that this language is also "anathema" to Christian views of the individual as well, but for different reasons.) And even though he admits that humans have a unique place within Buddhism, in that only from the human condition can one reach enlightenment, he argues that still humans "have no *right* to become enlightened" (ibid.).

Peter Junger concurs that "the test of being a 'person' seems to be that one must have a self-conscious self, a test that is difficult to reconcile with the teaching that all things are empty of self" (Junger 1998, 63). And Raimundo Panikkar asserts as well that "the individual as such is an abstraction, and an abstraction as such cannot be an ultimate subject of rights" (Panikkar 1982, 98). This is the primary argument against the use of the term human rights within Buddhism: the doctrine of anatta. The above arguments are representative in seeing a general conflict between the anatta doctrine and the concept of human rights.

---

2   Keown, however, suggests a solution to this problem which will be presented in the next section.

3   Clasquin is building on the claims of Martin Prozesky's article, mentioned in Chapter One, which argued against the compatibility of human rights theory with theistic religion.

Clasquin also points out that while the Buddhist system "as a whole is intimately concerned with the eradication of suffering," and while "the Buddhist is encouraged to do everything in his power to decrease the amount of suffering in his immediate environment," still he argues that "this is a matter of compassion and personal choice: it has nothing to do with 'human rights'" (Clasquin 1993, 96). He maintains that the Buddhist ethical system is based on compassion, and is voluntary, and is not based on the notion of inherent rights or even of justice. (Clasquin draws on the comments of Masao Abe that "Buddhism emphasizes wisdom and compassion rather than justice and charity" [Abe 1986a, 191]. While Abe is an outspoken Buddhist advocate for the concept of human rights, he is also somewhat critical of the Christian concept of justice. Abe argues that in the Judaeo-Christian tradition, "the wisdom aspect of God has been neglected in favor of the justice aspect of God" [Abe 1986b, 208]. He continues along this line that "the Buddhist notion of wisdom evokes the sense of equality and solidarity," whereas the Christian view of justice causes tension because of the duality and split between the righteous and unrighteous [Abe 1995, 149]).

The Buddhist emphasis on compassion is noted by others as well. Jay Garfield observes that "Liberalism and Buddhism are apparently at odds," because "to the extent that we define the moral landscape by rights and duties, we appear not to define it through compassion" (Garfield 1998, 117). Craig Ihara adds that "it probably would be a mistake to introduce the notion of rights into Buddhist ethics," because "as an ethic of compassion there is an ample basis for a rich social ethic even without invoking the notion of rights." He contends that "invoking rights has the inevitable effect of emphasizing individuals and their status, thereby strengthening the illusion of self" (Ihara 1998, 51).

Junger concurs that "the Buddha's ethical teachings are concerned with virtues and right conduct, they are not concerned with rights, and certainly not with rights against the state." Following the line of reasoning that we saw in Chapter One, he recalls that "the concept of human rights is a recent product of the history of Western Europe and of the civil law and common law traditions." On the other hand, he asserts that "the Buddha, and the successful followers of the Buddha's teachings, having wisdom and compassion, have no need for rights for themselves." He concludes that "that is why the Buddha has no rights" (Junger 1998, 86).

Ihara uses the analogy of a dance to explain that, in traditional societies, one can have responsibilities without also having corresponding rights. In a dance routine, one has a responsibility to catch one's partner, or they will fall and get hurt. Yet, we do not use "rights language" and argue that the person has a "right" to be caught. He emphasizes that it is a flaw "to assume that every kind of 'ought' or 'duty' entails a corresponding right" (Ihara 1998, 44).

Ihara maintains "that the notion of Dharma may be part of a vision of society in which human life is ideally a kind of dance with well defined role-responsibilities," and that "such a system does not entail or require having or using the concept of rights in order to be intelligible" (ibid. 47). He asserts as well that "rights in the sense of subjective entitlements are conceptually incompatible with classical Buddhist ethics" (ibid. 48). Finally, Ihara concludes that "if duties in Buddhism are best understood in terms of Dharma, and Dharma is the same kind of cooperative enterprise as dance or soccer, then it is impossible for rights to be introduced without changing Buddhist ethics in a very fundamental way" (ibid. 49).

Junger argues that the concept of human rights runs counter to the Buddhist concept of the impermanence of all things. He asserts that Buddhism views "a world that is continually in flux and that has no room for unchanging absolutes like 'human rights' that are deduced by a rigidly ahistorical rationality" (Junger 1998, 55). Therefore, he emphasizes that "anyone who tries to fit the concept of human rights into a tradition that recognizes that everything in this ocean of birth and death is arising and fading away ... is also going to have similar difficulties with such timeless absolutes" (ibid. 79).

Junger also maintains that the concept of human rights seems to conflict with the Buddhist perception that all life is suffering, and that "clinging" to things of this world is a cause of this suffering. He observes that there seems to be an "implicit denial of the fact of *dukkha* [suffering]" (ibid. 60), in that "rights seem more like an incitement to clinging than a cure for suffering." He points out that "surely it does not profit a man to tell him that he has a right to security in this world of impermanence" (ibid. 61), adding that even the right to property seems "hard to reconcile with the basic teaching that ignorant clinging to things is the cause of *dukkha*" (ibid. 83). Along this line, given the concept of *dukkha*, he argues that concepts such as "fairness" or "justice" do not seem to be central to the Buddhist tradition (ibid. 82).

Finally, given the concepts of anatta and impermanence, Junger articulates the primary problem in the discussion of human rights within Buddhism. From the Buddhist worldview, "the whole idea of 'grounding' the concept of human rights seems pretty problematical" (ibid. 65), because "there is no ground upon which rights could be founded, there is no ground at all" (ibid. 66). Without concepts such as God as the source of all creation, or as the source of goodness, or humans as the "image of God," or the concepts of "being" or "essence," there appears to be nothing upon which modern human rights theory can be grounded within the Buddhist system. Thus, some would concur with Clasquin that "the outcome of all this is that the Buddhist cannot logically use the term 'human rights' without involving himself in a contradiction in terms of his own religio-philosophical system" (Clasquin 1993, 98).

However, there are a number of scholars from within Buddhism and from without who argue that the term "human rights" can be used within Buddhism and that it can also express fundamental truths and concerns from within that tradition. I address these arguments next.

B. SUPPORT FOR THE CONCEPT OF HUMAN RIGHTS WITHIN BUDDHISM

Despite difficulties which some see in the Buddhist concept of anatta as it relates to human rights, others see potential in it as a positive contribution to the concept of human rights overall. One important factor is to consider how interrelated the concept of *anatta* is to the concept of *paticca-samuppada*. Another important factor to consider, which I articulated in Chapter One, is that the fact that the term "human rights" has not been present within the Buddhist tradition does not mean that Buddhism is not concerned with ethical principles behind human rights talk, or with the goals of human rights language. Buddhist scholar and translator Taitetsu Unno affirms that "the fact that Buddhist tradition in its past history has had little to say about personal rights in the current sense of the term does not mean that Buddhists were not concerned with human well-being, with the dignity and autonomy of the spirit" (Unno 1988, 129).

General Buddhist support for human rights relates to these concepts and flows along these lines. In addition, these Buddhist concepts are seen as offering potential to expand on the modern, Western, autonomous concept of human rights. (It must be noted that I am not equating the modern Western view of the individual with the Christian view. While the modern Western view developed in a Christian society, and was influenced by it, it jettisoned or at least downplayed the concepts of God and community, as well as the corresponding duties toward both.) For example, Traer agrees with Unno that "the key to the Buddhist contribution ... is its notion of the human person. The human person is a part of the interdependence of all life." He continues that "the Buddha's teaching of no-self (*anatman*) makes possible an appreciation of persons as more than entities or individuals" (Traer 1991, 136). Therefore, Traer emphasizes that "from a Buddhist perspective, human rights need to be grounded in what today might be described as an ecological view of nature and humanity" (ibid. 137).

In addition, the Buddhist communities of monks and nuns, the Sangha, have traditionally functioned as concrete examples of Buddhist commitments and ideals. Traer argues that "the principles of human rights were all there in the Buddha's earliest teachings and were embodied in the Sangha" (ibid. 138). Macy concurs that "the interdependence of person and community is an assumption reflected in the institution of the Sangha and in its symbolic value as model of social ideals" (Macy 1979, 47).

Along these lines, what is important in the discussion on human rights is Buddhism's check on the extreme individualism within the Western notion of human rights, since Buddhism sees the interconnectedness. Unno asserts that it is "imperative that as we affirm our own individual rights we must also be willing to give up ourselves in order to affirm the rights of others" (Unno 1988, 140). He cautions that "the most difficult problem in considering the nature of personal rights is the ego-centeredness that lurks in its background" (ibid. 144). In regard to this, Buddhism states that "what is necessary is a new understanding of reality, a new vision of the ideal community, based on the interdependence and interconnectedness of life" (ibid. 145).

This offers a general introduction to discussion of the concept of human rights within Buddhism. In addition, I would like to note that Buddhist leaders such as the Dalai Lama himself are key advocates for the concept of human rights. While not a representative of all of Buddhism, the Dalai Lama serves as an example of a Buddhist leader, recognized on a global scale, who strongly supports the concept of human rights.

His address delivered at the United Nations World Conference on Human Rights on June 15, 1993, in Vienna, Austria was entitled "Human Rights and Universal Responsibility" (Dalton 1999, 39). Dalton emphasizes that "the Dalai Lama ... endorses the *Universal Declaration of Human Rights* and rejects the positions of Asian nations (especially China) who reject the *Declaration*," and that he also "rejects the argument from cultural relativism that maintains the inapplicability of these principles to Asian cultures" (ibid. 40). The Dalai Lama states that "human rights, environmental protection and great social and economic equality, are all interrelated" (Cited in ibid.), and he asserts that "diversity and traditions can never justify the violation of human rights" (Cited in Strain 1998, 156).

Given the above general observations, I now examine more specifically how the concepts of *anatta* and *paticca-samuppada* are interpreted in favor of using the concept of human rights within Buddhism. Keown appeals to the Buddha's critique of the caste system, as well as his doctrine of anatta, to affirm that in Buddhism "all individuals are equal in the most profound sense" (Keown 1998, 23). In addition, he emphasizes that "human beings, like everything else, are part of the relational process described in the doctrine of dependent-origination;" and that therefore, "since no-one exists independently we should look out for one another; looking out for one another means respecting each other's rights" (ibid. 27).

Despite this view of interconnectedness, it is important to point out that the human condition was still the preferred one in Buddhism. Schumann explains that human embodiment "in Buddhist opinion is the most favourable one for liberation," because "only when reborn as human beings are they capable of grasping the teaching of the Buddha and of following the way to emancipation." Therefore, he concludes that "a human embodiment ... is preferable to all other forms of existence" (Schumann 1974, 51).

In this sense, then, Buddhism shares an anthropocentrism with other religions, since it is concerned with human liberation (Abe 1986b, 203). This is important to assert in counteracting the simplistic view that Buddhism is completely relative in its view of the human person as related to the rest of reality. Thus, even in Buddhism, there is somewhat of a hierarchy of life forms, with humans occupying the highest position in the natural order of things.

Strain suggests that the initial question "how can a tradition that preaches the doctrine of the not-self or of Buddha nature have any concept of human rights at all," is probably not the best place to start. He argues as well that the concepts of anatta and Buddha-nature need to be viewed in a soteriological sense rather than in an ontological sense. He observes that "as a soteriological concept in the Theravada tradition, *anatta* charts a middle path between the roles of avidity and despair generated by eternalist and nihilist concepts of the self." On the other hand, "in the Mahayana tradition Buddha Nature functions equally as a soteriological concept referring to the radical capacity for liberation" (Strain 1998, 164).

Keown sees this human capacity for liberation as the key to the human rights discussion with Buddhism. He argues that, in Buddhism, it is the *goal* (Buddha-nature as a goal), rather than any intrinsic nature of the person, which lays the ground for why individuals have human rights. This acknowledges the fact that while there is no ontological ground for human dignity within Buddhism, there is the goal of Buddha-nature, which all humans have the potential to achieve, and this goal provides the reason why their human rights should be respected. He asserts, in Western terms, that "the source of human dignity in Buddhism lies nowhere else than in the literally infinite capacity of human nature for participation in goodness" (Keown 1998, 29), or in Buddhist terminology that "all beings are potential Buddhas or possess the 'Buddha-nature'" (ibid. 41). This argument is key in countering the objection that within Buddhism there is no "person," "soul," or inherent "human dignity" present to which the concept of human rights could apply. By focusing on the goal, or Buddha-nature, rather than an absence of self, the value of the human person and hence of their need for human rights is affirmed.

Along these lines, Keown implies that, in discussions of human rights within Buddhism, too much focus has been placed on the first two of the Four Noble Truths, which deal with suffering and impermanence. He argues that, given the human potential for liberation, emphasis should be placed on the third and fourth Noble Truths, which deal with this. He asserts that "since all schools of Buddhism affirm the third and fourth noble truths and the vision of human good they proclaim, the required common ground for a pan-Buddhist doctrine of human rights is present" (ibid. 34).

In addition, he suggests that "modern doctrines of human rights are in harmony with the moral values of classical Buddhism in that they are an explication of what is 'due' under Dharma." Therefore, he concludes that "it is legitimate to speak of both rights and *human* rights in Buddhism" (ibid.).

Other elements within Buddhism also contribute toward the affirmation of the value of the individual person[4], and hence towards the affirmation of the concept of human rights. Robert Thurman observes that "the doctrine of 'selflessness' (*anatmata*) was a powerful critical tool that enabled many persons in those role-ridden, hierarchical ancient societies to awaken to their unique individualities beyond social, cultural, and religious stereotypes" (Thurman 1988, 150).

He notes that, even in the process of conception, the person was seen as more than a product of their parents. He explains that they described the act of conception "as involving three sets of genes: those of the mother, those of the father, and those of the person being born." This was expressed "in the tantric literature by the image of conception as the union of three drops (*bindu*)" (ibid. 151). Thurman argues that all of this "provides a metaphysical base for a responsible individualism," asserting that "one cannot belong totally to one's parents, tribe, nation, or even culture" (ibid. 152).

He also recalls the importance of the sangha in affirming the value of the individual and of that individual's quest for enlightenment. He stresses that "individualist monasticism answered a need to create a space for individualism and the individual's rights to liberty and enlightenment within an excessively holistic society" (Thurman 1996, 104). In addition, given the system of karma and rebirth, individuals have, on their own, earned certain "rights" based on their past lives. While these "rights" are not innate, he contends that "they have earned their own rights through suffering and transcending egotism in the sea of evolution, and no one can deprive them of such rights, since no one conferred these rights upon them" (ibid. 110). Thus, Thurman argues that much in Buddhism stressed an emphasis on the individual which ran against traditional societies' communal tendencies.

---

4   Perhaps the best way to phrase this is that, from a Buddhist perspective, one does not affirm the individual, but rather one affirms the *value* of what is perceived at the given moment to be an individual.

One can also argue for the concept of equality among human beings within Buddhism. Sallie B. King suggests that "since all humans are equal in their ability to become a Buddha, Buddhism is committed in principle to human equality" (S. King 1995b, 75). Padmasiri de Silva explains that some features in the Buddhist concept of equality are as follows:

- Rejection of artificial and arbitrary distinctions among human beings, rejection of caste distinctions based on birth, and emphasis on character.
- Common human potentialities (spirituality and moral transformation, rationality, ability to sympathize with the suffering of others, free will).
- All beings (including animals) are subject to the common predicament, described as a state of unsatisfactoriness (*dukkha*). This is the great leveller.
- The concept of human dignity and equal respect for all (*samanatata*).
- The Buddhist notion of benevolence and compassion shows that equality as a human rights orientation in Buddhism rests on a humanistic rather than a legalistic conscience (P. de Silva 1995, 135).

The importance of the element of compassion has been previously noted, and within Buddhist ethics compassion constitutes a strong contribution to the Buddhist perception of human rights. De Silva emphasizes that "the vibratory base of Buddhist ethics is the doctrine of compassion and it brings into play a wide variety of virtues" (ibid. 138). In fact, de Silva goes so far as to contend that "if we look at compassion across religions … it provides one of the lasting bases for the preservation of human rights and their neutral vocabulary" (ibid. 139). Donald Swearer points out as well that, while some argue "that the concepts of Not-self (*anatman*) and Emptiness (*sunyata*) undermine a sense of intrinsic nature and are not compatible with the language of rights," others argue just as vehemently "that the Buddhist critique of inherent self-nature coupled with an emphasis on compassion (*karuna*) provides a unique basis for an ethic of responsibility based on a distinctive sense of intrinsic mutual worth" (Swearer 1997, 87).

Jay Garfield agrees that the concept of rights needs to be grounded in compassion. He notes that Buddhism can contribute much to this, an area where, he argues, the modern liberal theory of rights is lacking. Garfield emphasizes that as "valuable as rights are … and broad as their scope is," still "it is not broad enough to encompass all that is morally significant" (Garfield 1998, 120). He observes that modern liberal theory creates a distinction between the public and private sphere of morality, with rights being associated with the more public aspect. Yet, grounding rights in compassion breaks down this distinction and leads to a more integrated connection of rights with morality. He maintains that, when this happens, "institutions and practices are not deemed wrong because they violate some right, ... but rather simply because they are harmful to people" (ibid. 122). Therefore, Garfield contends that "to begin from compassion is to begin by taking the good of others as one's own motive for action" (ibid. 123), and that "compassion can certainly provide the motivation for constructing a system of rights" (ibid. 127).

Other elements within Buddhist ethics can contribute to and relate to human rights theory. Reynolds and Campany note that "both the monks and the laity were called upon to show sympathy (anukampa) to their fellow human beings," as well as "to cultivate, through meditation, the mental attitudes of love (metta), compassion (karuna), sympathetic joy (mudita) and equanimity (upekkha)" (Eliade 1987, 500). The proper frame of mind, and the moral conduct which flowed from it, were seen as very important, since they determined one's rebirth. Alex Wayman explains that "the theory is that once having obtained human birth, one should take care to keep the stream of consciousness human" (Wayman 1990, 346). Therefore, by thinking and acting in ways that are subhuman, such as in feeding on the weak, one's "stream of consciousness is that of the animal kingdom" (ibid. 344), which would lead to a rebirth in that form.

Wayman points out that there are three types of rights: Rights in Law, Moral Rights and Natural Rights. He contends that while "both Natural Rights and Moral Rights are exposed and promoted in Buddhism, ... the Moral Rights appear to predominate" (ibid. 358). And, given the doctrines of karma and reincarnation, while people are seen as being in their social situation because of a past life, still the rule of conduct in Buddhism is to treat all people equally (ibid. 342). Kenneth Inada summarizes that "there will be mutual respect of fellow beings. It is on this basis that we can speak of the rights of individuals" (Inada 1982, 71).

In October, 1995, the *Journal of Buddhist Ethics* sponsored an Online Conference on "Buddhism and Human Rights." Based on the conference papers, some of which are mentioned in this study, it produced a *Declaration of Interdependence* to affirm the general support for the concept of human rights within Buddhism. It begins that "those who have the good fortune to have a 'rare and precious human rebirth,' with all its potential for awareness, sensitivity, and freedom, have a duty to not abuse the rights of others to partake of the possibilities of moral and spiritual flourishing offered by human existence." It observes that "the doctrine of Conditioned Arising shows that our lives are intertwined, and abusing others can only be done when we are blind to this fact." The document continues that "as vulnerable beings in a conditioned world, our mutual dependency indicates that whatever can be done to reduce suffering in the world should be done."

This *Declaration of Interdependence* also acknowledges that "the Buddhist teaching that we lack an inherently existing Self (*anatman*) shows that suffering does not really 'belong' to anyone." It asserts that "to try and reduce it in 'my' stream at the expense of increasing it in another life-stream is folly, both because this will in fact bring more suffering back to me (karma), and because it depends on the deluded notion that 'I' am an inviolable entity that is not dependent and can treat others as if only they are limited and conditioned." (*Declaration of Interdependence* 1998, 221). In addition, the document affirms "the inalienable dignity which living creatures possess by virtue of their capacity to achieve enlightenment in this life or in the future." It concludes by affirming that "every human being should be treated humanely both by other individuals and governments in keeping with the Buddhist commitment to non-violence (*ahimsa*) and respect for life" (ibid. 222).

The document affirms what scholars also assert, that the concept of human rights can be used within the Buddhist context. It is in keeping with key Buddhist ideals and teachings, and these teachings also enhance elements that are often neglected in Western human rights discussions. The concept of *anatta* cautions against a selfish view of human rights that sees the individual as a completely autonomous entity, and the concept of *paticca-samuppada* emphasizes the communal aspect of rights language, including a concern for other species and the environment.

But, in this study on Buddhism so far, I have focused primarily on theory. To close this chapter, brief mention also needs to be made of Buddhists who are not only convinced of the validity of the concept of human rights, but who are actually helping to bring that about by their involvement in social activism in the name of Buddhism.

2.5: BUDDHISM, SOCIAL JUSTICE AND HUMAN RIGHTS

Earlier, I acknowledged the perception that the concept of social justice is more prevalent and apparent in the Western religious traditions than it is in the Eastern traditions. Buddhism is no exception to this. However, Buddhism does offer unique concepts which have, and still can, add to modern theories of justice. In addition, in Chapter One, I examined general perceptions of "the poor" in Judaism, Christianity, Islam and Hinduism. In this next section, I briefly acknowledge some Buddhist perceptions of the poor, mention key Buddhist concepts which add to the current discussion of social justice and human rights, and take note of "socially engaged Buddhists" who are currently working toward these ideals.

A. BUDDHISM AND THE POOR

While not containing a strong social critique, Buddhist ethical teachings and practices can offer much to current understandings of human rights. Historically in Buddhism, the rejection of the caste system and the denial that many lives were necessary to achieve liberation altered the traditional Hindu view. Neville Gunaratne states that the first Buddhists "ushered in a new revival of values in an India tyrannized by the haughty brahmins. And they made no distinction between rich and poor, high and low" (Gunaratne 1981, 101). Unno concurs that the Sangha was "a society of equals – regardless of birth or lineage or whether one was rich or poor, man or woman" (Unno 1988, 131).

In addressing the issue of the poor within Buddhism, K. Anuruddha Thera maintains that "the Buddha has left no room for the view that poverty is an unavoidable burden that has come to us in consequence of our past *kamma*" (Thera 1980, 100). Thera explains that "it is emphatically stated that what one earns must be borne out of righteous means. When one earns by such right and just means, one is in a position to perform his *balis* (duties)" (ibid. 101). In regard to these material possessions, Thera notes that what is necessary is "the cultivation of the attitude called *appicchata*. The control over desires is the spirit of the practice" (ibid.).

This control over desires and an emphasis on charity is contained within various Buddhist texts. The *Sutta Nipata* explains that "The impulse 'I want' and the impulse 'I'll have' – lose them. That is where most people get stuck" (*Sutta Nipata* 706, cited in Wilson 1995, 667). Shantideva observed that "'If I give this, what shall I enjoy?' – Such selfish thinking is the way of the ghosts; [on the other hand] 'If I enjoy this, what shall I give?' – such selfless thinking is a quality of the gods" (Shantideva, *Guide to the Bodhisattva's Way of Life*, 8.125, cited in ibid. 696). (Shantideva was a representative of the Madhyamika school of Mahayana Buddhism, 7th/8th centuries, C.E. See Schuhmacher and Woerner 1994, 315.)

The Buddha emphasized that "When you see someone practicing the Way of giving, aid him joyously, and you will obtain vast and great blessings" (*Sutra of Forty-Two Sections* 10, cited in ibid. 695). In the *Itivuttaka*, it states that "If beings knew, as I know, the fruit of sharing gifts, they would not enjoy their use without sharing them, nor would the taint of stinginess obsess the heart and stay there" (*Itivuttaka* 18, cited in ibid. 695).

The *Garland Sutra* emphasizes that "enlightened beings are magnanimous givers, bestowing whatever they have with equanimity, without regret, without hoping for reward, without seeking honor, without coveting material benefits, but only to rescue and safeguard all living beings" (*Garland Sutra* 21, cited in ibid. 696). In addition, the *Dhammapada* states that "One should give even from a scanty store to him who asks" (*Dhammapada* 224, cited in ibid. 699).

Yet, in addition to this emphasis on renunciation and charity, the realization of poverty in the social setting does exist as well. Thera describes the *Cakkavatti Sihanada Sutta* in the *Digha Nikaya*. This legend presents "an analysis of how poverty can lead society to moral degeneration" (Thera 1980, 101). Thera explains that in Buddhism, poverty "mainly is a phenomenon which has socio-political causes rather than moral (*kammic*) causes" (ibid. 102). Phra Rajavaramuni notes that "poverty is regarded as the main source of crime and disorder as well as greed" (Rajavaramuni 1990, 39. He cites the *Dhammapada* III, 65; III, 92). He observes that the "absence of poverty, the accumulation of wealth or economic sufficiency, is a prerequisite for a happy, secure, and stable society, favorable to individual development and perfection" (ibid.).

Thera continues that, in the *Kutadanta Sutta,* the story about a king reviving a poverty stricken country seems to suggest that "the State is in a position to abolish poverty." He concludes that "the story shows the desirability of socio-political measures against poverty for Buddhists" (Thera 1980, 102). Macy agrees, noting that "the material welfare of the people, their need for hospitals, roads, wells and jobs, the importance of an economic base, are stressed in many a *sutta* and *jataka* of the Pali scriptures and have inspired Buddhist social service through Asoka's era to our present time" (Macy 1979, 46).

Asoka is a key figure in Buddhist social practice, held up as a primary example of one who ran an empire based on Buddhist principles. Asoka went so far as to erect stone pillars throughout the empire which were inscribed with Buddhist ethical teachings. It is noted that "Buddhist societies throughout Asia have looked back, at one time or another, to the image of King Ashoka (third century B.C.) as a righteous protector and defender of the Buddhist community" (J. Smith 1995, 166).

However, Asoka's era is one of the few times in Buddhist history when Buddhist teachings are closely wedded to political and social thought and practice. Thus, it is common to contend, as Winston King does, that when a Westerner "confronts Buddhist Asia and searches for a social ethic or philosophy, he finds himself aimlessly groping" (W. King 1964, 176). Thurman reflects as well that the idea "that the system itself is wrong, as our American founders insisted, never occurs in Buddhist literature" (Thurman 1988, 156).

While charity toward the poor and compassion are common throughout Buddhist history, a social advocacy toward the poor, and a general socio-political theory, are less pronounced. However, key concepts within Buddhism can currently make contributions to the discussion of human rights. In contrast to Winston King, Rajavaramuni points out that "in keeping with the Buddhist doctrine of dependent co-arising, individual betterment and perfection on the one hand and the social good on the other are fundamentally interrelated and interdependent" (Rajavaramuni 1990, 31). It can be emphasized as well that

> the virtue of compassion and the vision of society as a network of interdependent relationships have implications for the 'just' distribution of society's benefits and for the protection of the ecosystem that have made Buddhist teaching a popular resource for

contemporary thinking about the structure of society and the environment (J. Smith 1995, 166).

Thus, many argue that just because Buddhism has not had a history of strong social advocacy does not mean that it cannot do so today. They argue that one can build a strong case for human rights advocacy based on foundational Buddhist teachings. (They would also acknowledge, however, that some of the impulse for this comes from exposure to the modern West and also Christian Liberation Theology. See Chapter 5.) This is illustrated by the fact that practicing Buddhists *are* involved in actively working toward the cause of human rights. In this final section, I offer a brief example that the concept of human rights is not only compatible with Buddhism in theory, but also in practice.

B. SOCIALLY ENGAGED BUDDHISM AND HUMAN RIGHTS

Winston King observes that "the basic social axiom of Buddhism. . . may be stated as follows: 'the individual progress is, after all, the social progress.' In other words the goodness of society is but the sum of the goodness of its component individuals" (W. King 1964, 181). This has been the traditional Buddhist focus, on the transformation of the individual. Hence, there is the lack of a detailed social theory within Buddhism. However, the concept of *paticca-samuppada* (interconnectedness), or of *sunyata* (emptiness), qualifies this. Therefore, it is overly simplistic to say that Buddhism is "merely" concerned with the individual. Keiji Nishitani notes that "most people think that to transform society is one thing and to transform man is another," but asserts that "in reality, these two aspects cannot be separated from each other so easily" (Nishitani 1966, 1).

In addition, the example of the Buddha himself has profound social ramifications. Nishitani recalls that

> the first disciples who gathered around the Buddha came from various castes. They must have been fully conscious of the fact that their own establishment of 'brotherhood' was an historical event of revolutionary character and that it was made possible only by a wholly new basis of human relationship (ibid. 3).

Lankaputra Hewage points out that, upon the Buddha's enlightenment, he "devoted forty-five years of his life thereafter until the very moment of his death to an education service for the welfare of all humankind, regardless of sex, color, creed, caste, race, age and even intellectual and socio-economic status" (Hewage 1978, 212).

Sunanda Putuwar acknowledges that "some people misinterpret the Buddha's teaching as completely other worldly," but he cautions that this is incorrect. He contends that "the Buddha's advice concerning worldly possessions is only a warning on not clinging too much to possessions" (Putuwar 1989, 94). Hewage emphasizes as well that "basic human needs for food, clothing, shelter and medical care are accepted in the Buddhist traditions as essential even for spiritual growth" (Hewage 1978, 216).

Thus, despite the lack of a specific Buddhist socio-political theory or ethic, modern Buddhists have drawn from concepts and examples from within their tradition to become socially and politically involved. Traer observes that "Buddhists have begun to speak of human rights in various ways." He points out that "Buddhists protest 'human rights violations' in China, Tibet, Laos, and Korea. Buddhists join with other members of religious traditions in conferences concerned with human rights." And, he notes that "Buddhists participate in resolutions on human rights, such as the Seoul Declaration of the Asian Conference on Religion and Peace, which declared: 'Human dignity must be safeguarded by human rights, through which human dignity can be fully manifested'" (Traer 1988, 16). Traer concludes that "in Buddhist thought human rights may be seen not only as the fruits of wisdom and compassion but as a means of attaining both" (ibid. 18).

Sallie B. King observes that, "taking as their model the Buddha, who refused to lecture until a hungry man was fed," are many contemporary Buddhist social activists. These Buddhist activists "recognize an implicit hierarchy of needs." These are: first, "the protection and maintenance of life is most basic," secondly are "human physical necessities such as peace and reasonable security, an adequate material base to life, including food, shelter, etc.," thirdly come "human psychological and social necessities such as education," and finally is spiritual liberation. This last one is the "most difficult to attain, and rests upon an essential base of social, economic, psychological and political requisites" (S. King 1995a, 125).

Sallie King explains that "Buddhist social activists in the modern world are already working for human rights by the millions." She cites the following examples:

- In India, many millions of ex-Hindu untouchables have converted en masse to Buddhism primarily as a social-political act – to renounce the Hindu caste system and repudiate the larger social and political system that allows it to continue.
- In Thailand, the activist Sulak Sivaraksa has stimulated the development of countless non-government activist organizations and publications, and organized the International Network of Engaged Buddhists.
- In Burma, in 1988, Buddhist monks and students filled the streets calling for democracy. ... Their leader, Aung San Suu Kyi ... has spent years in house arrest.
- In Tibet, ... the Dalai Lama heads the Tibetan Liberation Movement (ibid. 126).
- In Japan and elsewhere many millions have joined the Soka Gakkai, a lay Buddhist organization which strives through education, dialogue and cultural exchange to put an end to the constant threat of war, to build international and interreligious understanding, and protect the environment (ibid. 127).
- Buddhist nuns in both the East and West ... have organized themselves to overcome millennia of institutional sexism on the part of Buddhism itself (S. King 1995b, 78).

She asserts "make no mistake: Buddhism has turned a historic corner," and emphasizes that "Buddhism in the modern world is a force with the proven ability to inspire millions to risk everything in nonviolent efforts to gain human rights" (S. King 1995a, 127).

Sallie King explains that "Engaged Buddhism," a term used by Buddhist social activist Sulak Sivaraksa, means "socially and politically engaged Buddhism" (S. King 1995b, 77). Hence, one could say that Engaged Buddhism equals Buddhism plus prophecy. King emphasizes that "millions of people working at the grassroots level ... inspired by their own Buddhist principles ... fall within the purview of the human rights agenda" (ibid. 78).

Sivaraksa, a lay Thai activist and author, is an outspoken figure in modern Buddhism. He notes that, prior to Western colonial expansion, Buddhism had "no vision for global problem solving," and was divided into many schools, "all of which were attached to national cultures and/or nation states" (Sivaraksa 1990, 81). He explains that, generally, official Buddhist organizations are still wed too closely to nation states and are therefore uncritical of those states. Sivaraksa set up the International Network of Engaged Buddhists to tackle social justice issues which the World Fellowship of Buddhists does not address (ibid. 91).

Sivaraksa maintains that "scattered communities of Buddhists continue in a radical disregard, and sometimes fiery condemnation, of the official 'State Buddhisms.'" He asserts that "it is imperative that those of us who are lay intellectuals should support the radical clergy in maintaining this critical perspective of the Buddha" (ibid. 86). He affirms that "a socially engaged spirituality is needed" (ibid. 87).

Sivaraksa notes that, while establishment Buddhism explains oppression "as the working of karma," non-establishment Buddhism is "against this trend of wrong teaching" (Sivaraksa 1998, 65). He emphasizes that the most important question "is how the ethical inspiration of Buddhism can enlighten politics by being courageous enough to question social structures themselves and not simply the individual acts of persons" (ibid. 66).

He contends that this falls within the Buddhist tradition, because "to ignore social aspects of human beings would indeed be contrary to the basic teaching of the Buddha, which stresses nonselfishness, love, peace and brotherhood of all beings" (Sivaraksa 1983, 123). He emphasizes that "Buddhists have been involved with social action all along, because Buddhism is in fact a prescription for the restructuring of human consciousness as well as the restructuring of human society," noting that "without one the other [will] be ineffective" (ibid. 124).

Sivaraksa also notes the work of Vietnamese monk Thich Nhat Hanh, who "teaches us to pay close attention to the minute particulars in our actions, as well as to the giant web of all life." His Tiep Hien order, translated as "Order of Interbeing," was created in Vietnam during the war. Sivaraksa explains that "the Order of Interbeing is designed explicitly to address social justice and peace issues" (Sivaraksa 1990, 88).

Thus, as Sallie King explains, "Buddhists are squarely in the human rights camp" (S. King 1995b, 78). And while some of this reprioritizing of Buddhism comes as a result of contact with the West, still much of the motivation and formulation comes from within the Buddhist tradition itself. These Buddhists feel that social activism in the cause of human rights expresses age-old Buddhist concepts and concerns.

In developing a more socially activist approach, and a more global vision, many Buddhists are finding sympathetic partners among Christian scholars and activists. Sivaraksa acknowledges that "liberation theology and engaged Buddhism may have more similarities than differences" (Sivaraksa 1992, 79), and admits that "Buddhists can support the kind of grassroots theology in the Christian liberation tradition and take inspiration from it" (ibid. 84). Sivaraksa points out that "our common enemies are consumerism, oppression, and militarism." Therefore, he asserts that "Buddhists and Christians should join hands in working for peace and social justice, and in liberating themselves from our geocentricity, selfishness, and intolerance" (ibid. 91). Robin Lovin observes also that in both Christian and Buddhist traditions "[the] insistence on a human destiny that transcends any possible social achievement provides the basis for a flexible social ethic that takes social relationships seriously but does not make the creation of any particular social order the first goal of religious life" (Lovin 1990, 204).

Charles Strain agrees, noting that "those of us who root ourselves in Catholic social teachings find common ground with engaged Buddhists in a fundamental distrust of the individualistic assumptions underlying the Western, liberal tradition which spawned the struggle for human rights." He emphasizes that "both groups share an instinctive sense … that the human rights tradition resonates with something absolutely fundamental in our religious commitments" (Strain 1998, 163). Strain asserts that the concept of human rights "remains a major bridge concept linking many who struggle for a transformed global community." Therefore, he argues that, since "both traditions have much to contribute to the design and construction of this bridge, … we would do well to work together" (ibid. 171).

In this chapter, I have examined the concept of human rights within Buddhism, and have shown that that concept can legitimately be used within that tradition. The next chapter addresses the concept of human rights within Roman Catholicism, before moving on to look at how both traditions interact on the concept of human rights and the implications of that for social justice and a global ethic.

CHAPTER 3

HUMAN RIGHTS AND THE INDIVIDUAL IN
CURRENT ROMAN CATHOLIC THOUGHT

3.1: INTRODUCTION TO ROMAN CATHOLICISM AND HUMAN RIGHTS

A. INTRODUCTION

I would now like to examine the concept of human rights within the Roman Catholic tradition. In doing so, I focus primarily on the development of Catholic teaching on human rights over the past century since Leo XIII's encyclical *Rerum Novarum*. This encyclical is generally acknowledged as the beginning of the contemporary Catholic understanding of human rights.

In Chapter One, I acknowledged the connection between the concept of human rights and the Judaeo-Christian tradition in general and emphasized the strong affirmation of justice and the concern for the poor within that tradition. These elements do not need to be reiterated in detail again here, yet they form a backdrop for this chapter's more specific examination of the Roman Catholic tradition's concept of human rights. This first section, then, briefly notes the general affirmation of the individual within the Roman Catholic tradition historically, previous to the twentieth century. Scriptural concepts such as human beings created in the "image of God," and the general concern for justice and the poor will once again be affirmed. Then, the more traditional, and philosophical, Catholic approach to "rights" as rooted in the idea of "natural law" will be examined. Finally, this section concludes with the acknowledgment that the Roman Catholic tradition generally stood in opposition to the concept of human rights historically. Given this general pre-twentieth century overview, the chapter will then specifically turn its attention to the shift in Catholic thought over the past century on human rights, from *Rerum Novarum* to the current day.

Section Two examines how Roman Catholicism comes to terms with the concepts of human rights and social justice in the pontificates of Leo XIII, Pius XI and Pius XII, as well as how historical events influence the Roman Catholic shift in thought. Section Three emphasizes the Roman Catholic affirmation of human rights as seen in John XXIII's *Pacem in Terris*, the Second Vatican Council, most notably in the documents *Pastoral Constitution on the Church in the Modern World* and in the *Declaration on Religious Freedom*, in the work of Paul VI after the Council, and in other historical influences on the church in the late 1950's and 1960's. These watershed years form the basic shift in Catholic thought toward advocacy on the behalf of human rights.

Section Four examines Roman Catholic development on human rights since Vatican II, noting such events as the '71 Synod of Bishops, the U.S. bishops' pastoral letter *Economic Justice for All*, and the pontificate of John Paul II. It will also note additional developments such as the Campaign for Human Development and Liberation Theology in general. Finally, Section Five offers conclusions on the Roman Catholic interpretation of human rights.

The strong ties between the concept of human rights and the Christian tradition in general have previously been noted. John Langan affirms that the Christian tradition is "the tradition within which and in criticism of which the most influential affirmations of human rights, both practical and theoretical, have been made" (Langan 1986b, 120). More specifically today, within Roman Catholicism, David Hollenbach observes that "the central institutional organ of the Catholic church, the Holy See, has adopted the cause of human rights as the prime focus of its ethical teaching and the pastoral strategy in the domain of international justice and peace." He emphasizes that "this rapid change in the Catholic church's stance toward global human rights is a crucial fact which must be taken into account in any effort to understand current church theory and practice in the rights field" (Hollenbach 1986, 366).

Hollenbach reflects on the past century of Catholic documents on human rights, and notes that "the thread that ties all these documents together is their common concern for the protection of the dignity of the human person" (Hollenbach 1979, 42). And Langan contends that, today, "Catholic human-rights doctrine emerges as a comprehensive and generous structure within which religious believers can both share and address the moral dilemmas of a religiously pluralistic and increasingly secular world." He observes that contemporary Roman Catholic theory on human rights "is able to offer shelter to those who are repelled both by the neglect of social and economic rights for the disadvantaged in liberal societies and by the repressiveness of authoritarian and totalitarian regimes" (Langan 1986a, 116).

Given this strong support for the concept of human rights within Roman Catholicism today, what brought about such a shift in a tradition that had opposed the concept throughout most of the modern era? And, how does it now understand the concept of human rights as being consonant with the foundational principles of its two thousand year tradition? These are some of the issues which I currently address.

B. GENERAL AFFIRMATION OF THE INDIVIDUAL IN ROMAN CATHOLICISM THROUGHOUT ITS HISTORY

1. HUMAN DIGNITY: THE "IMAGE OF GOD", THE MARGINALIZED, AND JUSTICE

In the discussion of the concept of human rights, Vatican II marked a profound shift in Catholic thinking from the traditional language of "natural law" to that of "human dignity." However, this does not imply that Roman Catholicism did not hold to the value of human dignity or to the value of the individual previous to that time. As discussed earlier, the Judaeo-Christian tradition saw the value of the individual person as rooted in the Genesis creation account, where human beings are seen as being made "in the image of God." Catholicism, as a part of that tradition, vehemently argued for the transcendent dimension and value of the human person based on that origin.

Todd D. Whitmore emphasizes that in Catholic teaching, human rights "are grounded philosophically in the concept of the dignity of the human person. All persons have an inherent dignity that transcends social structures." He continues that "this idea of human dignity is further backed by the theological doctrine of *imago Dei*: all persons are born in the image of God." He argues that "it is this theological grounding that gives force to the claim that persons have transcendent worth" (McBrien 1995, 643). Robert Traer agrees that "as 'a transcendental characteristic of persons' human dignity is the source of all moral principles, and this is 'the foundation of human rights'" (Traer 1991, 44 [Quotes from R.J. Henle in Traer]).

James P. Scullion expands on these concepts, by noting that "the prophets, including Jesus, challenged those (especially the powerful) who tried to falsify the story of creation by denying the dignity and worth of the marginal (e.g., widows and orphans, outcasts and sinners)" (Scullion 1999, 8). He points out that, "while the Torah affirmed human dignity, the prophets called the people to particularize their recognition of this dignity through their compassion for the marginalized" (ibid. 20). For example, he observes that "Jeremiah concretizes the vision of the Torah," noting that "since all human beings are created in the divine image, the dignity of all human beings, especially the resident alien, the orphan, and the widow, must be recognized and respected." Therefore, for Jeremiah, "it is not enough to trust in the Temple; one must act as God acts by doing righteousness and justice" (ibid. 21). And, for Isaiah, Scullion reminds us that "recognition of the dignity of the marginalized meant the concrete acts of giving food to the hungry, drink to the thirsty, and shelter to the homeless" (ibid. 22).

Daniel Maguire observes that "as the agents of *sedaqah*, the prophets had a preferential option for the poor. Their animating genius was sensitivity to the *anawim*, the benighted poor, the powerless, exploited base of society" (Maguire 1993, 174). He contends that "the prophets' religion was intrinsically moral and their morality was thoroughly political." Therefore, he reminds us that "Judaism and Christianity are political religions, not mystery cults for the solace of the pious" (ibid. 176).

Maguire also makes the point that "essential needs create rights," and he explains that "basic needs issue into rights when their neglect would effectively deny the human worth of the needy" (Maguire 1992, 70). Therefore, Maguire contends that "in Hebrew and Christian thought, meeting essential needs is the soul of justice" (ibid. 71). These perceptions of the Hebrew Scriptures are assumed into Christian ethical thought as well.

In addition, in Christianity itself, the creation concept of human dignity is given added emphasis through the earthly ministry of Jesus, and in the concept of the incarnation. Scullion points out that "Jesus recognized the divine dignity of all people, especially the outcasts of his society, lepers (Mk 1:39-45; 14:3), toll collectors (Mk 2:15-17), and Samaritans (Jn 4:4-42)" (Scullion 1999, 13). He maintains that "just as the creation story affirms the dignity of humanity, so the incarnation, the Word becoming flesh, reaffirms and even intensifies this dignity" (ibid. 14).

David Hollenbach agrees that "a second explicitly Christian warrant for the principle of human dignity" lies in "the beliefs that all persons are created in the image of God, that they are redeemed by Jesus Christ, and that they are summoned by God to a destiny beyond history" (Hollenbach 1986, 376). In this, he observes that "the Catholic tradition does not hesitate to claim a universal validity for the way it seeks to ground human rights in the dignity of the person" (ibid.).

Hollenbach also reminds us that, historically, the Catholic Church has always operated institutions which sought to protect the human dignity of persons and which were often the only agencies available to the downtrodden in those time periods. He notes that "the church has long been deeply involved in responding to pressing social ills through direct Christian service. Hospitals, orphanages, schools, and efforts to aid the poor have historically been part of the church's understanding of its own mission" (Hollenbach 1988, 3). Thus, as James E. Hug contends, "the longing for justice has been a central element in the Christian tradition from earliest biblical times to the present. Without work for justice, declared the 1971 Synod of Catholic bishops, we do not have true Gospel living" (Hug 1997, ix).

Charles Curran points out that the concept of human dignity is also affirmed by the "Christian understanding of love," the concept of "love of neighbor." Curran explains that this concept is universal, all inclusive, and emphasizes going out of one's way for another, even the stranger and the outcast. In addition, Curran explains that the Catholic Church's own ecclesiology points to a universal morality, that "our concerns are universal," since the Church is not only concerned with itself as an institution but with society as well. As Curran points out, "what goes on in God's world is a concern of ours" (Curran, 1999).

Thus, there is much throughout the Catholic tradition historically which argues for the value of the individual person and the concept of human dignity. However, the concepts of "person," "nature," and "rights," as in "natural rights," were most often traditionally explained within the framework of natural law. The next section of this chapter examines the concept of natural law in Roman Catholicism, before moving on to explain why the Catholic Church initially rejected the modern concept of human rights in light of the natural law framework. This will form a precursor to the shift in Catholic thought within the past century on human rights.

2. NATURAL LAW AND HUMAN RIGHTS

J. Bryan Hehir observes that "in Catholic theology the dominant mode of moral discourse concerning human rights has been the natural law tradition" (Hehir 1980b, 109). However, as we shall see later, while John XXIII's *Pacem in Terris* in 1963 employed the language of "natural law," Vatican II moved more in the direction of using the language of "human dignity." This shift in Catholic thought was a conscious move to place a greater emphasis on biblical language as well as to place less of an emphasis on its philosophical framework, a move which assisted dialogue with other Christian denominations. Yet, despite this shift in language and approach, Langan admits that while there has been "a tendency in more recent Catholic teaching to put less explicit reliance on natural-law categories," he emphasizes that "there is no sharp change in the underlying anthropology" (Langan 1986a, 112). Thus, natural law is a foundational category for understanding human rights in Catholicism.

Hehir explains that a "distinguishing mark of a natural law theory of human rights is its stress on the social nature of the person." He continues that "the person is radically social; society precedes the person historically and the person is dependent on a social context for full human development." Hehir points out that "this [implies a] correlation of rights and duties in Catholic teaching [that] sets it apart from the liberal philosophy which speaks of rights but seldom has an articulated theory of duties" (Hehir 1980b, 111). I now offer a brief historical sketch of the concept of natural law in Roman Catholicism as it relates to human rights.

William R. Garrett maintains that "the natural law theories appropriated from Stoicism by medieval churchmen were integrated into the teachings of the Roman Catholic Church as a basis for the Church's social ethic – especially after the papal revolution in the eleventh to thirteenth centuries, when canon law was codified and rationalized." He continues that "embedded in these natural law formulations was a theory of individual rights, familial organization, the nature of the state, economic regulations, and principles for the proper order of slavery." However, Garrett notes that "individual rights were relatively underdeveloped," since "the primary concern – especially among lawyers trained in canon law – was the interrelation between the church as a corporation and the state as a countervailing institutional, corporate structure" (Garrett 1988, 129).

John Mahoney acknowledges that "in accepting, and indeed appropriating, Stoic teaching on the moral life as an exercise of man's reason in subordination to a higher principle of reason which pervades all of reality, early Christian thinkers were to adopt a principle of divine cosmic and human order ... which ... has been a major intellectual feature of the history of Christian moral thinking" (John Mahoney 1989, 72). He recalls that "it is to Justin that Christian theology is primarily indebted for the Stoic idea of natural law" (ibid. 73), yet emphasizes that the Stoic influence "is most clear in Augustine in his systematic exploitation of the concept of order in the whole of God's creation." For Augustine, "underlying everything is an eternal law of God" (ibid. 74).

Mahoney explains that, added to the ethics of Stoicism was the concept from Roman law of *ius naturale*, or "'the just by nature' of the Roman jurists, which as the expression of universal reason was considered to be the basis of the *ius gentium*, the law of peoples." Isidore, the seventh-century archbishop of Seville, "explained that ... the *ius naturale* is the law observed everywhere by the prompting of nature." Thus, Mahoney observes that "the Church's canonists developed and perpetuated the idea of natural law as of divine origin and as the basis for all justice, described by Rufinus as 'the divine power which nature implants in man, impelling him to do good and avoid evil'" (ibid. 77). (Rufinus was the first systematic commentator on the *Decree* of Gratian.)

Yet, Mahoney acknowledges that "it was in the Dominican friar, the Italian Thomas of Aquino, that in the thirteenth century moral theology was to find its first fully and systematically articulated expression of natural law theory" (ibid.). Thomas defined law as an order or arrangement of reason for the common good (ibid. 78). Mahoney explains that, for Thomas, "all creatures have 'impressed' in their very being inherent tendencies which reflect the ordering and orientation which God their creator wishes for them." Therefore, "man as a rational being sharing in God's providential activity is aware of what God has impressed in his nature and he is capable of freely accepting and embracing the order of his being and his place in the divine scheme of things." Mahoney explains that, according to Thomas, "this knowing and free acceptance of his nature as created and destined by God is man's observance of the law of his nature, or of the 'natural law'" (ibid.).

Mahoney observes that, for Thomas, "the first thing which strikes us about anything is that it is a thing, a being," yet "there is a similar first principle in the area of action, based now not on being and not-being but on good and not-good" (ibid. 79). Thomas himself argued that "this is the first precept of law, that good is to be done and pursued, and evil is to be avoided. All other precepts of the natural law are based upon this" (Thomas Aquinas, *Summa theologiae* in Curran and McCormick 1991, 104).

Overall, Thomas maintained that "there belong to the natural law … certain most general precepts that are known to all" and that "as to those general principles, the natural law, in the abstract, can nowise be blotted out from men's hearts" (ibid. 112). (However, Thomas did insist that there was less certainty the more one moved to particulars, and that therefore it could be "blotted out" in the case of a particular action. This insight of Thomas, which acknowledged a lessening degree of certainty in moral areas as one moved from generalities to specific action, was often lost in the historical appropriation of Thomas by Roman Catholicism.) Therefore, Mahoney acknowledges that "in the centuries following Aquinas his teaching on natural law was to become an authoritative and central feature of moral theology and the outstanding example of its respect for, and expectations from, the power of human reasoning in the moral sphere" (John Mahoney 1989, 80).

In regards to society, David O'Brien and Thomas Shannon remind us that "Aquinas defined society as a system of mutual exchange of services for the common good." They explain that "society and government were part of nature, operating according to laws that reflected the universal structure of creation." They continue that, "on this basis Aquinas envisioned an organically unified universe in which there were transcendent norms to assist in understanding and evaluating human experience." Therefore, this implied that "what held society together and gave it ethical discipline and coherence was a theory of social obligation that sprang from the very nature of society and was related to a hierarchical universe presided over by God." O'Brien and Shannon note that, because of this, "social obligations thus took priority over individual desires and wants" (O'Brien and Shannon 1998, 3).

Along these lines, Brian Tierney points out that "when Aristotle or Aquinas sought to define *dikaion* or *ius*, they did not proclaim the rights and powers of individuals. They were concerned rather with a harmonious structure of relationships, right proportion, *juste partage*" (Tierney 1997, 22). Thus, while Roman Catholicism advocated a universal morality, which would seem to push for universal human rights, its communitarian vision of society and of the universe took precedence over the individual in the areas of rights. This becomes apparent in the next section on Roman Catholicism's historical opposition to the concept of human rights.

But first, a word on terminology. I have used the term human rights throughout, yet this section on "natural law" requires a note on the term "natural rights." In addition, the term "rights of man" has been used in the literature previous to the more inclusive "human rights." From the framework of "natural law" comes the concept of "natural rights." Tierney explains that "the term 'human rights' is often used nowadays to indicate a lack of any necessary commitment to the philosophical and theological systems formerly associated with the older term, 'natural rights.'" However, he asserts that "the two concepts are essentially the same," noting that "human rights or natural rights are the rights that people have, not by virtue of any particular role or status in society, but by virtue of their very humanity" (ibid. 2).

Tierney contends further that "the idea of natural rights is a *moral one.*" He explains that "it does not refer to the rights that people can *actually exercise* in any given society but to rights that *ought to be recognized* in all societies because they are necessary for the fulfillment of some basic human needs and purposes" (ibid. 5 [italics mine]). Therefore, he observes that "when medieval thinkers reflected on the nature of human beings, one fact they perceived … was that human rationality included a capacity for moral discernment" (ibid. 6), which included the area of natural rights. In addition, he suggests that "in medieval thought, there existed, not just some vague idea of a natural right, but many of the specific themes that we encounter in modern works on rights – a distinction between natural rights and positive rights, rights considered as protected choices and as protected interests, active rights and passive rights, alienable natural rights and inalienable natural rights, adventitious rights, rights that were also duties" (ibid. 7).

Thus, this medieval view of natural rights and natural law, particularly as articulated by Thomas Aquinas, formed the Roman Catholic Church's interpretation of natural or human rights. Examples of the strong ties between natural law and human rights in Roman Catholicism can be seen in the writing of Jacques Maritain in the past century. Maritain asserted that "the philosophical foundation of the Rights of man is Natural Law" (Maritain 1951, 80 [see also Maritain 1943]), and that "the history of the rights of man is bound to the history of Natural Law" (ibid. 81).

Maritain argued that natural law is the only solid basis for the language of natural rights, since this implies "that there is a human nature, and that this human nature is the same in all men" (ibid. 85). He acknowledges that, historically, "in ancient and mediaeval times attention was paid, in natural law, to the *obligations* of man more than to his *rights*," yet he reminds us that the great achievement of the 18th Century was "to bring out in full light the *rights* of man as also required by natural law" (ibid. 94). Thus, he observes "how could we understand human rights if we had not a sufficiently adequate notion of natural law?" He emphasizes that "the same natural law which lays down our most fundamental duties ... is the very law which assigns to us our fundamental rights" (ibid. 95).

Maritain points out the necessity of a philosophical and moral base for human rights, arguing "how, then, can one claim rights if one does not believe in values? If the affirmation of the intrinsic value and dignity of man is nonsense, the affirmation of the natural rights of man is nonsense also" (ibid. 97). He notes the tie between the concept of human rights and natural law with Aquinas' first principle, maintaining that "*natural law* deals with the rights and the duties which are connected in a *necessary* manner with the first principle: 'Do good and avoid evil'" (ibid.).

In addition, Maritain spoke of specific rights, and the connection between rights and the common good, all based on the concept of natural law. He asserts that "man's right to existence, to personal freedom, and to the pursuit of the perfection of moral life, belongs, strictly speaking, to natural law" (ibid. 100), and that "just as every law – notably the natural law ... – aims at the common good, so human rights have an intrinsic relation to the common good" (ibid. 101). Thus, Maritain serves as a prime example of the traditional Catholic framework for human rights discussion, which is based on natural law, and includes duties corresponding to rights, and the common good.

John Courtney Murray serves as another example of a major Catholic theologian within this past century who grounded the philosophy of human rights within natural law. Murray was instrumental in Vatican II's emphasis on human freedom and he drafted the *Declaration on Religious Freedom*. He is dealt with more extensively in the section on Vatican II, yet his emphasis on natural law is important to note here. In his *We Hold These Truths: Catholic Reflections on the American Proposition*, Murray's last chapter is entitled "The Doctrine Lives: The Eternal Return of Natural Law." He argues that modern society has not adequately rejected the true concept of natural law, but only "caricatures of the doctrine of natural law" (Murray 1960, 296).

In regard to human rights, Murray observes that "our problem is not simply to safeguard human rights, in the sense of fortifying each discrete individual in the possession of a heterogeneous collection of social empowerments." But rather, he argues that the purpose is "to erect, and secure against all assault, an *ordo juris*, an order of law that will be in consequence an order of rights and hence by definition an order of freedom." Thus, he contends that "if this is so, ... the new 'age of order,' of just law and true freedom, must look to natural law as its basic inspiration" (ibid. 302). Murray and Maritain stand as examples of Catholic teaching on human rights as rooted in the concept of natural law.

In this section, I have briefly shown the strong emphasis on natural law in Roman Catholic tradition, historically as well as within the past century. As we shall see, even when a shift takes place in Vatican II, to the stress on human dignity, the underlying philosophical base is still natural law. Today, as Walter Kasper points out, in the Roman Catholic tradition regarding human rights, "two traditions come together ... namely, a natural law foundation ascending 'from below,' and a ... salvific-christological-foundation descending 'from above.'" He reminds us that "the foundation of human dignity is derived from human nature itself, more precisely from the endowment of men and women with reason and free will." Kasper asserts that "the natural law foundation-the foundation 'from below'-can thus provide a foundation for the universal validity of human rights," and he notes that "it enables the Church to address itself beyond the confines of Christendom, listening to the voice of conscience of all people of good will, and to work together with them" (Kasper 1990, 157). While this is true more so today, at least in theory, the Church's universalist stand was not always so willing to embrace the modern notion of human rights, nor those who were its primary proponents. Having established the Roman Catholic tradition's strong ties with the concept of natural law for human rights, one must also acknowledge that tradition's rejection of human rights in the modern era.

C. ROMAN CATHOLICISM'S OPPOSITION TO THE CONCEPT OF HUMAN RIGHTS IN THE MODERN ERA

Charles Curran admits that "the natural law tradition associated with Roman Catholicism would seem in theory to be quite congenial with universal rights ontologically grounded in the human person. However, the Catholic tradition was slow to embrace the terminology of human rights" (Curran 1987, 153). Here, I will briefly acknowledge those tensions, before moving on to the acceptance of human rights within Catholicism in the past century.

Charles Wackenheim offers the following broad historical hypothesis. He suggests that "the message of Jesus and of the primitive Church helped to give men a powerful awareness of their true dignity. During the first three centuries of the Christian era, the Church ceaselessly asserted the rights of man and this in the face of the claims of the imperial power." However, he continues that "after 313, the need for the cohesion and survival of human institutions took precedence over the proclamation of 'the truth that makes men free' (Jn 8:32)." He observes that "once she gained the social and cultural leadership of the West, the Roman Church espoused as a matter of course the ideology of the established order," and that therefore, "from this point of view the claim for individual rights necessarily appeared subversive" (Wackenheim 1979, 52).

Later, forces shaping the modern world would threaten the Catholic view of Western Civilization. O'Brien and Shannon note that "one of the major consequences of the breakup of the medieval unity of civilization was the perception that individuals stood in an adversary relationship to the larger society," which "fostered a deeper sense of individual autonomy and personal worth." As pointed out in Chapter One, "this was provided over several centuries by the elaboration of contract theories of society, the most famous associated with Hobbes and Locke." O'Brien and Shannon remind us that, "while presenting diametrically opposed pictures of human nature, both theories emphasized individual rights as claims against society, and both looked at the individual as the bearer of certain rights that society should not contravene" (O'Brien and Shannon 1998, 4).

They observe that while "there was continuity with the medieval tradition in that contract theories were related to natural law," there was also "discontinuity with medieval philosophy in that this theory of natural law based itself on inalienable rights inherent in each individual, with social and political obligations arising not from nature but from voluntary consent" (ibid.). Thus, they explain that "the individual, not society, became the locus of natural law," and this "gave rise to a situation in which there could be continual and inherent conflict between individuals and society." Therefore, O'Brien and Shannon acknowledge that "again and again the Catholic Church faced a choice of adapting to new ideas of individual autonomy ... and almost always it chose to assert the need for order and hierarchy" (ibid. 5).

In addition, some key proponents of the individualism and autonomy of human rights theory were also key adversaries of Roman Catholicism. Knut Walf asserts that "the aversion of Catholic Church authorities to these formulated human rights can be traced back primarily to the expressly anti-Catholic (and anti-absolutist) orientation of the English Bill of Rights of 1689" (Walf 1990, 35). He also points out that "up till the middle of the twentieth century the Christian Churches as a whole experienced great difficulties in coming to acknowledge human rights ... (s)ince these rights had been proclaimed by the advocates of the anti-church French Revolution" (ibid. 36).

Walf recalls that "the Catholic Church viewed these ideas as a 'doctrine of unbridled freedom'" (ibid.). And Jack Mahoney points out that, "as Pope Pius VI exclaimed in a papal brief to Louis XVI of France, human rights was a monstrous idea." He notes that "Bentham, in his diatribe on the same French Declaration of the Rights of Man, expostulated that it was terrorist language and dangerous nonsense" (Jack Mahoney 1990, 313).

Thus, from a political as well as a philosophical perspective, Roman Catholicism was confronted by a concept which it openly rejected or at least dismissed. John Langan explains that "the Church, especially in France, experienced the proclamation of human rights in 1789 as a very cold and hostile wind," and he admits that "it cannot claim for itself a significant place in either the theoretical or the practical struggle for human rights in the eighteenth and nineteenth centuries." Therefore, Langan concludes that "human-rights theory in an explicit and politically dynamic form confronted Catholicism as an alien force, and it has taken Catholicism a long time to appropriate it" (Langan 1986a, 117).

Charles Curran concurs that, in general, "mainstream Western Christianity has taken a long time to work out a way of respecting human rights and liberty while holding on to the truth-claims of Christianity" (Curran 1987, 142). He sums up that "the heavy emphasis in Catholic thinking was on objective truth and the natural law," and that "at best one had to freely accept truth in the speculative order and natural law in the moral order, but freedom was never an ultimate value." Curran emphasizes that "the most important realities were the objective realities themselves," noting that "this emphasis was the basis for the famous statement that error has no rights" (ibid. 150).

But, what brought about the shift in Catholic thinking on the concept of human rights? Curran observes that "the Catholic Church, which was the great enemy of freedom in the nineteenth century, gradually came to champion freedom in the twentieth century." Again, politics comes into play. Curran explains that "as the twentieth century progressed, a new problem appeared on the scene – totalitarianism." Pointing out that "Catholic social ethics has always tried to find a middle path between individualism and collectivism," he observes that "against the collectivism of Fascism, Nazism, and Communism ... Catholic teaching defended the dignity and rights of the human person" (ibid. 151). This brings us to the past century, in which Roman Catholicism slowly accepted, then embraced, and finally advocated, the concept of human rights.

3.2: ROMAN CATHOLICISM COMES TO TERMS WITH THE CONCEPTS OF HUMAN RIGHTS AND SOCIAL JUSTICE

A. LEO XIII AND *RERUM NOVARUM*

David Hollenbach points out that "the history of modern Roman Catholic teaching about human rights begins with the pontificate of Leo XIII (1878-1903)" (Hollenbach 1979, 43). Spurred on by capitalism's abuse of its workers, on one hand, and the rise of totalitarianism on the other, Leo argued for the rights of workers, including the right

to private property, based on natural law. Thus, Roman Catholicism
entered into the human rights camp.

Hollenbach notes that "for several decades prior to the date when
Rerum Novarum was issued, groups of 'social Catholics' had been for-
mulating an approach to the new economic realities of industrial capitalism which sought to ameliorate the frequently appalling conditions
of the lives of workers" (ibid. 46). Peter J. Henriot, Edward P. DeBerri
and Michael J. Schultheis concur that "the terrible exploitation and
poverty of European and North American workers at the end of the
nineteenth century prompted the writing of *The Condition of Labor*,"
and that "the document was inspired by the work of the Fribourg
Union, a Catholic Social Action movement in Germany, and by re-
quest from the hierarchy in England, Ireland, and the United States"
(Henriot, DeBerri and Schultheis 1997, 33).

Within the political climate of the time, the Catholic emergence on
the side of human rights was often unsuspected or suspect at best.
O'Brien and Shannon reflect that "when one considers the background out of which *Rerum Novarum* emerged, it is a wonder that
the document was written at all." They point out that "the nineteenth
century began and ended amid hostility toward the Roman Catholic
Church," and that "anticlerical movements fueled the fires of an already
heated nationalism, leading to conflict with the church in many countries." Given that, they contend that "the issue now confronting the
church was to understand the new reality of a secular state" (O'Brien
and Shannon 1998, 12).

In coming to this new understanding, O'Brien and Shannon suggest
that "Leo attempted to persuade Catholics to concentrate less on politics and more on the 'social question'" (ibid.). They emphasize that "in
a remarkably evenhanded manner the pope laid anathemas on both
liberal capitalism, which released the individual from social and moral
constraints, and socialism, which subordinated individual liberty to
social well-being without respect for human rights or religious welfare." Instead, Leo argued that "economic life, like political life, should
reflect the dualistic nature of the person," which involved "providing
for bodily needs and facilitating the quest for salvation" (ibid. 13).
Thus, they concur that "Leo initiated modern Catholic discussion of
human rights in the economic order" (ibid.).

In *Rerum Novarum*, Leo himself wrote that "some remedy must be
found, and quickly found, for the misery and wretchedness which press

so heavily at this moment on the large majority of the very poor." He observed that "the ancient workmen's guilds were destroyed in the last century, and no other organization took their place" (*Rerum Novarum*, no. 2).[1] Given these circumstances, Leo argued for the economic rights of workers, including the right to private property, based on natural law. He asserts that "every man has by nature the right to possess property as his own." Observing that "man alone among animals possesses reason" (ibid. no. 5), Leo contends that "private ownership is according to nature's law" (ibid. no. 7), and that therefore "it is clear that the main tenet of socialism, the community of goods, must be utterly rejected" (ibid. no. 12).

Langan acknowledges that Leo represents "the first stage in the development of Catholic human-rights doctrine," pointing out that "along with a vehement affirmation of the natural rights of property and a denunciation of the Marxist notion of class struggle, Leo affirmed 'the natural right' of each person 'to procure what is required in order to live'" (Langan 1986a, 118). Langan observes that "in taking this position, Leo XIII was following the teaching of Thomas Aquinas, *Summa theologiae*, 2a 2ae, 66, 7" (ibid. 128).

In *Rerum Novarum*, Leo writes that "'It is lawful,' says Thomas of Aquinas, 'for a man to hold private property; and it is also necessary for the carrying on of human life'" (*RN*, no. 19 [From Thomas Aquinas, *Summa theologiae* 2a 2ae Q.lxvi. art. 2]). In addition, he continues that "in the words of the same holy doctor: 'Man should not consider his outward possessions as his own, but as common to all, so as to share them without difficulty when others are in need" (ibid. [From Q.lxv. art. 2]). Thus, Leo affirms the right to private property, based on Thomas' understanding of natural law, as well as affirming the Catholic middle ground between the rights of the individual and one's duties toward the common good.

Mahoney elaborates on the role of natural law in Leo's thinking. He observes that "it was with the pontificate of Pope Leo XIII that the doctrine of natural law was to flourish, partly as the result of another Scholastic and Thomistic revival," and "partly in its being considered a particularly apt instrument in the development of the Church's social and political teaching in a world which might listen to reason." Therefore, he asserts that "against full-blooded socialism, the right of property and ownership was based on human nature and on 'the most

1   All citations for *Rerum Novarum* will be from O'Brien and Shannon.

holy law of nature'" (John Mahoney 1989, 81). In addition, Mahoney points out that "the application of natural law thinking by Leo XIII in his teaching on working class conditions and the rights of workers was to be echoed in later social encyclicals of further Popes" (ibid. 82).

Leo continued that "all men are the children of the common Father" and that "all have the same end, which is God himself" (*RN*, no. 21), affirming the classical *exitus et reditus* , that God is the source of all humanity, as well as its final destination and purpose. Regarding the duties of rulers, he emphasized that "the first and chief is to act with strict justice-with that justice which is called in the schools *distributive*-toward each and every class" (ibid. no. 27 [italics in original]). Leo asserted that "when there is a question of protecting the rights of individuals, the poor and helpless have a claim to special consideration," since "the richer population have many ways of protecting themselves," but the poor "must chiefly rely upon the assistance of the State" (ibid. no. 29).

Leo affirmed that "it is the soul which is made after the image and likeness of God," pointing out that "in this respect all men are equal; there is no difference between rich and poor, master and servant, ruler and ruled, 'for the same is Lord over all'" (ibid. no. 32 [End citation from Romans 10:12]). Therefore, he emphasized that "no man may outrage with impunity that human dignity which God himself treats with reverence," noting that "it is not man's own rights which are here in question, but the rights of God" (ibid.).

Arguing against the modern concept of society as a contract between individuals and between individuals and the state, which was reflected in current economic claims concerning "free contracts," Leo asserted that "there is a dictate of nature more imperious and more ancient than any bargain between man and man, that the remuneration must be enough to support the wage earner in reasonable and frugal comfort." And, since "each one has a right to procure what is required in order to live," and since "the poor can procure it in no other way than by work and wages," it follows that if "the workman accepts harder conditions because the employer or contractor will give him no better, he is the victim of force and injustice" (ibid. no. 34). Along these lines, Leo concludes by citing Thomas:

> Human law is law only in virtue of its accordance with right reason: and thus it is manifest that it flows from the eternal law. And in so far as it deviates from right reason it is called an unjust law; in

such case it is not law at all, but rather a species of violence (*RN*, Footnote #36 [*Summa theologiae* 1a 2ae Q.xciii. art.iii]).

In *Rerum Novarum*, Leo argued for the rights of individual workers, against the oppression of their employers or the State. The words of that document, "Man precedes the State," have been repeated many times in later documents (Hollenbach 1979, 43). And, Leo's arguments were based on natural law, on the concept of the universality of humanity and justice, and the human dignity common to all. David Hollenbach observes that "the positive influence toward equality exerted by his writings came chiefly from his treatment of the economic and social rights of workers," and that it was on this "economic flank of the Church's engagement with modern society" that Leo "made the most substantial advances" (ibid. 46).

Hollenbach concludes that "Leo's encyclicals laid the groundwork for the modern Catholic theory of human rights" and that "human dignity is the foundation of this theory" (ibid. 49). With *Rerum Novarum*, Roman Catholicism entered into the human rights camp. Yet it did so cautiously, if not begrudgingly. Given the political and economic climate, it sided with the individual, yet repeatedly stressed the individual's duties toward the common good. And, it still continued at this point to argue for a Christian society (*RN*, no. 22), and in general for a "hierarchical and traditionalist model of social organization" (Hollenbach 1979, 49). However, the seeds were sown for the modern Roman Catholic understanding of the concept of human rights, which it would later advocate in Vatican II in recognition of a pluralistic society.

B. TRANSITION: PIUS XI AND PIUS XII

While *Rerum Novarum* marked the first stage in modern Roman Catholic thought on human rights, the second stage is a transitional period which includes the contributions of Pius XI and Pius XII. Langan notes that this second stage "consists in Catholicism's acceptance of the values, procedures, and norms of Western constitutional democracy as the appropriate framework for modern societies" (Langan 1986a, 119). This phase also includes the emergence of Christian Democratic parties and the work of Jacques Maritain on natural law and human rights. Langan explains that "the end of this second phase of Catholic development coincided with the internationalization and universalization of human rights in the declarations of the Allies," and "ultimately in the Universal Declaration of Human Rights in 1948" (ibid.).

After Leo XIII's successors, Pius X (1903-1914) and Benedict XV (1914-1922), who "made few notable advances in the Catholic rights theory," Pius XI (1922-1939) resumed the development which Leo XIII began. Hollenbach explains that these years "were dominated by three new social developments of massive significance-the great depression, the consolidation of the Russian Revolution into a successful communist regime, and the emergence of Fascist dictatorships in Italy and Germany." He observes that "the Roman Catholic understanding of human rights developed rapidly during this period under the pressure of these events" (Hollenbach 1979, 50). Unlike the years of Leo XIII, where "liberal capitalism was at the zenith of its power," Pius XI issued *Quadragesimo Anno: After Forty Years*, in 1931 after "World War I had shattered liberal confidence" (O'Brien and Shannon 1998, 40).

Pius XI's primary contribution was the introduction of the term "social justice" into the Roman Catholic vocabulary of human rights. O'Brien and Shannon explain that "a new phrase – *social justice* – appeared in *Quadragesimo Anno* to describe the type of justice that demanded due recognition of the common good, a good which included, and did not contradict, the authentic good of each and every person" (ibid.) They assert that, because of this, "the church could lift up both human rights and human solidarity as the basis of its response to the extremes of totalitarianism and capitalism," and that this also "provided the foundation for the balancing of political and civil with social and economic rights" (ibid. 41).

Hollenbach points out that Pius XI developed the term "social justice" "into a key ethical concept in Catholic social thought," explaining that the term "is a conceptual tool by which moral reasoning takes into account the fact that relationships between persons have an institutional or structural dimension" (Hollenbach 1979, 54). Therefore, Pius XI's use of this term "indicates the emergence of a new sensitivity in Catholic thought to the possibility of conscious institutional change," which was "an important departure from Leo XIII's frequent appeal to traditionalist justifications for a hierarchical social order" (ibid. 55).

Hollenbach concludes, then, that "in *Quadragesimo Anno* Pius XI reaffirmed the rights stated in *Rerum Novarum*, but with a new sensitivity to their social conditions and limits" (ibid. 56). In the concept of "social justice," "human dignity is a social rather than a purely private affair," and therefore "human rights have a social as well as individual foundation" (ibid. 55).

These themes were picked up and continued with Pius XII (1939-1958). Hollenbach maintains that "the central theme of respect for the dignity of the person as the foundation of all moral order was taken up and vigorously affirmed" by Pius XII, and that he "spoke more frequently and more systematically of the moral roots of social, political and economic order than had any of his predecessors" (ibid. 56). In arguing for "a community of morally responsible citizens," Pius XII contended that "human rights cannot be understood apart from social interdependence, nor can social well-being be understood apart from personal rights" (ibid. 61).

J. Bryan Hehir also sees Pius XII as a transitional figure, who "moved beyond economic rights to address political-civil rights and Catholic teaching on democracy" (Hehir 1996, 101), as well as moving beyond the concept of nation to a focus on the international community (ibid. 102). In doing so, he "set the stage for John XXIII" (ibid.), whose *Pacem in Terris* would become the definitive Roman Catholic document on human rights, and whose initiation of the Second Vatican Council would truly give the Roman Catholic Church a global focus.

3.3: ROMAN CATHOLIC AFFIRMATION OF THE CONCEPT OF HUMAN RIGHTS

A. INTRODUCTION TO JOHN XXIII, *PACEM IN TERRIS*, AND VATICAN II

Marvin L. Krier Mich observes that "by the late 1950's the Roman Catholic church in the United States had established itself as an institution whose theology and tone were generally introspective, defensive, and self-righteous toward 'the world'" (Mich 1998, 90). This tone would change on a global scale with the pontificate of Pope John XXIII. And it would be influenced by the American experience of democracy and Catholicism, particularly in the work of the American Jesuit John Courtney Murray on the Second Vatican Council's *Declaration on Religious Freedom*. Mich contends that the work of

these two individuals "signaled the end of an era – the era of thinking that had lasted too many centuries, which held that 'error has no
rights'" (ibid. 91). This section examines the legacy of John XXIII for
the Roman Catholic tradition on human rights, including his encyclical *Pacem in Terris*, the Second Vatican Council, its continuation in
the work of Paul VI, and influences within the American church.

This time period represents a third phase in the development of
Roman Catholic thought on human rights, according to John Langan
(Langan 1986a, 120). He maintains that "*Pacem in Terris*, together
with the decrees of Vatican II, is the resolution of a crucial stage of
Roman Catholicism's long struggle with the modernizing and secular-
izing culture of the West." Although "the issue of religious freedom
was central," the wider notion of human rights "provided a basis for the
transformation of Catholicism from an ally and ward of traditionalist
regimes to a critic of repression by both reactionary and revolutionary
regimes" (ibid. 110). Begun by Leo XIII, this process reaches its full
transformation in the pontificate of John XXIII.

Hollenbach asserts that "the brief years that John XXIII was pope
(1958-1963) were watershed years for the Roman Catholic human
rights tradition" (Hollenbach 1979, 62). Hehir agrees, pointing out
that "John XXIII made a double contribution to the Catholic human
rights ministry: the first was his encyclical *Pacem in Terris*; the second was his role in calling the Second Vatican Council." He emphasizes that the Vatican II document on religious freedom, *Dignitatis
Humanae* (1965), should be "read in tandem" with *Pacem in Terris*, and
that "taken together, these texts establish John XXIII as the pivotal
figure in the development of Catholic human rights theory" (Hehir
1996, 102).

Yet, even between these two documents, there is a shift in the underlying philosophy. *Pacem in Terris*, despite being the fundamental
Catholic document on human rights, is still operating from a philosophy of natural law. In the documents of Vatican II, a shift takes place
to focus on the human person and the concept of human dignity. This
shift attempts to be more biblically based, as well as to facilitate discussion with other Christian denominations and the modern world in
general. Traer notes that "Hollenbach indicates that modern Catholic
social teaching has shifted from natural law to human dignity, as a basis for human rights, which allows for development of a more realistic
and universal doctrine of human rights" (Traer 1991, 46). O'Brien

and Shannon note that the "new focus is the category of the person, which represents a major shift of emphasis from the traditional use of natural law categories." They point out that "the Second Vatican Council centers on a doctrine of individual rights that focuses on the person and validates the claims of the person over and against society" (O'Brien and Shannon 1998, 164).

Hehir reminds us, in regards to *Pacem in Terris*, that "it is necessary to indicate the significant shift away from natural law argument in Catholic teaching which occurred just after its publication." He contends that "the shift is represented in the Vatican II document the Pastoral Constitution on the Church in the Modern World (1965) published just two years after *Peace on Earth*." Hehir explains further that "what one finds in the conciliar text is not a rejection of natural law but a move to incorporate its philosophical view of human rights in a much wider theological framework" (Hehir 1980b, 113), which includes the greater use of scripture in its argumentation.

However, Hehir points out that an additional shift takes place here as well, a shift which refocuses how the Church sees itself. He suggests that, in *Pacem in Terris*, "there was no direct connection drawn between the moral teaching on human rights and the understanding of the Church's ministry and mission," but that "the Pastoral Constitution of Vatican II ... ties the ministry of the Church to the pursuit of human rights." Therefore, Hehir strongly asserts that "in its central ecclesiological affirmation, *the Pastoral Constitution describes the Church as a community of faith whose social role involves it directly in the promotion of human dignity and the protection of human rights*" (ibid. 114 [italics mine]). Having introduced this significant period in the development of Roman Catholic theory on human rights, and the corresponding shifts in thought, I now examine these documents and events in greater detail.

B. JOHN XXIII AND *PACEM IN TERRIS*

John XXIII's first social encyclical, *Mater et Magistra* (Christianity and Social Progress), was issued in 1961. In it, he "'internationalizes' the Catholic social teaching by treating, for the first time, the situation of countries which are not fully industrialized," addressing "the severe imbalances between the rich and the poor which exist in the world" (Henriot, DeBerri and Schultheis 1997, 42). Thus, issues were raised here which would be more systematically addressed in *Pacem in Terris*.

Hollenbach explains that, "in a significantly new emphasis within the tradition John XXIII moved toward a definition of human dignity in social and structural terms" (Hollenbach 1979, 64).

Langan affirms that "the central and classical document for the doctrine of human rights in the Roman Catholic tradition is *Pacem in Terris* (Peace on Earth)" (Langan 1986a, 110), issued in 1963. While rooted in the philosophy of natural law, its stress on human dignity initiated the shift toward that concept which would be embraced by Vatican II. Hehir describes *Pacem in Terris* as "the clearest exposition of a contemporary Catholic view of both natural law theory on human rights and the political order necessary to sustain human rights, from interpersonal relations through international relations" (Hehir 1980b, 112). And Charles Curran concurs that *Pacem in Terris* is "perhaps the most explicit affirmation of natural law as the basis of papal social teaching and the best illustration of its explication in social morality" (Curran cited in ibid.).

Pacem in Terris was groundbreaking in its actual listing of specific rights and duties. Hollenbach observes that "*Pacem in Terris* gives the most complete and systematic list of these human rights in the modern tradition," and that these include "both those rights stressed by the liberal democratic tradition and those emphasized by socialists" (Hollenbach 1979, 66). In addition, he points out that "this list of human rights is a systematic recapitulation of the rights claims made by the tradition since Leo XIII" (ibid. 67). Therefore, in addition to the wide range of rights articulated in *Pacem in Terris*, the overall concept of human rights itself is seen as being fully rooted in and consistent with earlier Catholic tradition. Hollenbach maintains that "the advance contained in *Pacem in Terris* is its attempt to show that there has been a logic operating throughout the development of the tradition which links these rights together," and that "the thread which ties all these rights together is the fundamental norm of human dignity" (ibid. 68).

Henriot, DeBerri and Schultheis point out that *Pacem in Terris* "was the first encyclical addressed to 'all people of good will,'" and that "its optimistic tone and development of a philosophy of rights made a significant impression on Catholics and non-Catholics alike" (Henriot, DeBerri and Schultheis 1997, 47). O'Brien and Shannon observe that "four major themes stand out in *Pacem in Terris*: the rights proper to each individual, the relation between authority and

conscience, disarmament, and the development of the common good"
(O'Brien and Shannon 1998, 129).

The encyclical states early on that:

> Any human society, if it is to be well-ordered and productive, must
> lay down as a foundation this principle, namely, that every human
> being is a person; that is, his nature is endowed with intelligence
> and free will. Indeed, precisely because he is a person he has rights
> and obligations flowing directly and simultaneously from his very
> nature. And as these rights and obligations are universal and invio-
> lable, so they cannot in any way be surrendered (*Pacem in Terris*, no.
> 9, cited in O'Brien and Shannon 1998).

It continues with a full section on rights, including the following:
the right to life and a worthy standard of living, rights pertaining
to moral and cultural values, the right to worship God according to
one's conscience, the right to choose freely one's state of life, economic
rights, the right of meeting and association, the right to emigrate and
immigrate, and political rights (ibid. nos. 11-27). Included in this section is the argument that "by the natural law every human being has
the right to respect for his person, to his good reputation; the right to
freedom in searching for truth and in expressing and communicating
his opinions, and in pursuit of art, within the limits laid down by the
moral order and the common good" (ibid. no. 12). In addition, it notes
the "equal rights and duties for man and woman" (ibid. no. 15). Pope
John concludes that section by appealing to Pius XII, that "every individual has a claim to the protection of his rights" and that "there is assigned to each a definite and particular sphere of rights, immune from
all arbitrary attacks," which is "the logical consequence of the order of
justice willed by God" (ibid. no. 27).

The following section of *Pacem in Terris* deals with duties, and includes: rights and duties necessarily linked in the one person, reci-
procity of rights and duties between persons, mutual collaboration,
an attitude of responsibility, social life in truth, justice, charity, and
freedom, and God and the moral order (ibid. nos. 28-38). In this section, John XXIII argues that "rights as well as duties find their source,
their sustenance and their inviolability in the natural law which grants
or enjoins them" (ibid. no. 28). He continues that "every fundamental
human right draws its indestructible moral force from the natural law"
(ibid. no. 30). This natural law argument emphasizes that the moral
order, "whose principles are universal, absolute and unchangeable, has

its ultimate source in the one true God, who is personal and transcends human nature" (ibid. no. 38).

Pacem in Terris continues by noting that "the conviction that all men are equal by reason of their natural dignity has been generally accepted" (ibid. no. 44). It emphasizes that "when the relations of human society are expressed in terms of rights and duties, men become conscious of spiritual values, understand the meaning and significance of truth, justice, charity and freedom, and become deeply aware that they belong to this world of values" (ibid. no. 45). In addition, it promotes the concept of the common good, arguing that "the common good is chiefly guaranteed when personal rights and duties are maintained" (ibid. no. 60), and that civil authorities must protect the rights of citizens as well as promote them (ibid. no. 65).

Arguing that natural law regulates the rights and duties of individuals, it also emphasizes that this same application applies to nation states (ibid. no. 80). Therefore, citing Augustine, it argues "What are kingdoms without justice but large bands of robbers" (ibid. no. 92 [Augustine, *De Civitate Dei* (*The City of God*), Book IV, Ch. 4; *Patrologia Latina*, 41, 115]). Given this international outlook, John XXIII acknowledges the United Nations, and affirms that "an act of the highest importance performed by the United Nations Organization was the Universal Declaration of Human Rights, approved in the General Assembly on December 10, 1948" (ibid. no. 143). While acknowledging that there are some objections and reservations about that document, he emphasizes that it "represents an important step on the path toward the juridical-political organization of all the peoples of the world," since "in it ... the dignity of a human person is acknowledged to all human beings" (ibid. no. 144).

By affirming and supporting the United Nations, John XXIII brought the modern Catholic understanding of human rights into alignment with the political view articulated in the U.N. documents. Hollenbach affirms that John XXIII's *Pacem in Terris* "includes all the rights enumerated in the UN Universal Declaration and its two accompanying Covenants," as well as "all the rights emphasized on each side of [the] East/West and North/South debates" (Hollenbach 1986, 374).

Hehir concurs that "in endorsing this spectrum of rights, including rights which are immunities and those which are empowerments, the pope took the Catholic church into the heart of the United Nations human rights debate." He points out that, while "the U.N. documents also encompass this broad range of rights," those documents fail "to provide a systematic foundation illustrating how these two distinct kinds of moral claims are coherently held together." However, *Pacem in Terris* does attempt to do this, and that "for *Pacem in Terris*, the foundation and purpose of all rights is the dignity of the human person" (Hehir 1996, 103).

Thus, John XXIII brought the Roman Catholic tradition into the modern discussion of human rights, acknowledging the importance of the U.N. and the Universal Declaration of Human Rights and viewing them as one of the many "signs of the times" (Traer 1991, 38). (That phrase itself is one of the key concepts of *Pacem in Terris*.) Traer observes that "in *Pacem in Terris* ... he affirmed that the protection of human rights was the basis for world peace" (ibid. 36). This landmark document set the stage for the continued discussion of human rights in Vatican II, in which the argumentation shifted away from natural law to the emphasis on human dignity and the individual, historical person. It also set the stage for the Catholic Church's advocacy for human rights, and for its viewing human rights as a major part of its own ministry and purpose. John XXIII's legacy on the issue of human rights in contemporary Roman Catholicism cannot be overemphasized. The Church was brought into the modern world, and it would fight for human rights along with "all men of good will" (*Pacem in Terris*, Introduction).

C. VATICAN II

1. INTRODUCTION TO VATICAN II

Reflecting on the changes in Roman Catholicism since Vatican II on the issue of social justice, Bernard Haring "noted that the five confessor's manuals most used by Catholic priests before Vatican II listed more than 300 sins related to the sacristy, but only 5 related to offenses against peace and social justice" (Jennings 1974, 2). Such an illustration shows the profound shift in Catholic thinking from the pre- to the post-Vatican II church. In the Church's renewed focus on social justice as an agenda for its ministry, the concept of human rights was a key ethical concept.

Hollenbach explains that "Vatican II was the occasion of a fundamental shift in the church's understanding of its social and institutional place in a pluralistic world" (Hollenbach 1986, 367). He suggests that "the Council had an impact on Catholic thought similar to the influence which the founding of the United Nations exerted on the content of secular political thought." Hollenbach maintains that both organizations "had a common concern with the problem of the unity of the human community and the task of finding norms and structures for world peace in the face of ideological pluralism and conflict," as well as "the need to find consensus on a normative basis for international justice and peace." Therefore, this "led both bodies to a human rights focus" for their endeavors (ibid. 371).

This acknowledgement of pluralism and of global concerns also led the church to reflect on itself. Hollenbach points out that "at the Council the Catholic church became, at least incipiently, a genuinely transnational body rather than a European one with missionary outposts" (ibid.). He explains that "the impetus for the rapid development of a human rights ethic in the Catholic church came in large part from the non-European regions of the transnational church," with the poor countries of the Third World raising the issues of social/economic rights and the United States raising the issues of civil/political rights, "especially the right to religious freedom" (ibid. 372).

In addition, O'Brien and Shannon point out that "Vatican II replaced the juridical, hierarchical definition of church with more biblical and symbolic images." More important for the concept of human rights, however, is another "shift marked by the Second Vatican Council [which] resulted from the long, agonizing effort of church leaders to come to terms with liberal, democratic principles." This is most evident in the document on religious freedom. They emphasize that "this new stress on human liberties and human rights occupied a central place with Pope John XXIII and Pope Paul VI" (O'Brien and Shannon 1998, 163).

In particular, though, two documents from Vatican II stand out in their development of the Catholic concept of human rights. Hollenbach recalls that "two years after the publication of *Pacem in Terris*, during its last session in 1965, the Second Vatican Council approved and promulgated two documents which carry the Catholic understanding of human dignity and human rights a step further." He emphasizes that "the *Pastoral Constitution on the Church in the Modern World (Gaudium et Spes)* and the *Declaration on Religious Liberty (Dignitatis Humanae Personae)* were the two most significant

statements of the Council related to questions of social morality."
Specifically, Hollenbach observes that *Gaudium et Spes* made "a number of significant contributions to the discussion of the foundations of
a theory of human rights," while *Dignitatis Humanae* concerned itself
"with a very particular and important human right: the right to religious liberty" (Hollenbach 1979, 69). I examine these two documents
next.

2. PASTORAL CONSTITUTION ON THE CHURCH IN THE MODERN WORLD (*GAUDIUM ET SPES*)

Henriot, DeBerri, and Schulteis contend that "Vatican II's *The
Church in the Modern World* is seen by many to be the most important document in the Church's social tradition." They point out that
"it announces the duty of the People of God to scrutinize the 'signs
of the times'" and acknowledges that "change characterizes the world"
(Henriot, DeBerri, and Schulteis 1997, 51). In addition, the "Church's
duty in the world" is now seen to be "to work for the enhancement of
human dignity and the common good" (ibid. 52).

The approach to putting the document together was unique to the
Church as well. O'Brien and Shannon observe that "*Gaudium et Spes*
was a powerful document, more powerful perhaps than the encyclicals
because it represented the opinion of the overwhelming majority of the
world's bishops." They summarize that it "embodied the incarnational-
ist theology that brought the church into the heart of human life," that
"it spoke in humble and sincere terms to Catholics and non-Catholics
alike," and that it "offered a systematic and synthetic ethical framework
for dealing with world problems." Thus, *Gaudium et Spes* gave "strong
and forceful voice to Pope John's vision of a church in service to real
people in the concrete circumstances of human history" and "set new
directions for Catholic social thought" (O'Brien and Shannon 1998,
165).[2]

In regard to human rights, Traer observes that *Gaudium et Spes*
"reaffirms that human rights are the necessary conditions for human

---

2 Henriot, DeBerri, and Schulteis point out that "originally, the material contained here was not scheduled to be considered separately by the
Council," but that Cardinal Joseph Suenens of Belgium urged for "consideration of issues more 'external' to the Church." They observe that the final
document "represents a significant break from the rigid traditionalism of
the Council's preparatory commission" (Henriot, DeBerri, and Schulteis
1997, 52).

dignity" (Traer 1991, 39). Hollenbach elaborates further that "the Council's most important contribution to the human rights tradition was its important new acknowledgement that the demands of human dignity are historically conditioned ones." Thus, while acknowledging the transcendental worth of persons, it also realizes that human dignity "cannot be known or affirmed apart from the concrete conditions of an historical epoch" (Hollenbach 1979, 70). In affirming this historicity, then, the Council acknowledges that "bodiliness, interpersonal relationships and social organization are positive possibilities in and through which human dignity is realized" (ibid. 73).

Hollenbach concludes that "*Gaudium et Spes* thus suggests a fruitful way to combine the traditional view of human rights as rooted in human nature with modern historical consciousness." He asserts that, therefore, "from the perspective of the Council, social, economic and cultural rights, defined in relation to historical conditions, assume a new place of importance in the Catholic human rights tradition" (ibid. 75).

In the document itself, part one deals with the Church's view of the human person, while part two deals with aspects of modern life and society. Chapter One is entitled "The Dignity of the Human Person," and acknowledges that "by his innermost nature man is a social being, and unless he relates himself to others he can neither live nor develop his potential" (*Pastoral Constitution on the Church in the Modern World* 1966, no. 12). While admitting that one "is obliged to regard his body as good and honorable" (ibid. no. 14), it also affirms that "by his intellect he surpasses the material universe, for he shares in the light of the divine mind" (ibid. no. 15). In addition, in speaking of the dignity of the moral conscience, it asserts that "conscience is the most secret core and sanctuary of a man," and that in it "man detects a law which he does not impose upon himself, but which holds him to obedience" (ibid. no. 16).

The section on the Church's attitude toward atheism asserts that "the Church holds that the recognition of God is in no way hostile to man's dignity, since this dignity is rooted and perfected in God" (ibid. no. 21). In addition, it contends that states who unjustly distinguish between believers and unbelievers are "ignoring fundamental rights of the human person" (ibid.).

Gaudium et Spes argues for the interdependence of person and society, maintaining that "the progress of the human person and the advance of society itself hinge on each other" (ibid. no. 25). Thus, in addition to the concept of human dignity, it emphasizes the concept of the common good. It argues that promoting the common good to-day "takes on an increasingly universal complexion and consequent-ly involves rights and duties with respect to the whole human race." Therefore, it observes that "there is a growing awareness of the exalted dignity proper to the human person, since he stands above all things," and strongly asserts that this person's *rights and duties are universal and inviolable*" (ibid. no. 26 [italics mine]).

Emphasizing that "everyone must consider his every neighbor with-out exception as another self" (ibid. no. 27), it also notes that even the person in error "never loses the dignity of being a person" (ibid. no. 28). Therefore, it argues for "the essential equality of men," and for the importance of "social justice," in the section bearing those terms in its title. *Gaudium et Spes* contends that "since all men possess a rational soul and are created in God's likeness, since they have the same nature and origin, have been redeemed by Christ, and enjoy the same divine calling and destiny, the basic equality of all must receive increasingly greater recognition" (ibid. no. 29).

Having established the dignity of the person, it focuses on social jus-tice by asserting that "human institutions ... must labor to minister to the dignity and purpose of man" and must "safeguard the basic rights of man" (ibid.). Thus, in tying together the concepts of the individual, the common good, and social institutions, *Gaudium et Spes* argues that "the obligations of justice and love are fulfilled only if each person, contributing to the common good, ... also promotes and assists the public and private institutions dedicated to bettering the conditions of human life" (ibid. no. 30). This focus on social institutions, and their promotion of human dignity, would also challenge the Church to re-examine its own mission.

Hehir explains that "on an ecclesiological level, *Gaudium et Spes* lo-cated the social ministry of the Church and the protection and promo-tion of human rights solidly within the ambit of the Church's religious ministry." He observes that, in contrast to *Pacem in Terris, Gaudium et Spes* "makes an explicitly theological argument for the ministry of human rights" (Hehir 1996, 105), noting that "both the theological anthropology which grounds human dignity and human rights, and the eschatological destiny of the person establish a context for human rights different from the philosophical arguments of Pius XII and

John XXIII." Because of this, "the engagement of the Church in the struggle for human rights is not only a moral and political task," but it is now seen as "part of the work of preparing a new heaven and new earth" (ibid. 106).

Also different in *Gaudium et Spes* is the shift from the natural law argumentation of its predecessors. Hehir points out that "natural law is not forsaken, but it is developed in an argument joining constitutional ideas previously tolerated but not accepted by the church" (ibid. 105), as well as the re-emphasis on scripture. Hollenbach adds that, while "*Gaudium et Spes* reaffirmed the natural-law argument that human dignity is evident, apart from faith, in the intelligence, freedom, and conscience possessed by all persons," it also "sought to make the direct links between these philosophical considerations and the biblical and theological notion of the *imago Dei*" (Hollenbach 1988, 7). In addition, he maintains that, in *Gaudium et Spes*, "the church's social mission was more tightly linked to the Bible, to Christology, eschatology, ecclesiology, and other central doctrinal perspectives than at any time in recent centuries" (ibid.).

Admitting that sometimes the acknowledgement of pluralism is a step toward religious indifference, Hollenbach observes that this was not the case in Vatican II. He argues that, in *Gaudium et Spes*, "the 'social question' became a properly theological question," which is not merely a side issue "or extension of the church's real purpose but is integral or essential to this purpose" (ibid.). Therefore, in this, Hollenbach contends that "in defending and promoting human dignity, ... the church is engaged in a properly religious task" since the "social mission is part of the religious mission of the church" (ibid. 8).

In conclusion, the natural law argumentation for human dignity and human rights was maintained, but now heavily refocused with theological and biblical arguments from within the Church's tradition and constitutional arguments from without. Added to this was the Church's new enthusiasm for seeing human rights advocacy as a central part of its mission in this world, a world which it acknowledged by its renewed affirmation of historical circumstances. Yet another document would add to this development. This was the *Declaration on Religious Freedom (Dignitatis Humanae)*, which emphasized the importance of freedom to human dignity. Its argument for religious freedom, a specific human right, made a significant contribution to the Roman Catholic concept of human rights in general.

3. DECLARATION ON RELIGIOUS FREEDOM (*DIGNITATIS HUMANAE*)

The *Declaration on Religious Freedom (Dignitatis Humanae)* added to the Catholic understanding of human rights, by allowing for religious freedom as a human right and by its emphasis on freedom itself. Hollenbach explains that "in rethinking this one right, the Council brought Catholic social thought into a new relationship with the entire Western liberal tradition" (Hollenbach 1979, 75). A part of this new concession in Catholic thought was the acknowledgement of pluralism, and the abandonment of the idea that one type of government, intertwined with the Church, was the sole ideal of what a state should be. Hollenbach underscores the fact that "the reorganization of the normative foundations of the Catholic understanding of human rights was produced by the same social force which precipitated the Declaration on Religious Freedom, namely, the reality of pluralism" (Hollenbach 1986, 368). He emphasizes that "the option of a single normative social-religious system was rejected as the Catholic ideal in the Declaration on Religious Freedom" (ibid. 369).

Another significant admission by the Council in the document is the concept that doctrine, in this case on human rights, can develop. The Declaration reads "in taking up the matter of religious freedom this sacred Synod intends to *develop the doctrine* of recent Popes on the inviolable rights of the human person and on the constitutional order of society" (*Declaration on Religious Freedom*, no. 1, in Abbot 1966 [italics mine]). John Courtney Murray, the American Jesuit who was the chief architect of the document, notes that "in no other conciliar document is it so explicitly stated that the intention of the Council is to 'develop' Catholic doctrine." He explains that "this is significant, since it is an avowal that the tradition of the Church is a tradition of progress in understanding the truth" (Murray 1966, 677). Murray recalls that it was "the most controversial document of the whole Council," because "it raised with sharp emphasis the issue that lay continually below the surface of all the conciliar debates – the issue of the development of doctrine." He observes that "this was a doctrinal event of high importance for theological thought in many other areas" (ibid. 673). I would argue that its importance cannot be emphasized enough, in its affirmation that *Catholic doctrine on human rights can develop*, and in its acknowledgement that it has already done so in the past century. Catholics are all too well aware of the Church's reticence to acknowledge change and development in doctrine, especially on moral issues.

Also, the importance of the concept of freedom and its necessity for human dignity is central to the Declaration. Hollenbach explains that, in *Dignitatis Humanae*, "responsible use of freedom defines the very nature of social morality." He points out that "human rights are rights *within society*. They are both negative immunities and positive entitlements," and that, therefore, *Dignitatis Humanae* affirms that "it is the function of government to intervene to assure that all the rights and duties of citizens are brought into the harmony of a moral order, thus assuring public peace." Hollenbach emphasizes that, in *Dignitatis Humanae*, "the focus is on persons in interaction, not on theories or religions seeking adherents," and that, therefore, "the concern of the argument is ... for the person and his or her freedom to act in society" (Hollenbach 1979, 77).

The concept of freedom was of utmost importance to Murray, and he left his stamp on the Council. His biographer notes that "in every discussion, he always brought with him the conviction that freedom was 'the first truth about man, a positive value, both personal and social, to be respected even when it involves man in error and evil'" (Cited in Mich 1998, 110 [End quote Murray]). Murray himself wrote that:

> Freedom, in the deepest experience of it, is love, to be free is to be-for-others. The Christian call to freedom is inherently a call to community, a summons out of isolation, an invitation to be-with-the-others, an impulse to service of others (ibid. 118).

Mich observes that "Murray attempted to show the compatibility of the Roman Catholic social tradition with the American ethos as expressed in the consensus of the founding fathers" (ibid. 114), and that he "audaciously claimed that the Catholic social vision, rooted in the natural law, was necessary to rebuild and articulate" that lost consensus (ibid. 113). Murray himself addressed what he called the relativity of the "new rationalism." He asserted that "its ethical relativism destroys the only ground on which a stand can be made – the absoluteness of the order of human rights that stands irremovably outside the sphere of state power, and the absoluteness of the order of justice that stands imperiously above the power of the state" (Murray 1960, 326). Thus, Murray's own understanding of freedom, and the American understanding of religious freedom, entered into the conciliar documents in *Dignitatis Humanae*.

The *Declaration on Religious Freedom* begins with the observation that "a sense of the dignity of the human person has been impressing itself more and more deeply on the consciousness of contemporary man" (*Declaration on Religious Freedom*, no. 1 in Abbot, 1966). The document argues from the standpoint of human dignity, contending that human rights in general and therefore religious freedom as a particular human right, are necessary to uphold human dignity.

Murray, in his notes on the document, explains that "the issue of religious freedom arises in the political and social order," and that "this is the order of human rights, and in it the principle of freedom is paramount." He argues that there is another order, a spiritual order, which involves "what is objectively true and morally good," and that this is "the order of duty and obligation." Therefore, he asserts that "no man may plead 'rights' in the face of the truth or claim 'freedom' from the moral law." Murray brings this up "lest religious freedom be made a pretext for moral anarchy" (Murray 1966, 676).

The document states that "this Vatican Synod declares that the human person has a right to religious freedom" (*DRF*, no. 2).[3]4 It further states that "the right to religious freedom has its foundation in the very dignity of the human person, as this dignity is known through the revealed Word of God and by reason itself." It continues that "this right of the human person to religious freedom is to be recognized in the constitutional law whereby society is governed," and that "it is to become a civil right" (ibid.).

The Declaration also emphasizes the concept of the common good, citing "the duty of all toward the common welfare" (ibid. no. 6). Murray himself notes that this concept of the "common welfare" is a "pivotal notion," which was "put forward in *Rerum Novarum*, which Pius XII strongly developed, and which John XXIII defined with greater precision." Murray explains that the common welfare "chiefly consists in the protection of the rights, and in the performance of the duties, of the human person" (Murray 1966, Commentary on *DRF*, 684, note 14).

Murray also underscores the importance of freedom to Catholic social thought. He maintains that "Catholic thought had consistently held that society is to be based upon truth, directed toward justice, and animated by charity." He contends that, "in *Pacem in Terris*, John

3 Murray notes that "in making it formally a 'freedom from' and not a 'freedom for' … the Declaration is in harmony with the sense of the First Amendment to the American Constitution" (Commentary, 678, note 5).

XXIII added the missing fourth term, freedom," which he defines as "an end or purpose of society, which looks to the liberation of the human person" (ibid. 687, note 21).

Finally, the Declaration argues that the concept of religious freedom as a human right, based on human dignity, is rooted in divine revelation. The document reads that "the declaration of this Vatican Synod on the right of man to religious freedom has its foundation in the dignity of the person," and that "the requirements of this dignity have come to be more adequately known to human reason through centuries of experience." It continues by asserting that "this doctrine of freedom has roots in divine revelation, and for this reason Christians are bound to respect it" (*DRF*, no. 9). Later, the document again strongly reiterates that "the Church therefore is being faithful to the truth of the gospel, and is following the way of Christ and the apostles when she recognizes, and gives support to, the principle of religious freedom as befitting the dignity of man and as being in accord with divine revelation" (ibid. no. 12).

Thus, in the specific human right on religious freedom, the Declaration affirms that the concept of human rights is based on human dignity and that this concept and the support of it is in accord with divine revelation, as well as through reason as seen in the natural law. Hollenbach maintains that the document "asserted that a Christian understanding of the human person, rooted both in the Christian tradition and the tradition of reason, demands that human dignity be respected through the civil guarantee of religious freedom." In regard to the Second Vatican Council in general, Hollenbach contends that "it affirmed that there are basic rights in the social, economic, political, and cultural fields which all systems and all ideologies are bound to respect. These are the basic rights of the human person, derived from the fundamental dignity of the person" (Hollenbach 1986, 369).

Therefore, the *Declaration on Religious Freedom (Dignitatis Humanae)*, in its affirmation of the human right to religious freedom, adds to the general affirmation of human rights in the *Pastoral Constitution on the Church in the Modern World (Gaudium et Spes)*. Based on the concept of human dignity, the Roman Catholic understanding of human rights is *developed* and supported, and is seen as being in line with both reason and divine revelation. This groundbreaking work of the Council on human rights continued on after the Council in the pontificate of Paul VI.

D. PAUL VI

Overseeing the duration of most of the Council, Pope Paul VI continued the development and advocacy for human rights in the encyclical *Populorum Progressio (The Development of Peoples)* (1967), and the Apostolic Letter *Octogesima Adveniens (A Call to Action)* (1971). Hollenbach observes that "both of Paul VI's social statements begin with an acknowledgement that they belong to a new period of self-understanding within the Roman Catholic tradition." He points out that "the problems of economic development, international economic relationships, and, above all, the poverty of developing nations are the central concerns of these documents" (Hollenbach 1979, 78).

Henriot, DeBerri, and Schultheis explain that, in *Populorum Progressio* "Paul VI enlarges the scope of Leo XIII's treatment of the struggle between the rich and poor classes to encompass the conflict between rich and poor nations," noting that it "is the first encyclical devoted entirely to the international development issue." In addition, he emphasizes that "more so than any of his predecessors, Paul VI explicitly criticizes basic tenets of capitalism, including the profit motive and the unrestricted right of private property" (Henriot, DeBerri, and Schultheis 1997, 59).

Francois Refoule suggests that Paul VI was a strong advocate for human rights, observing that anyone reflecting on his writings "cannot but be impressed by the place occupied by the defense of the dignity and rights of man" (Refoule 1979, 77). The day after Paul VI died, the patriarch Dimitrios referred to him as a "defender of human dignity, herald of the rights of man and of the ending of all social discrimination" (Cited in ibid.). Refoule recalls that, in an address to the United Nations in 1965, Paul VI asserted that "we make our own the voice of the poor, the disinherited, the wretched, those who long for justice," and that in a letter to Kurt Waldheim, Secretary-general of the U.N. in 1972, he wrote that "the Church feels wounded in her own person whenever a man's rights are disregarded or violated" (ibid.). At the end of the Synod of Bishops in 1974, Paul VI urged that "we declare our determination to promote the rights of man and reconciliation amongst men, in the Church and in the world today" (ibid.).

Refoule emphasizes that it was Paul VI who chose the theme of "Justice in the World" for the Synod of Bishops in 1971, as well as creating the commission *Justice and Peace* in 1967. In addition, he notes that "Paul VI never failed to refer explicitly to the Universal Declaration of the Rights of Man," which he wanted to make "the corner-stone of all his work" (ibid. 78). Thus, the Catholic concern for and development of human rights which he oversaw at Vatican II was continued after the Council in his pontificate.

E. CONCLUSION TO VATICAN II

I have shown that John XXIII, with *Pacem in Terris*, brought the concept of human rights to the forefront of Catholic social teaching. This concept was further developed and advocated in the documents of the Second Vatican Council, which he initiated and which Paul VI oversaw. This advocacy and development continued in the pontificate of Paul VI after the Council adjourned. But Vatican II had further repercussions for human rights.

Jo Renee Formicola suggests that, in the U.S., "Vatican II reinforced and helped to accelerate the total integration of Catholics into the American mainstream." She points out that "by the mid-1960's, the American Catholic Church was no longer an alien, aggressive adversary" and that it "now had the potential to be a significant moral force in the American social and political arena" (Formicola 1988, 95).

Formicola emphasizes that "the years 1965-1978 saw human rights re-emerge as a significant international concern of both the American Catholic Church and the U.S. government," observing that "the Church's interest in human rights was renewed by its desire to help its persecuted brothers in Latin America." She concludes that "the American Catholic Church, particularly through the United States Catholic Conference, took measures in the mid-1960's to publicize repression in Brazil, to create a climate of concern for international human rights generally, and to develop an American constituency interested in the problem of religious and political repression around the world" (ibid. 147).

J. Bryan Hehir, a key player in U.S. Catholic advocacy for human rights, contends that Vatican II in general "defined a role for the church in the world of public affairs," and that that role "was to stand as 'a sign and safeguard of the transcendence of the human person'" (Hehir 1996, 288). He maintains that "Vatican II both legitimated a more activist Catholicism and provided resources for directing it" (ibid. 111).

I now turn to the developments on human rights that followed after Vatican II. So far, I have dealt largely with papal encyclicals, and, as official pronouncements of the Roman Catholic Church, that approach has been valid. However, one must also acknowledge that a variety of people and events contributed to the development of these encyclicals, and that papal encyclicals alone do not make the entirety of the Catholic tradition. In the spirit of Vatican II, a variety of additional documents and movements contributed to the post-conciliar development of the Roman Catholic understanding of human rights, and these are acknowledged next.

3.4: DEVELOPMENT ON HUMAN RIGHTS
SINCE VATICAN II

A. INTRODUCTION: HISTORICAL INFLUENCES
IN THE 1960's, '70's, AND '80's

Other historical developments in the 1960's, '70's and '80's left their mark on the post-conciliar Church's advocacy for human rights. O'Brien and Shannon remind us that, in the U.S., "only in 1963, when the civil rights movement was exploding across the country, did the bishops again systematically consider the moral aspects of domestic social and economic life." In addition, they point out that "in 1971 they publicly concluded that the American war in Vietnam could no longer be justified," and that in 1973, when the Supreme Court decriminalized abortion, "the bishops condemned the action and urged a constitutional amendment to reverse the decision" (O'Brien and Shannon 1998, 489).

Jo Renee Formicola recalls that "in 1970, the United States Catholic Conference and the National Council of Churches took their human rights concerns one step farther to the OAS [Organization of American States] and sought sanctions against Brazil for violations of human rights." She observes that "this was the beginning of Catholic and Protestant attempts not only to publicize, but to bring sanctions against governments that engaged in repression." Formicola emphasizes that "by 1973, the American Catholic Church became politically involved on behalf of international human rights," and that "the U.S.C.C. began to participate in the political arena to insure the fact that human rights became a factor in U.S. foreign policy" (Formicola 1988, 148).

Mich observes that one important development in the U.S. during this time period was the Campaign for Human Development, established by the U.S.C.C. in 1970. He maintains that "the impact of Vatican II and the social turmoil in the United States during the 1960's" served "as the backdrop for the establishment of the Campaign for Human Development" (Mich 1998, 337). Mich emphasizes that "what has been a distinctive feature of the Campaign for Human Development is that it *takes poor people seriously as agents of change* and not merely as recipients of the 'charity' of others," noting that "from the very beginning CHD has stressed an empowerment approach" (ibid. 338 [italics in original]).

In Latin America, Margaret E. Crahan suggests that "religion and human rights in Latin America have been strongly linked particularly since the 1960's," observing that "many of the principal human rights actors ... were started by churches during periods of severe repression and survived in large measure because of national and international ecclesial support." Pointing out that there "was a historical base for it as far back as the early sixteenth century when Dominican and Franciscan friars denounced the exploitation of Native Americans by Spanish and Portuguese colonists" (Crahan 1996, 262), she contends that today "support for the Catholic Church appears to have increased at the grassroots in large measure because of its championing of human rights and socioeconomic justice" (ibid. 273).

This approach in Latin America developed on a global scale as well. Hehir points out that "while many forces were directing the church toward human rights from within, clearly one of the strongest influences on the life of Catholicism in the 1970's and 1980's was the rise of authoritarian regimes, particularly in developing countries." Here, in these situations, the Catholic Church was often "the only institution capable of confronting unrestrained political power" (Hehir 1996, 112). Hehir observes that "the Church has emerged in several countries as a principal adversary of authoritarian governments of the right and left," and contends that "when it has risen to the challenge *the justification for its action has been made in terms of human rights as a dimension of the ministry of the gospel*" (Hehir 1980b, 116 [italics mine]).

In addition, Hehir points out that since Vatican II, the Holy See "encouraged the creation of 'Justice and Peace' units in each country," and that these "are charged with the task of mobilizing the conscience of the Church regarding issues of social concern, among which human rights is a preeminent question" (ibid. 118). He emphasizes that, in the 1970's, "the ministry of justice has moved steadily from the periphery of the Church's life toward the heart of her life," and that it also "has moved from being treated as the work of some specialists in the Church ... to being now regarded as a basic responsibility of every Christian" (Hehir 1978, 19). In the words of Richard McCormick, "the Church has grown increasingly conscious that the protection and promotion of human rights is central to her ministry" (Cited in Hehir 1980b, 115).

Given the above influences, I would like to briefly examine some key events: the 1971 Synod of Bishops, the 1986 U.S. bishop's Pastoral Letter *Economic Justice for All*, and the pontificate of John Paul II, before concluding with some general developments. All of these continue the development of the Roman Catholic understanding of human rights as articulated in *Pacem in Terris* and the documents of Vatican II and as advocated in the postconciliar Catholic tradition. The next two documents are particularly noteworthy in their collegial approach as well as in their concern for human rights.

B. *JUSTICE IN THE WORLD*: STATEMENT OF THE SYNOD OF BISHOPS, 1971

O'Brien and Shannon note that, "as a way of implementing the Second Vatican Council, Paul VI announced the regular convening of synods of bishops" (O'Brien and Shannon 1998, 287). In its second session, this Synod "turned its attention to concerns of special importance to the churches of Africa, Asia, and Latin America: the problems of justice and human rights" (Hollenbach 1979, 85). In the document, "the bishops focused on the necessity of structural change," and "made it clear that the Church must stand with the poor and oppressed if it is to be faithful to this gospel mandate." O'Brien and Shannon recall that "the most quoted statement of the document continues to serve as the foundation for the church's social justice mission: '*Action on behalf of justice and participation in the transformation of the world fully appear to us as a constitutive dimension of the preaching of the Gospel*' (Introduction)" (O'Brien and Shannon 1998, 287 [italics mine]).

Henriot, DeBerri, and Schultheis note that the document "illustrates the powerful influence of native leadership of the churches of Africa, Asia, and Latin America," and that the Synod was "the first major example of post-Vatican II episcopal collegiality." It also "reflects a forceful, concrete, and realistic refinement of previous papal pronouncements" (Henriot, DeBerri, and Schultheis 1997, 67). The document itself affirms development as a basic human right (#15) and speaks of human rights violations and specific injustices (#'s 21-26) (ibid. 68). It notes that "Christian love of neighbor and justice cannot be separated" (#34) (Cited in ibid. 69). Henriot, DeBerri, and Schultheis explain that it emphasizes that "the Gospel message gives the Church the right and duty to proclaim justice on all levels and to denounce instances of injustice (#36)," and that it also contends that "the role of the hierarchical Church is not to offer concrete solutions to specific problems, but to promote the dignity and rights of each human being (#37)" (ibid.). In addition, it called for the ratification of the U.N. Declaration of Human Rights by all nations (#64) (ibid. 70).

Hollenbach contends that the document itself "incorporates both the strength of the tradition's theory of human dignity and rights, on one hand, and differentiated understanding of social relationships characteristic of Paul VI's writings on the other." He emphasizes that it does this "through a recognition that human dignity implies a constellation of rights which must be understood, not singly, but in dynamic interrelation with each other" (Hollenbach 1979, 85). Hollenbach points out that "the relational quality of human dignity is spelled out by the Synod in terms of a fundamental right to participation which integrates all the other rights with each other" (ibid. 86).

Thus, Hollenbach asserts that "the introduction of the right to development in the Synod document *Justice in the World* ... is the most explicit acknowledgment of the interconnectedness of all these personal, social and instrumental rights." Given this, Hollenbach concludes that "the major breakthrough in the period since Vatican II has been the recognition that the relationship between the different rights affirmed by the tradition is a dynamic one" (ibid. 99).

In *Justice in the World*, the Synod of bishops, working in the collegial spirit of Vatican II, continued the Catholic development of the concept of human rights by emphasizing the "right to participation," which was seen as key to the realization that the various other rights are interconnected. In addition, it continued the Church's own introspection, in viewing human rights as part of its own agenda in proclaiming the gospel to the world. Hehir observes that whereas "the constitutive tasks of the Church traditionally have been understood as the celebration of the sacraments and the preaching of the Gospel," now "the teaching authority through the Synod has expanded this vi-

tal category of constitutive tasks to include the ministry for justice"
(Hehir 1978, 20).

Shortly after the Synod, additional support for the advocacy of human rights was voiced by U.S. bishops. In October, 1973, on the 10th
anniversary of *Pacem in Terris* and the 25th anniversary of the *U.N.
Declaration of Human Rights*, Bishop James S. Rausch contended that
"the Church's role in the international order is that of an advocate,
seeking to surface human rights issues which get submerged in much
of the traditional routine of foreign policy" (Jennings 1974, 7). And,
in November, 1973, in the "Resolution on the 25th Anniversary of the
Universal Declaration of Human Rights," the bishops observed that
"as bishops entrusted with the social teaching of the Church and as
leaders of the Catholic community in the United States, we wish to
express our strong endorsement for the United Nations' Universal
Declaration of Human Rights and for the institution of the United
Nations" (Cited in ibid. 4).

Thus, Catholic support for the concept of human rights, as articulated in the U.N. Declaration, continued. And, Catholic development
and advocacy for the concept of human rights continued beyond the
confines of the U.N. Declaration, in affirming the other social and economic rights and in arguing for the interconnectedness of all of these
rights. By 1986, the concepts of human rights, the common good, and
the poor would be key elements in the U.S. bishops' pastoral letter
Economic Justice for All, which used the concept of human rights to
offer a critical view of the U.S. economy at home and abroad.

C. ECONOMIC JUSTICE FOR ALL:
U.S. BISHOPS' PASTORAL LETTER, 1986

In 1983, when a committee of bishops chaired by Joseph Cardinal
Bernardin issued a pastoral letter on peace and nuclear arms, *The
Challenge of Peace: God's Promise and Our Response*, another committee
was meeting to address the U.S. economy. This committee was chaired
by Archbishop Rembert Weakland of Milwaukee, and would produce
*Economic Justice for All: Pastoral Letter on Catholic Social Teaching and
the U.S. Economy* in 1986. O'Brien and Shannon explain that this
letter "originated in the felt need to provide a moral commentary on
American economic life to balance a strong letter on Marxist communism issued in 1980." They note that it "attempted to follow Paul
VI's directive to apply Catholic social teaching to concrete problems

within the United States," and that while it was "less specific than the peace letter in its policy proposals," still it was "more sharply critical of national values and practices" (O'Brien and Shannon 1998, 491).

Another major contribution of the pastoral letter was the process itself, where bishops became participants and listeners as well as teachers. Henriot, DeBerri, and Schultheis explain that "the Bishops consulted widely among business leaders, academicians, government officials, and other segments of American society, as well as among theologians and Church leaders," and that after several hearings throughout the U.S., they "received almost twenty thousand written suggestions as they circulated three preliminary drafts." They emphasize that "the pastoral is significantly influenced by Vatican II's call to read the 'signs of the times,' the social teaching of the Council, and the social teachings of Pope John Paul II" (Henriot, DeBerri, and Schultheis 1997, 121).

Mich describes one of these listening sessions, in which "the visual image of the five bishops on the committee sitting in the front row of the audience, *listening and taking notes* as various economists, business and governmental leaders addressed the issues of the economy struck me at the time and stays with me," emphasizing that "the bishops were in their *listening and learning* mode" (Mich 1998, 315 [italics in original]). He notes that "Richard McCormick underscored that the content and process reflected a new collegial vision of church that is 'broadly consultative, questioning, critical, open, appropriately tentative'" (ibid. 316).

After the letter's release, Weakland received many critiques from Catholics who argued from a more "individualistic ethic," and from critics who found the "collectivist moral strain" of the letter "repellent" (ibid. 319). In addition, while some critics felt that the bishops should not be addressing issues like the economy, Mich points out that "the bishops, in keeping with the Catholic social teachings tradition, refuse to be limited to personal, sexual, and family values" (ibid. 325).

The letter begins by summarizing some of its major themes. It states that "*every economic decision and institution must be judged in light of whether it protects or undermines the dignity of the person*," and that this human dignity "comes from God, not from nationality, race, sex, economic status, or any human accomplishment" (United States Catholic Conference 1986, no. 13, ix [All italics in original except where noted]). It also points to the social aspect of human dignity, arguing that "*human dignity can be realized and protected only in community*," noting that "the human person is not only sacred but also social" (ibid. no. 14, ix). The letter emphasizes the importance and priority of the poor, contending that "*all members of society have a special obligation to the poor and vulnerable*," and that "the justice of a society is tested by the treatment of the poor" (ibid. no. 16, x). It also stresses the importance of the concept of human rights, asserting that "*human rights are the minimum conditions for life in community*," and explaining that "in Catholic teaching, human rights include not only civil and political rights but also economic rights" (ibid., no. 17, xi). The letter emphasizes that "society as a whole, acting through public and private institutions, has the moral responsibility to enhance human dignity and protect human rights" (ibid. no. 18, xi). Thus, the concepts of the human dignity of the individual, the social nature of the individual as seen in concern for the common good, the concern for the poor and marginalized, and the importance of human rights as a means of safeguarding these values, are seen as key concepts throughout the document.

Chapter One begins by stating three questions which must be asked: "What does the economy do *for* people? What does it do *to* people? And how do people *participate* in it?" (ibid. no. 1). These form the basic questions which run throughout the pastoral letter's critique of the economy. The letter argues that the Catholic social tradition "insists that human dignity … is the norm against which every social institution must be measured" (ibid. no. 25). Chapter Two emphasizes that because of "the transcendent worth – the sacredness – of human beings," humans are "ends" and "not means," since they are "created in the image of God (Gn 1:27)" (ibid. no. 28). This chapter, in the spirit of Vatican II, emphasizes the biblical perspectives on human dignity and also points out that "a constant biblical refrain is that the poor must be cared for and protected and that when they are exploited, God hears their cries (Prv 22:22-23)" (ibid. no. 49). It contends that the example of Jesus "imposes a prophetic mandate to speak for those who have no one to speak for them, to be a defender of the defenseless, who in biblical terms are the poor" (ibid. no. 52).

The pastoral letter also speaks specifically of human rights and duties. It outlines the points that there are "*duties* [which] all people have to each other and to the whole community," that "corresponding to these duties are the *human rights* of every person," and that "these duties and rights entail several *priorities*" (ibid. no. 62). The letter emphasizes that "these rights are bestowed on human beings by God and grounded in the nature and dignity of human persons" (ibid. no. 79). It further contends that "the full range of human rights has been systematically outlined by John XXIII in his encyclical *Peace on Earth*," and that this discussion "echoes the United Nations Universal Declaration of Human Rights and implies that *internationally accepted human rights standards are strongly supported by Catholic teaching*" (ibid. no. 80 [italics mine]).

Thus, the document is a key advocate in the Catholic support for the concept of human rights. In addition, it argues for the importance of government in protecting human rights, asserting that "*government has a moral function: protecting human rights and securing basic justice for all members of the commonwealth*" (ibid. no. 122). And, as mentioned earlier, it is critical of the current economic system, which does not offer a substantial safety net to protect the poor and marginalized, asserting that the Church "rejects the notion that a free market automatically produces justice" (ibid. no. 115).

Therefore, *Economic Justice for All* is a landmark document in the Roman Catholic tradition on human rights. First, it upholds the Catholic social teaching on human rights, and specifically places a priority on the poor and marginalized. Secondly, it moves from the abstract to the concrete, in critiquing the U.S. economy based on the concept of human rights. And thirdly, it recognizes and respects the human rights of those within the Church in general, by its collegial style and input. Ten years after the document was released, Weakland reflected that, in hindsight, while the document was probably too long, it was the *process* itself which was "unique" and one of its "finest features" (Mich 1998, 329-330).

While many Catholics would bemoan the lack of collegiality in the Church in the pontificate of John Paul II, his advocacy for the concept of human rights on a global scale cannot be overemphasized. I now briefly examine his pontificate as it relates to Catholic advocacy for human rights.

D. JOHN PAUL II

The pontificate of John Paul II has been viewed as a two edged sword by many Catholics, and time will tell how his legacy will be recorded. On the one hand, many Catholics saw the Church's human rights concerns inadequately applied to internal Church life, including a lack of response on the pedophile scandal. Yet, on a global and political scale, he was an exhaustive traveler in the cause of human rights and a fearless advocate in the face of oppressive regimes. Highly visible in his travels and in the media, he represented to the world the Catholic Church's advocacy for the universality of the concept of human rights.

Hollenbach points out that during John Paul II's travels "the most consistent and forceful theme of the pope's message has been the appeal for the protection of human rights and the denunciation of patterns of human rights violations" (Hollenbach cited in Traer 1991, 41). Traer adds as well that "John Paul II has not only forcefully spoken out against human rights violations, but explicitly identified human rights with the mission of the Church" (ibid. 42).

Hehir contends that "the most significant continuity with the theological case for human rights is provided by John Paul II," noting that "from the outset of his pontificate, human rights, in theory and in practice, have been a central characteristic of this pope's ministry." He emphasizes that "from his first encyclical *Redemptor Hominis* (1979) through *Sollicitudo Rei Socialis* (1987) to *Centesimus Annus* (1991) John Paul's social ethic-in which human rights are a central element-is rooted in a theological vision of the person, of history, and of the causes of injustice" (Hehir 1996, 106).

Coming from Poland himself, John Paul II's clashes with Communism in Eastern Europe would eventually lead to his greatest political contribution, the downfall of the Soviet Union. Hehir points out that "all analysts today ... count him as an essential figure in the dismantling of Soviet power" (ibid. 115). Mikhail Gorbachev himself admitted at the time that "everything that has happened in eastern Europe during these last few years would not have been possible without the presence of this Pope, without the leading role – the political role – that he was able to play on the world scene" (Gorbachev cited in Moniz 1996, 388). Responding to the statement that he is a political pope, John Paul II himself replied that "in the Gospel there is man, respect for man, and, therefore, human rights, freedom of conscience and everything that belongs to man. If this has a political significance, then, yes, it applies also to the Pope" (John Paul II cited in ibid.).

Reflecting on John Paul II, John Moniz points out that he was "the proponent of human dignity, basic human rights, religious freedom, cultural and social promotion of workers, option for the poor, solidarity between peoples, integrity and stability of families, value of culture in its role in social life, dialogue, reduction of arms, international peace, non-violence, unity of Europe and unity among nations of the world" (ibid. 377). Moniz emphasized that John Paul II "touches the life of 'suffering humanity,' especially the 'oppressed poor' who are victims of man-made systems," and that he "defends their rights and awakens the consciences of those who are responsible for such an unjust and dehumanized social order." Thus, Moniz asserts that "this commitment for a radical transformation of society is seen throughout his life" (ibid. 380).

For example, *Centesimus Annus*, promulgated in 1991 and commemorating the one hundreth anniversary of *Rerum Novarum*, "misses no opportunity to affirm human dignity and human rights" (Henriot, DeBerri, and Schultheis 1997, 94). It condemns rampant consumerism as well as totalitarianism, and observes that "since 1945, the awareness of human rights – with the United Nations as a focal point – has grown (#21)" (ibid. 96). O'Brien and Shannon note that the pope "concludes *Centesimus Annus* with a presentation of Christian anthropology which grounds the Church's social vision and mission on the basis of a transcendent human dignity" (O'Brien and Shannon 1998, 438). The encyclical itself asserts that "*the social message of the Gospel must not be considered a theory, but above all else a basis and a motivation for action*"(55) (Cited in ibid. [italics mine]).

Of all that can be said of John Paul II in his pontificate, he was definitely a man of action, outspoken in his advocacy for human rights on a global scale. He represented Catholicism's promotion of the concept of human rights in the global, political, and universal arena, although he failed to apply that same advocacy to the Church's internal structure.

E. ADDITIONAL DEVELOPMENTS AND ISSUES

Other developments could be added which contribute to the Roman Catholic concept of human rights since Vatican II, and I will not be exhaustive here. But a few examples are in order. For example, the "seamless garment" approach or "consistent life ethic," outlined by Joseph Cardinal Bernardin in a series of speeches in 1983, spoke of a "'seamless garment' of pro-life commitment that linked opposition to abortion, the arms race, capital punishment, and economic justice" (ibid. 490). This concept formed a framework for dealing with various human rights issues.

Organizations in the U.S. working for human rights advocacy include the previously mentioned Campaign for Human Development and also Catholic Charities. Mich explains that "these two movements reveal the activist side of the institutional church as it moves from works of charity to the social ministry of advocacy and empowerment." For example, Catholic Charities USA "is a national network of 630 agencies and institutions serving 11 million individuals and families regardless of creed, race, sex, or age through community-based social programs," and as such "is the largest nongovernmental provider of diverse social services in the United States" (Mich 1998, 333). Its original statement of purpose reads that it aims to become "the attorney for the Poor in Modern Society, to present their point of view and defend them unto the days when social justice may secure to them their rights" (Cited in ibid. 334). Other countless agencies, individuals, and programs could be cited as examples of the Catholic Church's advocacy for human rights since Vatican II.

One example of advocacy combined with scholarship is the movement of Liberation Theology. My investigation so far has purposely focused on Church documents rather than additional movements within the Church. This has been to show the development of and advocacy for human rights in the teaching of the Roman Catholic tradition. I have shown that this is the case, that the Roman Catholic tradition currently is a strong advocate for the concept of human rights. Given this, however, it should be noted that there are numerous movements, agencies, and individuals who add to the Church's advocacy for human rights. Liberation Theology is one of those movements and influences.

Most would argue that Liberation Theology, whether from its beginnings in Latin America, or from various viewpoints such as Black Theology, Feminist Theology or Womanist Theology, is a strong advocate of the concept of global human rights.[4] For example, Donal

<hr>

4   Exceptions to this do exist, however. For example, William R. Garrett argues that since liberation theology is based on Marxist assumptions, it rejects the modern, Western, universal approach to human rights. Also, he argues that it is unwise to give the poor favored human rights status, since no social category should be elevated above others (see Garrett 1988). Feminist theologians are also often critical of any "universal categories," since they are suspicious of what group (usually male) has been defining these categories. Despite intellectual differences, however, those aligned

Dorr argues that "with the advent of various forms of liberation theology churches have begun more and more to commit themselves in principle to the struggle for the fundamental rights of all." He explains that "liberation theology encourages people to struggle for their fundamental human rights," and notes that radical changes in Poland and Germany "were inspired by a radical Christian vision of a new society where human rights are respected" (Dorr 1991, 123). Hehir concurs that "the content of the Theology of Liberation focused on themes directly related to human rights issues," although he admits that the theological vision of liberation theology "was broader than simply a theology of human rights" (Hehir 1996, 113). Hence, despite different viewpoints within Liberation Theology, and despite Vatican critiques of it, those involved in liberation movements form a strong constituency for human rights in the Catholic tradition since Vatican II.

Liberation Theology also serves as an example of the fact that, in Roman Catholicism, by the time a teaching becomes "officially pronounced," it has often been brewing for some time previous to that among theologians and/or the laity. The lay quality of Liberation Theology is noteworthy, as theology from the point of view of the people. In addition, it reminds us that, historically, it was often the "magisterium of theologians" who were instructing the "magisterium of bishops." Hence, while I have focused primarily on Church documents, I recognize that much groundwork has been laid by theologians and the laity previous to a teaching being pronounced within those Church documents.

At the second meeting of the Latin American Episcopal Conference, held at Medellin, Colombia in 1968, "influenced by Vatican II, the social teachings of John XXIII and Paul VI, liberation theology, and the reality of life in Latin America, the Bishops made a seminal and fundamental criticism of society and a strong commitment to the poor" (Henriot, DeBerri and Schultheis 1997, 135). In addition, the pastoral conclusions reached at that conference were "to form the consciences of Latin Americans to peace, justice, and the rights of the poor (#'s 21-22), ... to encourage Catholic institutions to foster vocations of service (#25)" and "to urge an end to [the] arms race, violence, and domination" (ibid. 138).

---

with liberation movements have been strong advocates of issues which involve human rights.

The third meeting of the Latin American Episcopal Conference, held in Puebla, Mexico in 1979, "confirmed Medellin's mandate that the Church evangelize for the poor, for liberation, and for an end to unjust social structures" (ibid. 140). Henriot, DeBerri and Schultheis note, however, that "although many of the leading progressive Bishops of Latin America were not appointed delegates," and although "most of the region's prominent liberation theologians were not chosen as experts," still, in the end, "the conference's final document supported the basic thrust of the social significance of the Church's mission to the world" (ibid.). Thus, Catholic teaching is often based on the work of theologians and the laity, including the poor, who contributed to that theology from the grass roots level and base communities. Therefore, the role of Liberation Theology in recent Catholic teaching on human rights cannot be overemphasized.

I have sought to show that in the period since Vatican II, the Roman Catholic tradition has continued to develop the concept of human rights, and has increased its advocacy for human rights on a global scale. In addition, the Church has incorporated the concept of human rights into its own ministry, and has seen the concept of human rights as synonymous with the preaching of and living out the gospel message. Hehir agrees that these developments "provided the church with a renewed language of concepts, principles, and legitimation to engage the contemporary issues of human rights," and that further developments also "created a context for this ministry" of the Church (Hehir 1996, 107).

3.5: CONCLUSION

I have argued that, over the past century, the Roman Catholic tradition has moved from an acceptance of the concept of human rights to a full-fledged advocacy for human rights on a global scale. It has moved from an acceptance of workers' rights to a full integration of political, economic and social rights, and sees these various rights as interconnected. It has moved from its "natural law" language to a language of "human dignity," based on the scriptures, in its advocacy for the value of the individual. Yet, while moving away from its natural law view of a hierarchical society, it nonetheless argues that the individual is also a social being, and it forms a middle ground between purely "individualist" and "socialist" views of the person and society.

Its emphasis on the concept of the "common good" reminds us that there is a correlation between rights and duties, and it rejects a purely "individualist" view of rights which does not also recognize "duties" to the community. Therefore, I have illustrated three distinct marks of Roman Catholicism that contribute to the discussion on human rights: 1) communitarianism, 2) rights and duties being equally emphasized, and 3) an accent on the poor and marginalized.

Hence, in theory, Roman Catholic teaching on human rights offers a much needed middle ground between Western, liberal, consumer oriented, autonomous views of the individual and Marxist socialist views, and also recognizes the correlation between those human rights and duties. In practice, Roman Catholicism offers a global organization which supports other global organizations such as the U.N. and which is a strong advocate for human rights.

Therefore, Roman Catholicism is a key supporter of the concept of human rights on a global scale today. Its emphasis on the human dignity of all human beings, and therefore the universality of that dignity, forms a strong voice for the modern concept of human rights. While I would also argue that the Church needs to direct its attention inward, to the rights of its own members,[5] its commitment to human rights worldwide, and especially to the poor and marginalized, is vitally apparent. Hence, the Roman Catholic tradition today is a key player and advocate in the global struggle to promote and protect universal human rights. As Traer concludes, "in the Roman Catholic tradition one finds today that the discussion of human rights is central to ethical reflection. For human rights are understood in faith as the necessary social conditions for the human dignity which is God's gift to all peoples of the earth" (Traer 1991, 44).

---

5   Charles Curran argues that "contemporary Roman Catholicism needs to adopt structures and institutions which better protect the freedom and human rights of the believers" (Curran 1987, 169).

CHAPTER 4

ECO-JUSTICE: THE NECESSITY OF ECOLOGICAL DUTIES AS A CORRELATE TO HUMAN RIGHTS

The concept of human rights necessarily involves the concept of duties. These duties contain obligations to other human beings and emphasize the unity of the human family. But, as Buddhism so strongly cautions, an ego-centeredness which focuses too much on the individual in general or even on the human race exclusively can lead to a perverted and selfish concept of human rights which no religious tradition would uphold. Therefore, it is no longer possible to speak of "rights" without speaking of "duties," nor to speak of "human" without speaking of other species and the planet as well.

In this chapter, I argue for the necessity of ecological duties as a correlate to human rights. I begin by examining the concept of ecology and how that concept relates to religions in general, then briefly discuss the relationship between ecology and Christian theology. I then introduce the concept of "eco-justice," emphasizing the relation between social justice and ecological concerns. Having established these general terms, I next examine the traditions of Buddhism and Roman Catholicism for their own contributions toward the advocacy of ecological duties as a necessary correlate to a just and viable theory of human rights.

4.1: ECOLOGICAL DUTIES AND RELIGION IN GENERAL

A. INTRODUCTION TO THE CONCEPT OF ECOLOGY

Jürgen Moltmann writes that "being created in the image of God is the basis of the right of human beings to rule over the Earth and of their right to community with the Non-Human creation" (Moltmann 1984, 26). He continues that "if along with the right of human beings to the earth 'rights' of the earth over against human beings are recognized, then basic ecological duties are also bound up with these basic economic rights"(ibid. 27). In this section I will examine the issue of ecology in general, in religions and in Christian theology.

To begin, "ecology" cannot be seen as a side issue. Perhaps a better term would be "the environment" or "biological life-itself." Larry L. Rasmussen points out that "nature is not what is around us or where we live, but the reason we are alive at all," adding that "nature is the reason each and every society and culture that ever existed did so" (Rasmussen 1996, 9). Thus, he observes that "society and nature together – that is, earth – is a community, without an exit" (ibid.). In observing the current ecological crisis, Rasmussen agrees that it is not the environment that is unsustainable, but our current way of life. It is "a virile, comprehensive, and attractive way of life [which is] destructive of nature and human community together" (ibid. 7). Therefore, he argues that what is necessary is "a new account of responsibility," which "requires moralities and ways of life that extend responsibility to include everything that has life and is necessary to life" (ibid. 5).

So, it is a comprehensive endeavor, in which religion must play a part. In regard to current global trends, Maguire observes that "if current trends continue, we will not," and argues that "if religion does not speak to [this], it is an obsolete distraction" (Maguire 1993, 13). In this section, I examine ties between religions and ecology and argue that ecology is not a subset of theology, a new type of theology, but an approach to theology in general. In addition, I contend that if religion is not involved, other ideological systems will be, often to the detriment of the environment. Harold Coward has concluded, as one example, that "the global market economy, with its teleology constantly to increase consumption, was as strong, if not a stronger, threat to the earth's ecology than population increase" (Coward 1997, 265). (This is addressed later in this chapter by David Loy.) Overall, I argue from a position of "eco-justice," where human rights are seen as one interconnected element within a global and ecological perspective.

B. RELIGIONS AND ECOLOGY

It is almost impossible to discuss the issue of human rights in Buddhism without also addressing ecological duties and concerns. Buddhist notions of the interconnectedness of all reality and of all living beings necessarily bring the conversation on human rights into the arena of ecological duties. However, the perception that Eastern religions are in general "ecological" and that Western religions are "un-ecological" in their beliefs may be an oversimplification. I argue that all of these religions have resources to address the current ecological crisis and that the issue of human rights falls within that context.

Political Science scholar Hwa Yol Jung argues that "a Copernican revolution of the mind" is needed "to avert the impending ecologi-cal catastrophe," and that Zen Buddhism "could be the fountainhead of that revolution" (Jung 1972, 1153). He cites the words of D.T. Suzuki that "the problem of nature is the problem of human life itself" (Suzuki cited in ibid., 1154), thereby arguing for a more fluid rela-tion between humankind and nature than is currently assumed. Jung cautions against the danger of anthropocentrism in not observing this interconnection between humans and nature. He concludes that "con-ceived of as God's favored creature, man held a monopoly on spiritual-ity that enshrined him in the temple of arrogance" (Jung, 1153).

Joanna Macy agrees, asserting that "the crisis that threatens our planet … derives from a dysfunctional and pathogenic notion of the self. It is a mistake about our place in the order of things." She con-tends that "it is the delusion that the self is so separate and fragile that we must delineate and defend its boundaries, that it is so small and needy that we must endlessly acquire and endlessly consume, that it is so aloof that we can … be immune to what we do to other beings" (Macy 1990, 38). Macy explains that, in the past, the experience of the interconnectedness of life was "largely relegated to the domain of mystics and poets," but that now it is a "motivation to action" (ibid. 37). She cites the term "deep ecology," a term coined by Norwegian phi-losopher Arne Naess, which connotes "a basic shift in ways of seeing and valuing." This contrasts with "shallow environmentalism," which is described as the "band-aid approach applying technological fixes for short-term human goals" (ibid. 45).

Clearly, modern society is more comfortable with the latter, yet this human centered "quick-fix" will not address ecological duties. What is necessary is a more fundamental re-examination of values. In Hinduism, it is rooted in the fundamental notion of *dharma*. Harold Coward comments on the work of Vasudha Narayanan, where she "notes the close connections between the teachings in the Hindu epics and puranas on *dharma* (righteousness, duty, justice) and the ravag-ing of the earth." He explains that "it is in the *dharma* rather than the *moksha* or enlightenment texts" where positive resources can be found within Hinduism "for positive practices in the face of the problems of ecology, population pressure, and excess consumption" (Coward 1997, 269 [see Narayanan 1997]).

Raimundo Panikkar brings this overall worldview back to the concept of human rights in Eastern and Western religions. He reminds us that "human rights are not Human only. They concern equally the entire cosmic display of the universe." He contends that "the animals, all the sentient beings and the supposedly inanimate creatures, are also involved in the interaction concerning human rights" (Panikkar 1982, 98). Panikkar explains that "our right is only a participation in the entire metabolic function of the universe," emphasizing that "it is the universal harmony that ultimately counts" (ibid. 99).

Drawing on the metaphor of Indra's Jewelled Net from Buddhism, he explains that the East in general focuses on the net itself, symbolizing interconnectedness, while the West has focused on the separate knots of the net, symbolizing individuality. He argues for a coming together of these two worldviews, concluding that "perhaps we may now be prepared for a cosmotheandric vision of reality in which the Divine, the Human and the Cosmic are integrated into a whole, more or less harmonious according to the performance of our truly human rights" (ibid. 102).

However, the prevailing view that Western religions in general are not environmentally friendly may be naive and may represent an imposition of a modern worldview on the traditional sources of those religions. Kusumita Pedersen points out that "neither Judaism, Christianity, nor Islam is or could be anthropocentric, or human-centered; rather, all three traditions are theocentric, or God-centered, in their worldviews." She explains that, "given this starting point, a viable environmental ethic is available in each of the traditions" (Pedersen 1998, 260).

Theodore Hiebert observes that "the biblical Hebrew language possesses no terms for 'nature' or 'history' … in fact, wherever one looks in the Hebrew Scriptures, divine activity and human experience are so interrelated with the world of nature (as we call it) that traditional [i.e., nineteenth – and twentieth-century] dualistic and highly anthropocentric readings of the biblical texts become problematic" (Hiebert cited in Pedersen 1998, 260 [brackets Petersen's]). In addition, Pedersen notes that "'stewardship' (the responsible care of something one does not own but has been entrusted with) is a well-developed concept in Jewish law," which "stipulates that the inherent worth of what is 'possessed,' or borrowed, must be maintained or, if damaged, restored" (Pedersen 1998, 264).

This fundamental worldview of the Hebrew Scriptures, and the notion of stewardship in the Genesis creation account, are integral to Christianity's perception of nature as well. Pedersen also sees a positive resource in Christian asceticism and monasticism. Rather than a devaluation of the world, Pedersen sees monasticism as "an immense practical resource for environmental ethics." She explains that "monastic vows of poverty in the Christian tradition have sometimes aspired not only to the restraint of sensual indulgence and worldliness but also to solidarity with the poor and the oppressed, thus uniting environmental and social concerns in a monastic embodiment of eco-justice" (ibid. 267). St. Francis of Assisi is perhaps the best embodiment of this, as the "patron saint" of Catholic environmentalists.

In Islam, Pedersen suggests that "the Qur'anic vision embraces an environmental ethic on which Muslim writers on the environment appear to be in strong agreement" (ibid. 268). She concludes that "the biblical and Qur'anic testimony is clearly that nature's purposes are not limited to human uses and human meaning. There is a significant distinction between acceptable and unacceptable treatment of nature" (ibid. 270). Therefore, in the end, Pedersen argues that "the moral norms for human life" contained within Judaism, Christianity, and Islam "can be applied directly to environmental questions within an eco-justice perspective that embraces the well-being of both humans and the natural world" (ibid.).

Daniel Maguire acknowledges "the moral common ground of the world's classical religions," and argues that "the moral energies of the world's religions are renewable and applicable to the contemporary terracidal crisis" (Maguire 1998, 19). He explains that "the world's religions are and will be players in the population, ecology, and consumption issues," noting that "two thirds of the world population are mentally and emotively linked to these powerful symbol systems" (ibid.).

Maguire realizes that religions reach into "the motivational core where the sense of the sacred pulses," and that "no realistic study of power or social change can afford to miss that" (ibid. 21). Therefore, he concludes that "the population-ecology-consumption crisis will not be solved by nude rationality but only by truths that stir the flaccid collective will by touching the sacral core of human willing" (ibid. 24).

Hence, the role and necessity of religion in the ecological endeavor is clear. And, the importance of Western as well as Eastern traditions is affirmed. But, how does Christian theology and the concept of human rights fit within the broad context of ecological concerns?

C. CHRISTIAN THEOLOGY AND ECOLOGY

Jürgen Moltmann says that he sees "the greatest task of the church of Christ today as being the ecological reformation of the 'religion of modernity'" (Moltmann 1989, 15). He continues that "ecological justice, which is the basis of a symbiosis of humankind and nature capable of survival, will become just as important in the future as economic justice" (ibid. 14). Perhaps that future is now. For if it is not, we severely limit the possibility of that future at all. But how should the issue of ecology be incorporated into theology in general? Is it another type of theology or another issue to address? And, is it addressed *after* we take care of human concerns? Or, is it a different lens through which one does theology, a different mindset through which all of theology must be re-examined and re-applied?

John B. Cobb, Jr. offers the example of liberation theology. He states that "a theology of liberation is not asking what the church has said and now should say about liberation," but rather, "it is arguing that all that the church says about all topics should be rethought from the perspective of the centrality to its mission of the liberation of the oppressed" (Cobb 1990, 263). Thus, in like manner, a theology of nature is "not trying only to spell out what traditional theology implies about nature." Rather, Cobb explains, "we want to see the whole of theology influenced and reconceived in light of what we are learning about nature" (ibid.). This, therefore, makes the "theology of nature" something different from and broader than the "doctrine of creation."

Cobb argues that a theology of nature should not just become another "theology of," competing against the interests and problems of other theologies. Instead, he emphasizes that "the theology of nature has a particular and peculiarly important role to play in bringing out the deeper shared concerns on many (even all) of the 'theologies of.'" And, since these "theologies of" are anthropocentric, "representatives of the theology of nature are crucial for setting the discussion of human problems in the wider context" (ibid. 266) of the environment. Cobb concludes that this ecological perspective will liberate theology itself, asserting that "it is as important to liberate theology to pursue saving truth wherever it can be found as to liberate particular groups of people from oppression" (ibid. 272).

Pedersen as well sees the connection between liberation theology and a theology of nature. She suggests that "liberation theologies are belief systems which challenge the assumption, widely held in the West, that the earth is simply a commodity which can be exploited thoughtlessly by humans for the purpose of material acquisition within an ever-expanding economic framework." She proposes that "a liberation theology will develop in people a consciousness that all life on earth is sacred and that the sacredness of life is the key to human freedom and survival" (Pedersen 1998, 280).

This call for a "new theology," rather than just an additional type of theology, is echoed by Harold Coward as well. Coward relates his experience at the 1994 Cairo U.N. Conference on Population and Development, where the past emphasis on *fertility control* was replaced with a new approach of *reproductive health*. This holistic approach involved "reducing poverty, improving health, decreasing mortality rates, enhancing education, augmenting reproductive health services, achieving sustainable development, abating environmental degradation and excessive consumption, and attaining gender equity and equality" (Grist and Greenfield cited in Coward 1997, 262). Coward emphasizes that what was made clear for theologians of all religions at that conference was that "one can no longer deal with the challenges of population pressure, excess consumption, and environmental degradation as questions to be addressed separately." What is needed, he argues, is "new theology," where fresh and creative answers will be forthcoming, answers "that we could not get by asking about the ethics of reproduction, just consumption, and our relation to nature separately" (ibid.). Yet, he admits that "in no religion could we find this complex, multifaceted problematic already addressed. The task called for new theology from each religion" (ibid. 263).

Thus, many of these issues cannot be solved, nor even addressed, unless they are done so in connection with other related issues and within the larger environmental context. And religion *must* play a role in this, and must therefore develop its own ecological perspective. For, as Maguire reminds us, "religion, in [the] broad sense of a *response to the sacred* and religion in its various institutionalized forms, is and will be a major player in the planetary crisis ... *for good or for ill.*" This last word of warning cautions that "either you deal honestly with sacrality or you allow misplaced sacreds to achieve untested and unsuspected hegemony"(Maguire 1998, 36).

The religious dimensions and longings of human beings run deep, and it is no news that eliminating traditional religion may merely re-channel these longings and drives into areas and structures which are often far from sacred. Therefore, it is urgent that traditional religion finds a place within the environmental crisis, or other value systems will. A profound example of this is David Loy's argument that "our present economic system should also be understood as our religion, because it has come to fulfill a religious function for us." Loy argues that the discipline of economics is the theology of that religion, and "its god, the Market, has become a vicious circle ever-increasing pro-duction and consumption by pretending to offer a secular salvation" (Loy 1997, 275).

Loy contends that "ecological catastrophe is awakening us not only to the fact that we need a deeper source of values and meaning than market capitalism can provide but also to the realization that con-temporary religion is not meeting this need either"(ibid. 276). Under this current economic value system, he warns that "our humanity is reduced to a source of labor and a collection of insatiable desires; our communities disintegrate into aggregates of individuals competing to attain private ends; the earth and all its creatures are commodified into a pool of resources to be exploited to satisfy those desires." In response to this, he emphasizes that "here we are reminded of the crucial role that religions can serve: to raise fundamental questions about this di-minished understanding of what the world is and what our life can be" (ibid. 285).

Loy also recognizes that Eastern and Western religions will play a role in this. He notes that "the great sensitivity to social justice in the Semitic religions (for whom sin is a moral failure of *will*) needs to be supplemented by the emphasis that the Asian enlightenment tradi-tions place upon seeing-through and dispelling delusion (ignorance as a failure to *understand*)." Within this context, he admits that "we are unlikely ever to solve the problem of distributive social justice without also overcoming the value-delusion of happiness through individual-istic accumulation and consumption"(ibid. 286).

Loy's article is intriguing, for it points not only to the huge impact that the economy has on these issues, but also to the additionally huge shift in values and perceptions which is necessary and to which religion can be a key contributor. I argue that religion must be a key component in overcoming ecological problems and developing a more inclusive ecological perspective, and that theology itself must be re-examined and re-applied within the larger ecological context.

James Nash observes that "Christian responses to ecological problems should be developed in the light of biblical commitments to justice" (Nash 1991, 163). He emphasizes that "justice is too close to the core of the biblical message to be ignored or trivialized in the development of an ecological ethic. Justice is not an option for Christians, but a moral imperative" (ibid. 165). Yet, Nash goes further in observing that "there is no inherent reason, however, why the poor and oppressed cannot be extended to include nonhuman creatures – without implying equality of rights or denying human primacy" (ibid. 166).

This brings us back to the issue of rights, and the issue of ecological duties which we are currently addressing. And while I will not argue for the "rights" of animals, plants, or the Earth itself, I will argue for "human rights" and for a corresponding "ecological duty" to those other living beings. In the next section, I argue for those ecological duties and for the inclusion of the issue of human rights within that larger ecological context.

D. HUMAN RIGHTS AND ECOLOGY: THE CONNECTION

Maguire notes that the experience of the sanctity of life "undergirds all national constitutions and legal systems and grounds all claims of human and civil 'rights' and yet it remains ultimately beyond our powers of empirical analysis or description." He observes that "civilization depends utterly on this knowledge but we are humbled by the question of how we know this knowledge" (Maguire 1998, 34), arguing that this experience operates from a higher affective-symbolic level of knowledge, a level in which religion plays a major role. Maguire emphasizes that "religion in the general sense, as the experience of sacredness, *is at the core of ecological ethics and human rights thinking*" (ibid. 48 [italics mine]).

In this study, I affirm that religion needs to play a key role in human rights and ecological movements. I also affirm that human rights issues and ecological concerns are interconnected. But how are they related, and to what extent do human rights involve ecological duties? Does putting "human" rights in the ecological context water down those rights, and does it give equal rights to other species?

My answer here will be "no." As Nash argues, "nonhuman rights would be absurd if they were construed as equal rights with humans or as the same rights as humans." He cautions that "statements about nonhuman rights must be carefully constructed with appropriate qualifications and limitations" (Nash 1991, 174). Even Buddhism, with its strong emphasis on interconnectedness, does not avoid this hierarchy entirely. Pedersen argues that the view that Buddhism has a biocentric worldview as opposed to an anthropocentric one is subject to some qualification, since "humans are unique in that, according to traditional belief, only from a human birth can one attain liberation" (Pedersen 1998, 271). In the same vein, in this study, I affirm the priority of "human" rights, but will also argue that those rights contain a corresponding duty toward the environment and nonhuman species.

This priority of the human, however, has been extended too far in modern culture, at the expense of other species, the environment, and ultimately ourselves. Rasmussen asserts that "the world of 'modern anthropocentrism' is deeply, even fatally, flawed," and that "a moral universe limited to the human universe will not … even understand life, much less serve it" (Rasmussen 1996, 17). He argues from the perspectives of Vaclav Havel that "the basis for any new world order, including a universal respect for human rights and the democratic processes, is not laid unless the imperatives derive from respect for the miracle of Being, the miracle of the universe, the miracle of nature, and the miracle of our own existence" (ibid. 18).[1] Rasmussen asserts that "what is untenable for sustainability is a moral universe that circles human creatures only and does not regard other creatures and earth as a whole as imposing moral claims that we need worry over" (ibid. 344). He continues that "compassion and justice and the mending of community thus envelop more than human members" (ibid. 345). Yet, he argues that this "comprehensive communitarian ethic with nature" is not merely nature romanticism or an attempt by humans to imitate nature. Rather, it is necessary that humans go beyond nature, since "much of nature is simply *too casual about suffering*" and that "for human morality this is unacceptable" (ibid. 346).

The language of human rights and ecology come together at our most basic level of existence: the fact that we exist at all and are

---

1   Rasmussen is paraphrasing a speech by Vaclav Havel, "Address of the President of the Czech Republic, His Excellency Vaclav Havel, on the Occassion of the Liberty Medal Ceremony, Philadelphia, July 4, 1994."

dependent on the environment for our continued existence. The World Commission on Environment and Development states in *Our Common Future* that "all human beings have the fundamental right to an environment adequate for their health and well-being" (Cited in Nash 1991, 171). Thus, *the environment is one of our most basic human rights.*

Human rights movements, however, have often operated quite independently of environmental ones. That is currently changing, as the need to view human rights within the larger ecological context becomes more clear. In April, 1998, the Boston Research Center, the Center for Respect of Life and Environment, and Global Education Associates convened a consultation called *Practical Steps to Realize Environmental Justice: Drawing on 50 Years of Human Rights Developments.* The consultation involved ethicists working on the Benchmark Draft of the Earth Charter, environmental lawyers, and scholars and activists engaged in human rights. During the consultation, "the inseparability of environmental justice and human rights was a guiding principle for the discussions" (Casey 1998, 1).

Steven Rockefeller, coordinator of the Earth Charter drafting process and a representative from the United States on the Earth Charter Commission, notes that "when I use the term environmental justice, I am thinking about it as a human rights issue that has to do with the rights of people regarding the environment in which they live." He continues that "the idea is that human rights is one part of the larger tapestry, that issues of peace, of social justice, of economic development and environmental protection are all interdependent, and the Charter needs to weave them together" (Cited in ibid. 8). (This view is also advocated in the Environmental Justice Program of the United States Catholic Conference.)

Clarence Dias argues, from an Asian perspective, that "human rights are needed in order to ensure that most precious of all rights, the right to be and remain human." He observes that "if we think of human rights in that sense, we are coming very close to the concept of stewardship which really enshrines environmental thinking." Dias concludes by emphasizing that "the human right to development is not about *having* more but about *being* more" (Dias cited in ibid. 9).

Environmental lawyer Stephen Kass points out that "the environment is never going to be preserved if there are tremendous disparities in wealth," and adds that "we will never be able to deal with human

rights very effectively unless we address some of the issues of sustainable development." He admits that "I don't think we can begin to address any of these issues unless we address them all" (Kass cited in
ibid.).

The *Earth Charter Benchmark Draft* stated in its introduction that
"we must reinvent industrial-technological civilization" and that "the
challenges before us require an inclusive ethical vision." Principle 3 was
the first to mention human rights. It stated: "Live sustainably, promoting and adopting modes of consumption, production and reproduction that respect and safeguard human rights and the regenerative capacities of Earth." Principle 4 included the statement that "people have
a right to potable water, clean air, uncontaminated soil and food security" (*Earth Charter Benchmark Draft* 1997, EC-1). Principle 6 agreed
to "promote social development and financial systems that create and
maintain sustainable livelihoods, eradicate poverty and strengthen lo-
cal communities." Principle 10 agreed to "affirm that gender equality is
a prerequisite for sustainable development," and 11 to "secure the right
to sexual and reproductive health, with special concern for women and
girls." Principle 16 offered a spin on the Golden Rule: "do not do to the
environment of others what you do not want done to your environment." Finally, the last principle, number 18, included the statement
that "every person, institution and government has a duty to advance
the indivisible goals of justice for all, sustainability, world peace, and
respect and care for the larger community of life" (ibid. EC-4).

The final version of the Earth Charter was approved and released
by the Earth Charter Commission in Paris in March, 2000. In its
Preamble, the document emphasizes that

> We must join together to bring forth a sustainable global society
> founded on respect for nature, universal human rights, economic
> justice, and a culture of peace. Towards this end, it is imperative
> that we, the peoples of Earth, declare our responsibility to one an-
> other, to the greater community of life, and to future generations
> (*The Earth Charter*).

Thus, human rights and environmental issues are related, in fact
intertwined, not only on the level of theory but also at the level of
practice. And religion has a key, and also necessary, role to play in this
discussion. Pedersen affirms that "each religious tradition, whether
supposedly anthropocentric or biocentric in general orientation,

possesses resources for the construction of what is now often called an 'eco-justice' ethic." She defines this "eco-justice" ethic as "an ethic that holds together concerns for the natural world and for human life, that recognizes that devastation of the environment and social and economic injustice go hand in hand, and that affirms that *environmental rights and human rights are indivisible*" (Pedersen 1998, 254 [italics mine]).

Echoing John Cobb Jr.'s view that a "theology of nature" cannot be just one more type of theology, Pedersen explains that "eco-justice has developed as a conscious refusal to see the environmental crisis merely as a question of nature or as 'one more issue.'" She suggests that, instead, "it seeks to unite what is now recognized as the biblical valuation of nature with the biblical calls to justice and love of neighbor" (ibid. 266). As James Martin-Schram puts it, "the hallmark of an eco-justice approach is the attempt *to hold together the twin imperatives of social justice and ecological integrity*." He explains that "breaking down the traditional barriers between social and environmental ethics, an eco-justice approach attempts to discern and adjudicate various responsibilities owed to the poor, to future generations, to sentient life, to organic life, to endangered species, and to ecosystems as a whole" (Martin-Schram cited in ibid. [italics mine]). Pedersen asserts that all of these areas must be brought to bear on the ecological crisis, because "human actions are the cause of the crisis," and therefore "environmental issues must be seen in economic, political, and social terms" (Pedersen 1998, 258).

Pedersen concludes by arguing that the world's major religious traditions do agree on key issues regarding nature, and that an eco-justice approach has drawn out shared moral precepts of these religions that relate to environmental ethics. For example, Pedersen lists these key areas of agreement as:

> 1) The natural world has value in itself and does not exist solely to serve human needs. 2) There is significant ontological continuity between human and nonhuman living beings, even though humans do have a distinctive role. This continuity can be felt and experienced. 3) Nonhuman living beings are morally significant, in the eyes of God and/or in the cosmic order. 4) The dependence of human life on the natural world can and should be acknowledged in ritual and other expressions of appreciation and gratitude. 5) Moral norms such as justice, compassion, and reciprocity apply (in

appropriate ways) both to human beings and to nonhuman beings. 6) There are legitimate and illegitimate uses of nature. 7) Greed and destructiveness are condemned. Restraint and protection are commended. 8) Human beings are obliged to be aware and responsible in living in harmony with the natural world, and should follow the specific practices for this prescribed by their traditions (ibid. 281).

Yet, others have observed the connection between human rights and environmental issues from the more practical standpoint of the growing interaction between environmental and human rights advocacy groups.

Aaron Sachs points out that "environmental degradation ... usually carries a high human cost," and that "that cost is often borne disproportionately by the people least able to cope with it – people already on the margins of society" (Sachs 1995, 6). In observing social justice activist Chico Mendes' and environmentalists' battles to save the Amazonian rainforests in Brazil, Sachs observes that "one of the best ways of preventing deforestation was to use the human rights approach – to reform the law enforcement system and empower people to mount protests to defend their health and livelihoods" (ibid.).

Ashish Kothari, Lecturer in Environmental Studies at the Indian Institute of Public Administration, notes that "most mass movements at the grassroots are not just human rights, nor just environmental, but inevitably both." Kothari continues that "they have to be, if they are conscious of the role of natural resources in their lives, and of the dominant forces exploiting those resources" (Kothari cited in ibid. 9). Sachs also points out that "one additional reason for couching environmental justice concerns in the language of human rights is that the international human rights system is more accessible than most other international law frameworks, making its treaties inherently more enforceable" (Sachs 1995, 46).

Thus, the concepts of human rights and of ecological duties necessarily interact on the levels of theory *and* practice. In fact, to enforce ecological duties, human rights documents and advocates have served as the best resource. As Sachs observes, while environmentalists traditionally are good at developing scientific methods to reduce pollution and depletion, they still "need human rights activists to uphold people's ability to get such reforms implemented" (ibid. 54).

Overall, Sachs concludes that "the universal human rights framework provides all individuals with a practical means of defending themselves against environmental degradation," and that "the older, better-established human rights covenants are especially well designed to unite vastly different cultures in this common struggle" (ibid.). Former U.N. Secretary-General Javier Perez agrees, asserting moreover that international human rights law "has equal relevance and validity for every political or social system and also every cultural tradition" (Cited in ibid.).

Throughout this study, I have argued for the importance of the concept of human rights, and this chapter so far introduces the vital connection between human rights and ecological duties. As Sachs asserts, "protecting the rights of the most vulnerable members of our society ... is perhaps the best way we have of protecting the right of future generations to inherit a planet that is still worth inhabiting" (Sachs 1995, 55). Given the apparent universality of these two issues, human rights and ecological duties, what specific contributions are offered by Buddhism and Roman Catholicism?

In this study, I have argued for the importance of the concept of human rights in religions in general, and within Buddhism and Roman Catholicism in particular. In this chapter, I have also argued for the necessary connection between the concept of human rights and ecological duties in general. In the remainder of this chapter, I specifically examine the concept of ecological duties as they relate to human rights within the current traditions of Buddhism and Roman Catholicism.

As John D'Arcy May observes, "one of the most far-reaching religious developments of recent times has been the rise to prominence of what Christians call 'creation spirituality' or what Buddhists might describe as the ecological significance of spiritual practice" (May 1998, 213). Yet, he emphasizes that this "new ecological spirituality ceases to be mere pragmatism and discloses something of the unity at the heart of all traditions" (ibid. 215). And Paul O. Ingram strongly asserts that "dialogical encounter with Buddhist traditions ... and Western ecological models of reality, as seen emerging in the natural sciences and Christian process theology, may energize an already evolving global vision through which to refigure and resolve the current ecological crisis." He maintains that "what is at stake is nothing less than the 'liberation of life'" (Ingram 1997, 72). I next focus on specific contributions of Buddhism to the concept of ecological duties.

4.2: ECOLOGICAL DUTIES AND BUDDHISM

A. INTRODUCTION TO BUDDHISM AND ECOLOGY

Many elements within Buddhism seem to make it a very "good fit" for ecological concerns. Concepts such as non-self (*anatta*), the interconnectedness of all things (*paticca samuppada*), Buddha-nature, non-violence (*ahimsa*), compassion, liberation from suffering, and others, all offer an obvious contribution toward ecological concerns. Many of these concepts have been examined in Chapter Two in regard to Buddhism and human rights, and they will not need to be reiterated in great detail here. Yet, they will be looked at in light of their contribution toward ecological duties.

In addition, one needs to avoid an overly simplistic view which romanticizes Buddhism's connection with nature throughout its history and condemns Christianity's domination of it. As noted earlier, the Judaeo-Christian tradition developed out of societies which took for granted a closeness with nature. The rift between humans and nature is largely a contribution of modern thought and practice. Likewise, while Buddhism had resources within its tradition for a "oneness" with nature, it may not always have historically practiced it. Thus, Buddhism and Christianity may not be that far apart on ecological concerns as is popularly assumed. This may hold true for actual practice as well as ideological concepts.

Is Buddhism more concerned with nature? Ian Harris argues that "I find this attitude difficult to square with any actually occurring Buddhist tradition and shall argue that the Christian situation is more or less precisely mirrored in Buddhism." Harris suggests that the attitude of Buddhism and of Christianity is "an essentially negative attitude toward the environment, underpinned by an influential but minority position far more favourable to an environmental ethic" (Harris 1994, 9). Therefore, in Harris' eyes, neither of these traditions has been strongly concerned with the environment throughout their history.

Harris points out that "the typical follower of the Buddha in the early period is a *renouncer*." He contends that "in essence and theory, then, Buddhism cannot uphold an environmental ethic," because "there is nothing within the sphere of nature which can be said to possess any meaning or purpose," since "everything, without exception, is subject to decay"(ibid. 25 [italics mine]). However, he does admit that "Buddhism endorses a spirit of toleration and co-operation with the natural world"(ibid. 26), and points out as well that "the Buddhist analysis of things, be they animate or inanimate, is far more radical than that adopted by western ecology"(ibid. 15).

Feminist Buddhist scholar Rita Gross observes as well that "Buddhism has not been especially oriented to an environmental ethic historically," although she notes that "East Asian forms of Buddhism seem to be more nature-oriented than South Asian Buddhisms"(Gross 1997, 334). Lewis Lancaster sheds some light on this difference. He explains that Buddhism in India viewed nature, as in the forest, as hostile, while later Buddhism in China, where nature was the ploughed field, viewed nature as good. He points out that "in the Ganges Valley, Buddhism reported the perception that the forest was a source of pain, danger, and struggle," but that "when it moved into the Han cultural area, a quite different perception of nature was held by that society" (Lancaster 1997, 12). Lancaster maintains that "the great contribution of Buddhism to this collective perception about nature in China was the concept of Buddha-nature," noting that "what was of such importance to the Chinese was the teaching that insentient objects also have it"(ibid. 13). Thus, the Buddha-nature idea was added to the Chinese reverence for nature which already existed.

The point of this is to note that Buddhism has not always embraced nature in the course of its history, and that when it has emphasized this, it has been confined to certain cultures, time periods, and forms of Buddhism. Also, one needs to consider that Buddhism is a religion of renouncing the world, not embracing it. Having said that, however, one also needs to acknowledge that, in theory and in practice, Buddhism has much to offer today toward ecological concerns.

Gross contends that "Buddhism has many intellectual and spiritual resources that can easily support an environmental ethic"(Gross 1997, 336). This is the predominant view of most scholars today in the area of Buddhism and Ecology. Most scholars *do* acknowledge a strong compatibility between Buddhism and environmental concerns, and argue that Buddhism can make strong contributions to this issue today. Here we will focus on those resources within Buddhism which can contribute toward the advocacy for ecological duties within the human rights discussion.

One concept at the heart of Buddhism which speaks to ecological concerns is the concept of impermanence. Masao Abe speaks of that "profound realization of that *transitoriness* common to man and to all other beings, living and nonliving." He explains that "this realization, when grasped in its depth, entails a strong sense of solidarity between man and nature." However, Abe is quick to point out that this does "not imply ... any denial of the significance of individualized human existence," since "man alone can be aware of universal transitoriness as such" (Abe 1982, 151). In addition, since the human state is the only one which can achieve liberation, Buddhism still holds a priority on the human being. This needs to be emphasized, so as not to naively equate Buddhism with some forms of ecology which deny a priority to human existence above other life forms. For even in Buddhism, a hierarchy, although subtle, does exist.

But the concept of impermanence cautions humans not to place themselves apart from nature, since they are subject to the same laws, and possibly the same end, as the rest of nature. This concept of impermanence is at the root of the unique Buddhist concepts of non-self (anatta) and interconnectedness/interdependence (paticca samuppada).

Sunyana Graef explains that "the premise of Zen Buddhist ecology is this: When we understand what we really are, we will be at peace with ourselves and our environment" (Graef 1990, 43). She observes that "the goal of Buddhist ecology is much more than an unpolluted environment. It is a life of simplicity, conservation, and self-restraint" (ibid. 44). This lifestyle flows from a realization of non-self and the interdependence/interconnectedness with all of reality. She maintains that "once we discover the unreality of the ego-I, we no longer relate to the world from an individual, self-centered perspective, but rather from a universal perspective." This, she suggests, "is the *weltanschauung* of a true ecologist" (ibid. 46).

Graef emphasizes further that "one who believes in the law of causation, therefore, will be careful not to cause pain to people, animals, plants, or the earth itself, for harming them is simultaneously harming oneself" (ibid. 48). She observes that, just as "the wave and the ocean work as one, for in reality, they are one," so too "what affects the universe, affects each of us, since we and the universe are not two." Graef concludes, therefore, that "in a person of wisdom, compassionate concern for the world will instinctively arise," and emphasizes that "the expression of this universal compassion is ecology"(ibid. 50).

This summarizes the basic Buddhist ecological worldview, and the relationship between the concepts of non-self and interdependence. These two concepts are central to the Buddhist view of ecology. Having examined these two concepts in Chapter Two in light of the individual and human rights, let us now observe further what these concepts offer to a Buddhist view of ecology.

B. THE CONCEPTS OF NON-SELF (ANATTA) AND INTERDEPENDENCE (PATICCA-SAMUPPADA) AND BUDDHIST ECOLOGY

As we discussed in Chapter Two, the Buddhist view of *anatta* holds that the individual person is a collection of elements (groups of grasping), none of which are permanent. To cling to one of these, or to the concept of a permanent self, is what causes suffering, and is delusion. Flowing from this, "rooted" in impermanence, is the idea that all things, constantly changing, are interconnected and interdependent. So, these two concepts are interrelated.

Rita Gross asserts that "*anatman* is simply another name for interdependence," and observes that "because we are interdependent with everything else in the matrix of existence, we do not exist in the way we conventionally believe that we do." She emphasizes that "that imagined independent self that greedily consumes and reproduces itself is a fiction," and that therefore "giving up on it is not a loss but a homecoming." Gross points out that "this is the aspect of Buddhism that has been so inspiring to deep ecologists"(Gross 1997, 344). Macy agrees, suggesting that "as we awaken, then, to a larger, ecological self, we find new powers. We find possibilities of vast efficacy, undreamed of in our squirrel cage of separate ego"(Macy 1990, 47).

Stephen Batchelor points out that this perception of a separate ego is delusion, whereby "we feel separate from each other, separate from the environment that sustains us and separate from the things we use and enjoy." He observes that "we fail to recognise them for what they are: part of us as we are of them, and the context in which we must painstakingly work out our salvation"(Batchelor 1992, 32). Batchelor asserts that "the ecological crisis is at root a spiritual crisis of self-centered greed, aided and abetted by ingenious technologies run amok" (ibid. 33). And, he contends that "since greed and attachment are short-sighted, mentally deadening and dehumanizing, the environment will reflect back those very qualities we inject into it" (ibid. 36).

Lily de Silva agrees, asserting that "pollution in the environment has been caused because there has been psychological pollution within ourselves." She emphasizes that "if we want a clean environment, we have to adopt a lifestyle that springs from a moral and spiritual dimension" (Lily de Silva 1992, 29). This is a major contribution of Buddhism, the emphasis on right view and right mindfulness. De Silva points out that "generosity, compassion and wisdom produce purity within and without," and that therefore "this is one reason the Buddha pronounced that the world is led by the mind" (ibid. 21). This Buddhist emphasis on the state of one's mind offers a strong corrective to the general Western view on solving all problems based on technology alone. Only when individuals change their minds and their hearts, their intent, and therefore their lifestyles, can true change occur. Otherwise, our technologies offer an external band-aid approach, while the larger problem persists because we ourselves have not changed.

De Silva emphasizes that "man and nature are mutually related to one another, a change in one is apt to bring about a change in the other." She points out that "the *Cakkavattisihanadasutta* of the *Dighanikaya* and a discourse in the *Anguttaranikaya* further point out the appearance of unhealthy environmental changes with the deterioration of man's moral values" (Lily de Silva 1979, 8).

In addition, Buddhism does speak of individuals using nature for themselves without abusing it. De Silva notes that "according to the *Sigalovada Sutta* a householder should accumulate wealth as a bee collects nectar from a flower. The bee harms neither the fragrance nor the beauty of the flower." She observes that "similarly, a human being is expected to make legitimate use of nature so that s/he can rise above nature and realize his or her innate spiritual potential" (Lily de Silva 1992, 22).

As already noted, the Buddhist concept of non-self (*anatta*) is interwoven with the concept of interconnectedness, interdependence, or *paticca samuppada*. Gross observes that "when one brings the vast collection of Buddhist teachings into conversation with environmental concerns, one basic teaching stands out above all others in its relevance." She points out that "that is the Buddhist teaching of interdependence, which is also one of the most basic aspects of the Buddhist worldview, a view held in common by all forms of Buddhism" (Gross

1997, 337). Gross asserts that "given interdependence, our very identity as isolated, separate entities is called into serious question, and we
are invited to forge a more inclusive and extensive identity." Therefore,
she reiterates that interdependence is "the most commonly invoked
concept in Buddhist environmental ethics" (ibid. 338).

One of the most famous metaphors for the concept of interconnectedness and interdependence is that of Indra's Jewelled Net. Attempting
to describe the concept of dependent co-arising (*paticca samuppada*)
as described in the earlier Pali texts of Theravada Buddhism, this metaphor developed based on the Madhyamika and Yogacara philosophy
of Mahayana Buddhism and the *Avatamsaka Sutra*. This sutra appears
to have been composed mainly in China around the 3rd Century C.E.,
and refined by Chinese sages in the 6th – 8th Centuries C.E. (Jones
1989, 136).

Ken Jones explains that "Indra's Net was one of the favorite analo-
gies of Avatamsaka scholars attempting to depict the interdependence
and interpenetration of phenomena or, more precisely, their identity-
in-separateness, in time as well as space" (ibid.).
He describes it in this way:

> At each intersection in Indra's Net is a light-reflecting jewel (that is,
> a phenomenon, entity, thing), and each jewel contains another Net,
> *ad infinitum*. The jewel at each intersection exists only as a reflection
> of all the others and hence it has no self-nature. Yet it also exists as
> a separate entity to sustain the others. Each and all exist in their
> mutuality (ibid. 137).

Jones explains that "in other words, all phenomenon are identifiable
with the Whole, the One, just as the phenomena which make up a specific phenomenon are identifiable with it." Thus, he observes that "each
has no existence except as a manifestation of all, the Whole, the One,"
and that "contrariwise, the One exists only through the many" (ibid.).
Jones reflects that "ethically, Indra's Net suggests respect and gratitude
for all things which reciprocally sustain our being, including respect
for the things we must consume and destroy in order to live, and a
lean, aware frugality in our use of resources" (ibid. 144).

Noting that this point of view is very much in keeping with the
Zen tradition in Buddhism and the Franciscan tradition in Roman
Catholicism (ibid.), Jones also notes the similarities with deep ecology.
He observes that "deep ecology, and derivations such as permaculture

and bioregionalism, are instructive exemplifications of Indra's Net and useful entry points for exploring its social implications." Jones recalls that "deep ecology is about the cultivation of a consciousness so that, in Arne Naess's words, 'with maturity, human beings will experience joy when other life forms experience joy, and sorrow when other life forms experience sorrow" (ibid. 139).

Here, the words of Zen Master Dogen are appropriate:

> Delusion is seeing all things from the perspective of the self. Enlightenment is seeing the self from the perspective of the myriad things of the universe (Dogen cited in Habito 1997, 170).

Ruben L. F. Habito brings this topic back to Zen practice. He emphasizes that "to see one's true self *as* the mountains, rivers, and forests, and as the birds, dolphins, and all the inhabitants of the great wide earth, constitutes a solid basis for living an ecologically sound way of life." He contends that this vision of reality can come about through the Zen practices of *zazen* (sitting) and *koan* meditation. Habito explains that "nonseparation, opened to the practitioner in the initial awakening experience and cultivated in continued *zazen* and *koan* practice, enables one to feel, as one's very own, the pangs of hunger of those who are deprived of the basic necessities of life, the pain of the victims of violence and discrimination and injustice, in their different forms" (ibid. 172). Habito concludes that "the most significant contribution Zen can make toward supporting and fostering the earth's well-being and promoting an ecologically viable way of life is in offering a fundamental vision of reality that invites human beings to an experiential oneness with mountains and rivers and the great earth" (ibid. 173).

C. ADDITIONAL CONCEPTS WITHIN BUDDHISM FOR ECOLOGY

When discussing the concept of "nature," Lily de Silva explains that the Pali equivalents which come closest to it are the terms *loka*, which is "usually translated as 'world,'" and *yathabhuta*, which "literally means 'things as they really are.'" She notes that the words *dhammata* and *niyama* are also used in the Pali canon and mean "natural law/way" (Lily de Silva 1979, 7). But what other concepts and teachings within Buddhism contribute to its ecological worldview, its view of the relationship between humans and nature?

Rita Gross observes that the basic concepts of non-harming, and the Middle Way itself, which she says would come to mind for any

Buddhist, would themselves "be a sufficient basis for an environmental ethic that would encourage limited consumption and reproduction" (Gross 1997, 337). She notes that the concept of rebirth also contributes toward an environmental ethic, since "all sentient existence is thought to be interconnected and related by virtue of karmic ties from past lives, and rebirth in non-human realms is highly possible" (ibid.). This brings us to the Buddhist view of animals and other living beings.

Although "the world of plants is not one of the six destinies" (Harris 1994, 24),[2] the world of animals and other living beings are possible destinies in the Buddhist view of rebirth. Andrew Schelling describes a collection of Buddhist literature called the *Jataka Tales*, which he contends "register the first instance in written literature of what I'd call *cross-species compassion*, or Jataka Mind, an immediate and unqualified empathy shown towards creatures not of one's own biological species" (Schelling 1991, 11).

This ancient collection, written in Pali, "preserves 550 legends which tell of the Buddha's miraculous births in the aeons before he became enlightened." Schelling speculates that some of these stories originally came from "animal tales dating in all likelihood to Paleolithic times." One of these *Jataka tales*, for example, tells of the Buddha offering his body as a meal to a hungry tigress who is about to devour her own cubs (ibid.).

Compassion for other living beings is a strong theme within Buddhism. Schelling notes the *Diamond Sutra*, where "the Buddha announces an unqualified brother and sisterhood of all creatures" (ibid.). He points out that "Mahayana Buddhism charges one to regard every creature possessing a nervous system, however rudimentary, as 'motherlike,'" and observes that "in the beginningless round of birth and rebirth, say the intricate commentaries, in the perennially growing garland of *Jatakas*, every incarnate creature has at some point been one's own mother" (ibid. 18).[3]

---

2   Harris notes that, in Buddhism, "we can never be reborn as a tree or piece of grass," and that "this is noteworthy because some Hindu *dharma* texts do accept this as a possibility."

3   Harris argues, to the contrary, that "the Buddhist attitude toward animals is essentially instrumental. Its essential function is to aid the practitioner in his search for spiritual perfection," and that "for Buddhism, animals belong some way down the hierarchy of beings" (Harris 1994, 19-20). Still, I

Grace G. Burford notes a famous line from the *Metta Sutta* which states "Just as a mother would risk her own life to protect her child, even so let one cultivate a boundless heart toward all that lives." And the *Dhammapada* states "Shun evil, do good, purify one's mind – this is the teaching of all the buddhas" (*Dhammapada* 183, cited in Burford 1997, 29).

Other elements exist within Buddhism which can contribute toward an environmental ethic. Gross contends that "the Second Noble Truth, with its emphasis on desire as the cause of suffering, is the key to a Buddhist environmental ethic." Observing that "the usually-chosen English word 'desire' translates the Pali *tanha* and the Sanskrit *trishna*," she suggests that "'grasping,' 'attachment,' 'clinging,' 'craving,' and 'fixation' are also possible, more accurate translations, and the way the term 'greed' is now used when discussing some multinationals also could translate *trishna*" (Gross 1997, 342).

Burford concurs that "according to the Buddha's second Noble Truth, everything unsatisfactory about our lives derives from desire based on a fundamental ignorance about the nature of reality." She insists that "similarly, the cause of our environmental woes lies in our insatiable desire to possess and consume natural resources, an approach that reflects a fundamental ignorance of the limits of Earth's resources." Burford reflects on the third Noble Truth, that "one can eliminate all pain and suffering and disappointment in life by letting go of selfish desire," and concludes that "the Buddhist model suggests that if we hope to counteract the environmental crisis, we should attempt to undermine the selfish desire that causes it" (Burford 1997, 31).

Burford also cites the Eightfold Path, particularly the three which apply specifically to ethics: Right Speech, Right Action, and Right Livelihood. She contends that "we can apply these basic Buddhist teachings to the process of developing an environmental ethic" (ibid. 30). In addition, she points out that "the Buddhists' Five Precepts of Right Action contribute helpful guidelines for achieving environmental objectives." She notes that "the first four, virtually universal precepts relate to environmental concerns about human destruction of life, and human dishonesty and insensitivity in our actions toward the natural world and each other" (ibid. 32). She emphasizes that "in Theravada

---

would argue that use and hierarchy do not negate a compassion for other living beings, which is a strong theme throughout Buddhist tradition.

Buddhism, each Buddhist undertakes the Five Precepts of Right Action over and over again, within the context of the practicing community" (ibid. 34).

Along with Burford, Steven C. Rockefeller examines the ties between Buddhism and the Earth Charter, which was mentioned earlier in this chapter. Rockefeller notes that Buddhism has supported and made significant contributions to the environmental ethic contained in the Earth Charter. He observes that "a number of scholars have pointed out that there seems to be a significant convergence of Buddhist philosophy and contemporary physics, ecology, and environmental ethics." In addition, he points to the Four Noble Truths as well, which "focus attention on suffering as the fundamental problem from which sentient beings seek liberation," and reminds us that "Buddhist ethics regards compassion for the suffering of all sentient beings as the supreme ethical virtue" (Rockefeller 1997, 318).

D. CONCLUSION ON BUDDHISM AND ECOLOGY

There is much within Buddhism which can and does contribute toward an environmental ethic. The general worldview of Buddhism forces one to realize that being human involves ecological duties, and cautions against an anthropocentric view of human rights which does not acknowledge duties toward the environment and other living creatures. Buddhist concepts such as non-self, interdependence, Buddha-nature, ahimsa, compassion, and the impermanence of things contribute toward an interconnected view of reality, where humans are not isolated individuals. In practice, Buddhist ethics have strongly supported compassion toward all living beings. And today, Buddhism's support for the Earth Charter, and Engaged Buddhism's activist stance toward environmental and human rights issues stands as a testament to modern Buddhism's support of ecological duties. (The history and development of Engaged Buddhism will be dealt with later in Chapter 5.)

Yet, there is another contribution which Buddhism can make which is often overlooked. In an age of global, multinational corporations, Buddhism's stand toward the merchant class can offer some practical advice. Lewis Lancaster contrasts Buddhism with the West, where he notes that "from biblical sources onward, wealth – and its companion, mercantile activity – has often been denigrated." By contrast, "Buddhism has been the religion of merchants from its earliest days,

and the spread of Buddhism has been accomplished by the mercantile community" (Lancaster 1997, 9). He emphasizes that "if ecological discourse assumes a rejection of this particular group, then one
of the pillars of the Buddhist community will be under strong at-
tack." Therefore, Lancaster admits that "perhaps we can learn from
Buddhism in this regard," and he asserts that "we need to seek out the
merchants and the corporate leaders, include them in our conferences,
urge them to be active partners in the search for answers to the ecological crisis" (ibid. 10).

Buddhism, therefore, in theory and in practice, has much to offer toward an environmental ethic, which can help to overcome the current
ecological crisis. Ecological duties, as a correlate to human rights, are
strongly supported within the Buddhist tradition. In fact, one could
argue that Buddhism begins with ecological duties, with a view of the
whole, and adds human rights as an element of that. The modern West
would operate from the other direction, beginning with human rights
and adding ecological duties. I next address what resources Roman
Catholicism brings to the concept of an ecological ethic.

4.3: ECOLOGICAL DUTIES AND ROMAN CATHOLICISM

A. INTRODUCTION TO ROMAN CATHOLICISM AND ECOLOGY

Many factors today influence the discussion of ecology, religion, human rights, and ecological duties. One of these is the article published
by historian Lynn White in 1967, "The Historical Roots of Our
Ecological Crisis." Pamela Smith sums up White's thesis: "the Judaeo-
Christian tradition, with its emphasis on God's transcendence, the
other-worldly destiny of the human, its orientation toward 'progress,'
and its biblical notion of human 'dominion' over the Earth, bore much
of the blame for environmental devastation and degradation." She
continues that "the tradition fostered a perception of nature as 'other,'
White argued, and allowed for a very exploitive exercise of 'dominion'"
(P. Smith 1997, 72). This article still offers a strong historical critique
of Christianity and is one which Roman Catholicism must keep in
mind as it re-examines its own resources in light of current ecological concerns. For, as Alberto Munera observes, "like every major religion that has achieved tenure on this earth, Roman Catholicism has
historically manifested a rich variety of themes and accents, not all
of them complementary and not all of them helpful" (Munera 2000,

65). In this section, I examine those resources from within the Roman Catholic tradition which can make a positive contribution toward the concept of ecological duties as a correlate to human rights.

Another major factor in this discussion, which was mentioned earlier, is the philosophy and movement of "deep ecology" developed by Arne Naess. While influential and positive in its contributions, the deep ecology movement differs from Roman Catholicism in its view of rights and duties in an ecological sense, and this needs to be noted here. Smith explains that "as the deep ecology movement has developed, it has ... asserted a notion of rights which subsumes and supersedes several centuries of development in *human rights* theorizing." She observes that "deep ecology suggests that rights are not only the possession of human moral agents-of, that is, rational, articulate, ethically responsible beings-but also of beings which can be affected by moral agents" (P. Smith 1997, 12). In this book I have avoided that terminology throughout, arguing instead that the language of "rights" should be employed in regard to humans, and the language of "duties" in regard to humans' interaction with other species and the environment. In doing so, this study is in line with the traditional Roman Catholic response to these issues. Yet, the issue of "rights" for animals and for the biosphere itself remains a contested issue.

Smith summarizes, for example, the thinking of John Kultgen, who argues that "the treatment of 'subpersons' as persons serves only to add hopeless confusion to the project of morality and to the making of ethical distinctions and determinations" (ibid. 13). Smith observes that, in deep ecology, there seems "to be no clear standard for applying 'biospheric egalitarianism' when rights conflict" (ibid. 14). She cites the work of Thomas Derr, who proposes a new kind of humanism to counter "not only deep ecology's anti-anthropocentric tones but also what he perceives as a general unfriendliness to the Judaeo-Christian tradition characteristic of environmental ethical thought." Derr argues instead that "an obediential reading and application of the biblical notion of stewardship" can lead to a more positive view of humans' relationship with nature (ibid. 17).

Smith notes Henryk Skolimowski, who argues that "the human has an irrevocable 'exquisiteness,'" which "renders human quality 'more precious than the exquisiteness of the mosquito'" (ibid. 16). Leonardo Boff echoes similar sentiments, asserting that "there is no justification for anthropocentrism, but that does not mean ceasing to regard the human being as unique." He points out that it is the human being who "emerges as an ethical being assuming responsibility for bringing the entire planet to a happy fate" (Boff 1997, 106).

Having established a fundamental difference between a Roman Catholic ecological view and some other ecological worldviews, this distinction also raises two key concepts within Roman Catholic ecological thinking. Those are the concepts of "human dignity" and "the common good." These concepts form a key framework for Roman Catholic thought on ecological duties and human rights.

As Boff observes, we "face a new paradigm. The foundation is laid for a new age, the ecological age" (ibid.). Roman Catholicism has much to offer to this new age, and its involvement is critical. Thomas Berry warns that "the future of the Catholic church in America ... will depend above all on its capacity to assume a religious responsibility for the fate of the earth." He asserts that "only by assuming its religious responsibilities for the fate of the earth can the church regain any effective status either in the human community or in the earth process" (Berry 1994, xi). I next address what specific resources Roman Catholicism can, and must, offer for this ecological age.

B. HUMAN DIGNITY AND THE COMMON GOOD

If "non-self" and "interdependence" form the basis for the Buddhist worldview in regard to human rights and ecological duties, the equivalent in Roman Catholicism would be the concepts of "human dignity" and "the common good." "Human dignity" emphasizes the value of the individual and the priority of human beings over the rest of creation, while the concept of "the common good" acts as a check on that to emphasize that humans live in community. When applied to an ecological perspective, "the common good" calls for our ecological duties toward the biospheric community which we call Earth, and even beyond that to the entire cosmos which God has created. These two concepts were examined earlier in light of their impact on the concept of human rights. They are briefly noted here for their influence on an ecological perspective.

Christine Firer Hinze points out that "the pope and U.S. bishops have promulgated a strong claim that modern Catholic social teaching is, in fact, fundamentally compatible with religio-moral attention to ecology." Firer Hinze, "focusing on the much-emphasized theme of 'human dignity' in contemporary Catholic social thought," argues

4 ◊ ECO-JUSTICE: ECOLOGICAL DUTIES & HUMAN RIGHTS   191

that "this moral ideal necessarily includes interdependent responsibility within the physical environment, beginning with the environment bordered by one's skin" (Firer Hinze 1996, 166). (This collection of essays and documents itself was initiated by the United States Catholic Conference in 1993, and shows the Catholic Church's concern in the U.S. for environmental issues.) She notes that "Scripture and tradition (along with evidence of common experience) confirm the judgment that humanity is distinct from other aspects of nature," yet emphasizes that "humans, because of who we are within nature, have particular responsibilities in relation to nature" (ibid. 169). This is my contention as well.

Firer Hinze emphasizes that "a Catholic social and ecological ethics will affirm human dignity. But that dignity will be reinterpreted in light of humanity's complex relationships and responsibilities within the ecosphere." For, she contends, "human dignity can be realized only in the midst of ecological respect and responsibility, never apart from it" (ibid. 170). Therefore, Firer Hinze concludes that "if my ecological location includes my body, and my survival as an embodied, spiritual being depends on certain positive relations to my physical environment, then it is not possible to speak morally about human dignity apart from ecological concern." She asserts that "Catholic social thought need not jettison a commitment to personal dignity in order to focus on ecosystemic responsibility; the two, in fact, entail one another" (ibid. 176). The concept of human dignity, in this light, does not necessarily have to be regarded as an anthropocentric concept which is a threat to an ecological worldview. It can be viewed as a concept which is realistic in its perception of human uniqueness but also in the responsibilities which humans have because of that uniqueness.

A concept in Western thought which emphasizes the role of responsibilities is the concept of "the common good." Drew Christiansen reminds us that "through 2,500 years, the principle of the common good has served as a standard of social integrity demanding that all sectors of society have a stake in the welfare and well-being of the polity." This concept remains a strong one within the Catholic tradition. Christiansen points out, for example, that "Aquinas argued that tyranny and faction violated the unity of society and its common good because they placed the good of an individual or group ahead of the good of the whole society" (Christiansen 1996, 184). Noting that "historically, the common good was understood in the context of a limited political setting, a city-state or nation" (ibid. 190), it is now being viewed more in the context of the earth itself. Christiansen observes that, "as people have become more aware of the earth's ecology and the risks of unrestrained economic growth, Catholic social teaching has come to think of ecology as an essential component of the common good" (ibid. 185).

Pointing out that recent Catholic social teaching uses the term "the universal common good," he recalls that "in his 1963 encyclical letter *Pacem in Terris*, Pope John XXIII specified for the first time the notion of a universal or global common good," and that "in *Renewing the Earth*, the bishops of the United States termed this 'the planetary common good'" (ibid. 190). Therefore, Christiansen emphasizes that "Catholic social teaching has come to formally recognize the ecological nature of the common good" (ibid. [italics mine]).

These concepts of "human dignity" and "the common good" are key Roman Catholic contributions toward an environmental ethic, for they supply a context for the role of rights and responsibilities. As Munera reminds us, "in Catholic social-justice theory, government is not an evil to be minimized. It is the prime agent of distributive justice. Its natural role is the furtherance of the common good and the protection of the powerless and the poor." Yet, the current unfettered, global, capitalist, consumerist system "is at odds with Catholic justice theory because it dignifies greed, destroys God's earth, has no sense of companionship with the rest of nature, and has no effective concern for the poor" (Munera 2000, 69).

Munera also points out that the concept of human dignity "not only grounds human rights but encourages the followers of Jesus even to lay down their lives for others" and "at least to live lives marked by sacrificial sharing and solidarity" (ibid. 76). Daniel C. Maguire notes as well that "personal rights, however cherished, may need to be curtailed by the essential requirements of the common good" (Maguire 1998, 16). He reflects on the fact that, "strangely, American religions and other moral instructors have not tried to define *saving the planet* as a 'family value,'" and concludes that "again *individualism* and a diminished sense of the *common good* dim the optic nerve" (ibid. 18 [italics in original]). The stress which Roman Catholicism places on the concepts of "human dignity" and "the common good," and the relationship between the two, can offer a major contribution toward the current development of an ecological ethic and the discussion of the relationship between ecological duties and human rights.

C. SCRIPTURE, TRADITION, AND ECOLOGY

Despite Lynn White's thesis, the Judaeo-Christian tradition has much to offer toward an ecological ethic. Primary, of course, are the creation accounts in Genesis. These state that creation is good, that God has created all, that humans are to act as stewards of creation, and that the suffering of the world is caused by man's failures and sin, since God's intent is that all of creation should flourish. Throughout all of scripture, the fact that God intervenes in the natural, historical process speaks to a continuity between the "material" and the "spiritual," that the natural, historical world is of value. This is reiterated most profoundly in the incarnation, by God actually taking human form, and affirming the value of the natural world. Throughout scripture, images of nature speak to the glory of God.

Lynn A. de Silva observes that the book of Genesis "explains the nature of the universe, man's place in nature and God's Lordship over nature" (Lynn de Silva 1979, 16). Noting that a dualism is rejected, he reminds us that "the idea that the world is either God or an emanation from God is also rejected." But in regard to humanity, de Silva maintains that one "implication arising from the story of creation is that man is also created just as the material world is created and as such man shares the nature of the world." He emphasizes that "man is part of nature because he is created out of the 'dust' of the earth," that "man is subject to the same laws that nature is subject to," and that therefore "there is a kinship between man and nature" (ibid. 17).

De Silva argues that there are three ways "in which man can relate himself to nature: he can either *renounce, manipulate* or *transform* nature." He points out that "Christianity rejects the idea of renunciation of the world as evil because it considers the world to be good," and that it also "rejects manipulation or exploitation of nature, because the material world is God's creation and is accorded a value." Therefore, he asserts that "the right attitude to nature is that of transformation," and suggests that "the biblical view is that the transformation of personal life goes hand-in-hand with the transformation of nature" (ibid. 19). This can be a positive way of viewing the Fall, that human, moral actions have repercussions on all of nature.

De Silva also contends that, in scripture, nature is seen as a sacrament, that "the Genesis story of creation was written, not to recount how God created the universe, but to praise and magnify God as Creator" (ibid. 20). He adds that "central to the sacramental view of the universe is the Incarnation," and therefore concludes that "by the very nature of its central doctrine Christianity is committed to a belief in the ultimate significance of the historical process, and in the reality of matter and its place in the divine scheme" (ibid. 21).

Denis Edwards argues for a stronger connection between the creation and the incarnation, suggesting that "the theology of Jesus as divine Wisdom can undergird a Christian approach to ecology" (Edwards 1995, 69). He contends that there is a biblical structure in which the early Christian communities "could see Jesus as the Wisdom of God, present and active in all of creation, pitching a tent among human beings on earth" (ibid. 70). Edwards argues that the incarnation need not only be tied to the Fall, but that "an alternate Christian theology sees the incarnation as flowing from God's free love for creatures." This alternative vision can be seen in the work of Irenaeus in the early church, of Duns Scotus, and has been supported by Teilhard de Chardin, Karl Rahner, and others within the past century (ibid. 71).

In regard to Paul's theology, Edwards points out that "the identification between Wisdom and the cross has profound meaning for an ecological theology," explaining that "it suggests that the love revealed on the cross is the very same loving Wisdom that is at work in, and manifest in, an eco-system, a rain forest, and the Milky Way galaxy" (ibid. 72). Joseph Sittler concurs that "a doctrine of redemption is meaningful only when it swings within the larger orbit of a doctrine of creation" (Cited in ibid. 82). Edwards emphasizes as well that "the material universe is not just a stage on which we play out our own redemption, but it too will also be transformed" (ibid. 86).

Edwards concludes that "when Jesus is understood as the Wisdom of God, it becomes possible to glimpse the unity between God's self-expression in each creature and in Jesus of Nazareth." He contends that "the resurrection of Jesus crucified can be grasped as the beginning of the transformation of the whole universe" (ibid. 153).

In addition to this theological approach to Jesus, Munera simply reminds us that any Catholic approach to ecological issues "must be taken from the same perspective that Jesus clearly demonstrated in his daily dealing with the poor, the oppressed, the marginalized, the weak, the rejected, and those considered the debris of the world" (Munera 2000, 66). In this regard, Christiansen also points out that there is a "reticence about material accumulation" which is "very much a theme in the New Testament ... and among the fathers of the Church." This, along with the emphasis on community (*koinonia*) (Christiansen 1996, 187), offer contributions toward an ecological ethic. Yet, besides scripture, there are elements throughout the historical tradition which can make contributions.

The traditional Catholic view of the relationship between nature and grace is one contribution. Munera points out that the tendency generally was "to see grace as activating the potential of the natural," and that "this was a way of seeing the sacredness of nature as a gift from God." He concurs that "out of this there grew a sacramental view of nature," in which "a rich repertoire of natural elements thus wove themselves into Catholic liturgy." Munera recalls that "the Catholic tradition held that the Holy Mystery is perceived through the whole created world-*invisibilia per visibilia*, the invisible through the visible," which was "a sensuous, nature-friendly approach that saw the whole world as a mirror of God" (Munera 2000, 70).

The theology of Thomas Aquinas can also be seen as a contribution toward an ecological ethic. Munera reminds us that "each of us is in Thomas Aquinas's phrase 'a participant in divine providence,' charged to care for the earth as cocreators and coproviders with the caring God in whose image we are made" (ibid.). Firer Hinze notes the work of Jame Ehegartner Schaefer, who "advances the claim that between Thomism and ecologism, there exist multiple points for fruitful contact and mutual enrichment." She observes that encompassing "facets of Aquinas's theological ethics is a worldview which envisages the parts of creation as interrelated and places the meaning and telos of all within the pseudo-Dionysian schema of *exitus-reditus*, origination from and return to the divine source" (Firer Hinze, 172 [see Schaefer 1994]). Pamela Schaeffer also notes the work of Jame Schaefer, who gives "examples of patristic and medieval writings that provide new resources for a Catholic environmental theology: the writings of Basil of Caesarea, of Augustine, of Bernard of Clairvaux and Francis of Assisi" (Schaeffer 1999, 14). Schaefer observes that "we really have a treasure house in our tradition" (Schaefer cited in ibid.).

St. Francis of Assisi is regarded by many as the most prominent Catholic historical figure in regard to ecology. In the 1979 Apostolic

Letter *Inter Sanctos*, Pope John Paul II proclaimed him "the heavenly Patron of those who promote ecology," and reminded us of this again in his "The Ecological Crisis: A Common Responsibility," (John Paul II 1996).

Keith Warner contends that "Francis demonstrated a way of living in harmony with nature that provides a much needed basis for dialogue between ecology and Christianity" (Warner 1994, 226). He points out that "The Canticle of the Creatures" by Francis "speaks of the essential values of what is today loosely referred to as Franciscan Spirituality: the intrinsic goodness of all the created world, the interdependence of all life, a passion for beauty and for peace, and the personalism of Francis" (ibid. 231). He suggests that The Canticle's view of interconnectedness "is also suggestive of Paul's metaphor for the interdependence of the diverse members of the body in 1 Corinthians 12" (ibid. 232).

Warner also contends that Francis' view of chastity offered "a broader definition" which meant "the right ordering of relationships," which was expanded to include all aspects of creation (ibid. 229). This insight drawn from the vow of chastity can also be applied to monasticism within Roman Catholicism in general. An emphasis on discipline and moderation can offer much to a consumer society today which promises fulfillment of instant gratification. And while monasticism in general was world denying, it also offered examples of self-sufficient, ecologically sound communities. Thus, the traditional monastic communities, while appearing to deny the value of the material world, in actuality lived in harmony with it and did not harm it (see Pedersen above). This is in contrast to our current society, which affirms the value of the material world, often claiming it is the only reality, and yet continually harms it. The monastic lifestyle and values within the Roman Catholic tradition may offer needed values toward a more ecologically sensitive lifestyle today. Therefore, there is much within Roman Catholicism's past tradition, scripturally and historically, which can contribute toward an ecological ethic. Current teachings push this issue even further.

D. RECENT CATHOLIC TEACHING AND ECOLOGY

As I noted in the section on liberation theology in Chapter Three, by the time certain Catholic developments receive mention by the magisterium, they have probably been supported and developed by theologians and the laity. This applies to the issue of ecology as well. But the fact that *it has been noted* is still significant, since genuine developments are often slow in being acknowledged by the Roman Catholic Church.

Pamela Smith points out that "the Vatican II pastoral constitution *Gaudium et Spes* laid a foundation for environmental reflection." She summarizes that "called to attend to and advance the 'universal common good' (GS #84), humans bear reminding that caring for and 'cultivating' the Earth is a human obligation (GS #39)," and that "humane and fructifying 'development' of the Earth is part of 'the design of God' (GS #57)" (P. Smith 1997, 79).

Smith observes that there are some common threads in Roman Catholic teachings on ecology since Vatican II. She suggests that "the Catholic magisterial view is ... thoroughgoing in its anthropocentrism insofar as it focuses on the human as *imago Dei*, as the being charged with responsible 'dominion' over the Earth, as the moral agent capable of prudently using or flagrantly misusing other created beings and resources." Yet, she maintains that while "the human occupies a primacy of place in the created order in Catholic thought," still "other creatures have their own place and 'proper perfection' (an expression grounded in Thomas Aquinas)" (ibid.). She concludes, therefore, that "a theory of creaturely value and an ethic of creaturely respect (though not a concession of animals' or nature's 'rights') have marked magisterial writings" (ibid.).

Smith argues that the teachings of John Paul II, bishops' conferences, and even the *Catechism of the Catholic Church* "would seem to bear out these themes:"

1) a vision of the natural world that is theocentric and anthropocentric but also, in some senses, incipiently ecocentric out of a reverence for all of creation's expression of the divine being; 2) a sense that other-than-human beings possess 'intrinsic value' even while they fittingly have 'instrumental value' to humans; 3) an understanding that humans are obligated to use and care for animals and the whole Earth respectfully; 4) a morality which implicates human agency in consequences not only to present but to future generations; 5) a view of the human telos as not only God-driven but intertwined with other living beings, the planet, and the cosmos; 6) a life-ethic that prescribes care, prudent use, the exercise of foresight and restraint in environmentally impacting actions and that locates

responsibility for environmentally ethical attitude formation and
behavior in all manner of societal institutions (ibid. 80).

I next briefly examine these source areas. For example, regarding
Pope John Paul II, Firer Hinze points out that the 1987 encyclical
Sollicitudo Rei Socialis "remains a key document for those ... who approach ecological matters from the vantage point of social ethics." She
observes that "not only does the pope for the first time advert to ecological issues in a major encyclical (nos. 29, 34), ... but he also offers
rich reflections on the connections between environmental degradation and misuses of technology; poverty and exploitative international
trade policies; and underdevelopment in the southern hemisphere and
a 'harmful superdevelopment' fed by consumerism, economism, and
materialism in the north" (Firer Hinze 1996, 178).

But the most often cited document on ecology from John Paul II is
The Ecological Crisis: A Common Responsibility, from January 1, 1990.
In it, he argued that there is "a growing awareness that world peace is
threatened" by, among other things, a "lack of due respect for nature,"
and that "a new *ecological awareness* is beginning to emerge" (John Paul
II 1996, 215 [italics in original]). He affirmed that the various world
problems are interrelated, which presses the need even more for "a
morally coherent worldview" (ibid. no. 2).

Arguing throughout that "the ecological crisis is a moral issue" (ibid.
no. 15), he contended that the "lack of *respect for life*" (ibid. no. 7) is a
root of the ecological problem. He observed that "the dramatic threat
of ecological breakdown is teaching us the extent to which greed and
selfishness – both individual and collective – are contrary to the order
of creation, *an order which is characterized by mutual interdependence*"
(ibid. no. 8 [italics mine]). In addition, he contended that "*the right to
a safe environment* is ever more insistently presented today as a right
that must be included in an updated Charter of Human Rights" (ibid.
no. 9 [italics in original]), thus making the connection between human
rights and ecology.

John Paul II also specifically noted the connection between "*structural forms of poverty*" and ecology (ibid. no. 11 [italics in original]), and
maintained that modern society must take "*a serious look at its life style*"
(ibid. no. 13 [italics in original]). Ultimately, he concluded that "the
ecological crisis has assumed such proportions as to be the responsibility of everyone," and that "its various aspects demonstrate the need

for concerted efforts aimed at establishing the *duties and obligations* that belong to individuals, peoples, States and the international community" (ibid. no. 15 [italics mine]). He even went so far as to state that Christians must realize that "their responsibility within creation and their *duty toward nature* and the Creator are *an essential part of their faith*" (ibid. [italics mine]). This is a significant statement, for, in a papal document, *duties toward the environment* are not only addressed, are not only one issue, or side issue, but *are an essential part of one's faith as a Christian.*

In addressing Catholics specifically, John Paul II reminded them of "their serious obligation to care for all of creation," noting that this comes directly from their belief in God the Creator, the recognition of original and personal sin, and redemption in Christ (ibid. no. 16). Therefore, for John Paul II, *ecological duties for Roman Catholics are rooted in key creedal concepts of the faith.* He concluded by reiterating that "respect for life and for the dignity of the human person extends also to the rest of creation" (ibid.).

Similar themes can be seen in the writings of the bishops. One major document is the 1991 Pastoral Statement of the U.S. Catholic Conference entitled *Renewing the Earth.* In it, the bishops write that they "seek to explore the links between concern for the person and for the earth, between natural ecology and social ecology" (U.S. Catholic Conference 1996, 224). Acknowledging that "our tradition calls us to protect the life and dignity of the human person," they emphasize that "it is increasingly clear that this task cannot be separated from the care and defense of all of creation" (ibid. 225). Thus, the connection between human rights and ecological duties is affirmed by the U.S. bishops as well.

Noting that "the tradition of Catholic social teaching offers a developing and distinctive perspective on environmental issues," they list the following themes which are "drawn from this tradition" and are "integral dimensions of ecological responsibility" (ibid. 230). They are:

  – A *God-centered and sacramental view of the universe,* which grounds human accountability for the fate of the earth;
  – A consistent *respect for human life,* which extends to respect for all of creation;
  – A worldview affirming the ethical significance of *global interdependence and the common good;*

– *An ethics of solidarity* promoting cooperation and a just structure
of sharing in the world community;
– An understanding of the *universal purpose of created things*,
which requires equitable use of the earth's resources;
– An *option for the poor*, which gives passion to the quest for an
equitable and sustainable world;
– A conception of *authentic development*, which offers a direction
for progress that respects human dignity and the limits of material
growth (ibid. [italics in original]).

Given these themes, the bishops assert that they are "confident that
this developing tradition can serve as the basis for Catholic engagement and dialogue with science, the environmental movement, and
other communities of faith and good will" (ibid. 231).

Reiterating that "respect for nature and respect for human life are inextricably related," they also observe that respect for nature must also
include a respect for the *diversity* of nature. They remind us that "the
diversity of life manifests God's glory," and that "every creature shares
a bit of the divine beauty" (ibid. 232), and recall the words of Thomas
Aquinas in his *Summa theologiae* that God "produces many and diverse
creatures, so that what was wanting to one in representation of the divine goodness might be supplied by another" (Aquinas cited in ibid.).

Introducing the phrase "the planetary common good," the bishops
also contend that "the universal common good can serve as a foundation for a global environmental ethic" (ibid. 233). This expression of
the concept of the common good emphasizes the strong ties between
traditional social justice categories and ecological duties. They reiter-
ate that "the ecological problem is intimately connected to justice for
the poor" (ibid. 234), and assert that "a just and sustainable society and
world are not an optional ideal, but a moral and practical necessity"
(ibid. 242). The U.S. bishops conclude that "without justice, a sustainable economy will be beyond reach," and that "without an ecologically
responsible world economy, justice will be unachievable" (ibid.).

Worldwide, other groups of bishops have addressed ecological issues as well. Brennan R. Hill points out that "one of the most extraor-
dinary documents on religion and the environment has come from
the Catholic mountain churches in Appalachia" (Hill 1998, 162 [In
reference to Catholic Committee of Appalachia, *At Home in the Web
of Life* 1996]), and notes that it "links the two processes of creation
and redemption" (ibid. 163). He observes that the bishops of northern

Italy "strongly support the human right to live in an environment suit-
able for health and well-being" (ibid. 165 [In reference to "Ecology:
The Bishops of Lombardy Address the Community"]),[4] and that the
Guatemalan bishops "point to the desperate 'cry for land' from millions
of their people" (ibid. 168 [In reference to "The Cry for the Land"])
in a "powerful document" (ibid. 171). In addition, the bishops of the
Philippines "have written one of the most significant church documents on environmental issues" (ibid. 172) in "What Is Happening to
Our Beautiful Land?," which also includes a "willingness to listen to
feminine voices and to see women activists as role models" (ibid. 174).

Yet, environmental issues, by their very nature, extend beyond national borders. A recent pastoral letter on the Columbia River and
its resources in the Pacific Northwest is "the first to be developed by
bishops of two countries-the bishops of the Pacific Northwest in the
United States and British Columbia in Canada" (Schaeffer 1999, 14).
John Hart reflects that "the bishops are saying that national borders
are really artificial in terms of who we are, that the environment is a
totality" (Cited in ibid.).

In addition, the Catechism of the Catholic Church addresses ecological concerns as well. Pamela Smith points out that the Catechism does
"point to the 'particular goodness of every creature' (#339) and the necessity for human respect for that particular good," and that "diversity,
beauty, the 'interdependence of creatures,' and creaturely solidarity are
hailed as signs of the Creator and of the divine will (#340-#344)" (P.
Smith 1997, 84).

Thus, there is much within recent Catholic teaching which draws
on its own tradition as a resource for a developing Roman Catholic
ecological ethic. As is also apparent, there is a strong tie in Catholic
thought between the concept of human dignity, and therefore human
rights, and an ecological ethic. This has been seen above in official
Church documents. I examine this further from the perspective of
theologians within the context of liberation and social justice.

E. SOCIAL JUSTICE, LIBERATION, AND ECOLOGY

Within Catholic theology, there is a growing consensus that an ecological ethic is not a side issue, but an all-encompassing ethic which
necessarily includes an option for the poor. In this light, there is an

4   This and the following documents referred to by Hill are contained in
    "And God Saw That It Was Good", ed. Christiansen and Grazer.

202   A MOUNTING EAST–WEST TENSION

obvious link between an ecological ethic, social justice, and liberation theology.

Pamela Smith observes that "ecotheology from a liberation perspective links the ruination of ecosystems with oligarchic, demagogic oppression – with what it views as the skewed assertion and enforcement of power over the poor, the landless, the voiceless, and indeed over the bounty of nature itself" (ibid. 57). She affirms that "eco-ethical concerns, because the fate of the poor and their land are interwoven, are, then, part of the fabric of liberation theology" (ibid. 58). The concern for the poor and marginalized in liberation theology and in Catholic social teaching in general has further led to a realization that the "marginalized" may in some way include other life forms and the earth itself. It has also led to a realization of how environmental degradation often affects the human poor first. As Smith suggests, "liberation theology seems to be moving from implicit to explicit awareness of the linkage between the exploitation of peoples and the obliteration and exhaustion of Earth's other creatures and features" (ibid. 64).

So acute is this link, that Dieter Hessel contends that "we're at the front end of an ecological reformation." He asserts that "the eco-justice crisis, the link between environmental degradation and social injustice worldwide, will be the paramount problem of the 21st century" (Hessel cited in Schaeffer 1999, 16). Carol Dempsey concurs, stating that "no longer can we speak only of social justice," but that "we need a new ethical paradigm that speaks of care for all creation" (Dempsey cited in ibid.).

And this paradigm cannot come soon enough, for there is a strong tie between exploitation of the poor and exploitation of the planet. For example, Daniel C. Maguire points out that "of the world's one hundred largest economies, fifty are corporations … and these giants that now bestride the earth are not encumbered with democratic structure, constitutions, or Bills of Rights" (Maguire 2000, 8). As he observes, "the planet and the poor of the world are not experiencing this rampage as salvation" (ibid. 9).

Maguire emphasizes that "not surprisingly, people, in solidarity with the decedent earth, are dying too." Commenting that "when it comes to impoverishment, the rule seems to be *women and children* first," he notes that "women constitute 70 percent of the world's 1.3 billion absolute poor." In addition, given environmental pollution and disease, he suggests that "if one glass of pure water was the cure for AIDS, most people in the world would not have access to it" (Maguire 1998, 3).

Bryan Massingale examines the connections between environmental degradation and race and economic class, and concludes that "environmental racism" exists. He emphasizes that statistics contend that "environmental hazards are not randomly or evenly distributed across population groups, but rather are borne disproportionately by people of color and the poor" (Massingale 1997, 234). Citing Environmental Protection Agency reports which state that "racial minority and low-income populations are disproportionately exposed to lead, selected air pollutants, hazardous waste facilities, contaminated fish tissue and agricultural pesticides in the workplace" (ibid. 237), he also observes that poorer communities do not have the resources or contacts to fight potential environmental threats such as hazardous waste facilities moving near their communities. Thus, he concludes that since "people of color and the poor bear the brunt of the nation's environmental miseries," therefore "imbalances of social power are at the heart of disparate environmental burdening" (ibid. 239). Massingale contends as well that "the environmental crisis cannot be resolved in the absence of social-indeed racial-justice" (ibid. 240 [italics mine])

As environmental hazards are disproportionately borne by certain racial and economic groups in the U.S., similar patterns emerge on a global scale. Massingale points out that Third World countries are often the final destination for hazardous waste storage of the industrialized First World (ibid. 245). And, while these countries on a global scale and communities on a national level may be financially remunerated for their willingness to store hazardous waste, Massingale argues that "one must question the level of financial compensation that could be adequate for the compromise of this 'inalienable' right," since "the right to a safe environment is a fundamental human right" (ibid. 244). Emphasizing again this connection between human rights and ecological duties in Roman Catholicism, he contends that "what one finds, then, in Catholic social teaching is a declaration that respect for creation is not simply a concern for natural resources, but also a matter of social justice having immediate ramifications for the value and worth of persons" (ibid. 242 [italics mine]).

Liberation theologian Leonardo Boff points out that "liberation theology and ecological discourse have something in common: they start from two bleeding wounds," which are "the cry of the poor for life, freedom, and beauty (cf. Ex 3:7), and the cry of the Earth groaning under oppression (cf. Rom 8:22-23)." He asserts that "now is the time to bring these two discourses together" (Boff 1997, 104).

Boff reminds us that in its initial development, liberation theology "became aware that a perverse logic was at work," and that today there is the similar realization that "the very same logic of the prevailing system of accumulation and social organization that leads to the exploitation of workers also leads to the pillaging of whole nations and ultimately to the plundering of nature" (ibid. 110). Thus, he concurs that "liberation theology and ecological discourse need each other and are mutually complementary" (ibid. 114).

Denis Edwards connects this starting point of liberation theology, and the concern for social justice and an ecological ethic, with the fundamental category of discipleship. He maintains that "a Christian discipleship will need to recognize both the intrinsic value of all creatures and the unique dignity of human creatures," and that "it will need to be committed to both ecology and justice." Further, he contends that true Christian discipleship "sees economic oppression, sexism and the violation of the planet as radically interrelated." Thus, Edwards emphasizes that "social justice and care for the planet are not understood as competing options, but as part of one ethical stance" (Edwards 1995, 157).

Therefore, it is readily apparent that concerns for ecological duties are closely tied to the concerns of liberation theology and to Catholic social justice concerns overall. These approaches, which form a more "activist" stance in Roman Catholicism, will be helpful in forming a more activist and aggressive approach toward an ecological ethic. Thus, within Roman Catholic liberation theology and social justice teaching and advocacy, ecological duties are necessarily linked to the concept of human rights. No valid Roman Catholic theory of human rights can ignore this ecological dimension. As Munera observes, "in the Roman Catholic perspective of liberation theology," the myriad ecological problems and issues of consumption and population "must be considered and interpreted in terms of justice theory from the perspective of the poor and oppressed." He reiterates that "this perspective includes poor people and the poor embattled earth" (Munera 2000, 65).

F. CONCLUSION ON ROMAN CATHOLICISM
AND ECOLOGICAL DUTIES

I have sought to show the extent to which ecological duties are a growing concern within Roman Catholicism, from the position of the magisterium to activist liberation theologians. As Pamela Smith concludes,
"the Catholic Magisterium has begun, in the decades since Vatican II,
to develop and detail a theology of creation, an anthropology which
understands the human in relation to the 'web of life,' and a visional
ethic which is more profoundly aware of animals and ecosystems than
earlier Catholic moral thinking has been." In addition, for Smith and
others, this reexamination by Roman Catholicism is often seen as a
positive reflection on its Thomistic tradition (P. Smith 1997, 87).

Roman Catholicism thus brings much to an ecological ethic. It offers the views that creation is good, that humans are stewards of creation, and in the Incarnation it sees the value of the material world reaffirmed. Within its tradition, it maintains an intellectual and mystical
element which sees beauty in nature for its own sake and sees creation
as a reflection of the Creator. And, within current Roman Catholic
social justice theory, which has strongly supported human rights over
the past century, the recent concern for ecological issues and duties are
now seen as being necessarily linked with human rights issues.

Firer Hinze asserts that "a gift of environmentalism to the Church
has been to alert us to the fact that *no future Catholic social ethic may
legitimately ignore the ecosphere*" (Firer Hinze 1996, 180 [italics mine]).
Noting that a "gift to the Church from liberation theology has been
its treatment of the dynamics of class, gender, race, and ethnicity," she
maintains that "Catholic ecological reflection, too, will be flawed to the
degree that it proceeds in isolation from, or fails to seriously engage,
these social-ecological realities" (ibid.).

Therefore, while I earlier affirmed Roman Catholicism's support
and current advocacy for the concept of human rights, I now additionally affirm Roman Catholicism's concern and advocacy for an environmental ethic. And, from its overall social justice stance, and fueled
by the perspectives of liberation theology, it links ecological duties as
a correlate of human rights. Ecological issues and human rights issues
can no longer be addressed in isolation from each other. Thus, as a major advocate for human rights on a global scale, Roman Catholicism

is also emerging as a strong advocate for ecological duties within this human rights agenda.

In *Renewing the Earth*, the U.S. Catholic bishops "call upon Catholic scholars to explore the relationship between this tradition's emphasis upon the dignity of the human person and our responsibility to care for all of God's creation" (U.S. Catholic Conference 1996, 241). Given Catholicism's social justice stance, this relationship between human dignity of the person (and therefore human rights), and ecological duties, is now seen as a necessary relationship. In Roman Catholicism, ecological duties form a necessary component of human rights theory, and human rights advocacy is often the most effective way to address ecological concerns.

4.4: ECOLOGICAL DUTIES AND HUMAN RIGHTS: A CONCLUSION

I have examined the concept of an ecological ethic, within religions in general, Christian theology, and more specifically within Buddhism and Roman Catholicism. I have also argued that the concept of ecological duties is a necessary correlate to the concept of human rights. Within religions, including Buddhism and Roman Catholicism, a theory of human rights which does not include ecological duties is seen as overly anthropocentric, selfish, egocentric, irreverent to the sacredness of life, and irresponsive to the awareness of the interconnectedness of all of life.

Defining religion as a *"response to the sacred"* (Maguire 1998, 23 [italics in original]), Maguire observes that this "sense of the sacred may be more vibrant in the movements of ecofeminism, transnational human rights and peace activism, and the green revolution than in the traditionally assigned places" (ibid. 44). While that may be so, I have sought to show what the traditions themselves of Buddhism and Roman Catholicsm also bring to the concepts of human rights and ecological duties. I have shown that these two concepts are interrelated, and that these traditions can offer much to current discussions of both concepts.

Pamela Smith explains that "what appears to be emerging, among the many and diverse interreligious and ecumenical discussions of the environment, is an ethic that emphasizes a positive vision of the natural world and a conscientious commitment to pro-environment

action on the part of individual believers and religious organizations."
She continues that "humans, animals, fields, forests, jungles, rivers,
lakes, seas, and ecosystems *are all deemed*-in varying ways and to varying degrees-*worthy of moral consideration and respect*" (P. Smith 1997,
77 [italics mine]). As advocates of the sacredness of life and of moral
sensitivity, the world's religions can offer much to the current ecological crisis. Munera asserts as well that "the world's religions must unite
to confront the real causes of injustice and ecological collapse in the
world" (Munera 2000, 77).

Buddhism, with its concepts of interdependence, interconnectedness, and non-selfness, can obviously contribute toward a strong ecological ethic. But, as seen above, so can Roman Catholicism, with its
emphasis that creation is good, that creation can have its own beauty
and purpose apart from humanity, and that humans are stewards
of creation. Keith Warner reflects that the founder of deep ecology,
Arne Naess, "believes that almost every religious movement, from
Buddhism to Christianity, has some elements consistent with deep
ecology already present within it" (Warner 1994, 227).

For example, Lynn A. de Silva suggests that "in speaking about the
disorder in nature St. Paul uses the Greek terms-*mataiotes, pathemata*
and *phthora*-which have close approximations to the Pali terms *anicca,*
dukkha and *anatta*" in Buddhism. He argues that, in both Buddhism
and Christianity, "the picture that emerges ... is the interdependence
of the different parts of creation – matter, life, mind, spirit. The created order cannot be divided into distinct and independent sections."
De Silva emphasizes that "what happens on one level will have its repercussions on other levels ... . Man's folly affects nature" (Lynn de
Silva 1979, 22).

Both Buddhism and Roman Catholicism currently argue for ecological duties. In their distinct ways, both Buddhism and Roman
Catholicism currently support and advocate the concept of human
rights and the unique value of the individual human being. Both
Buddhism and Roman Catholicism argue that the concept of human
rights is shallow and perverse unless it also includes a recognition of
ecological duties. In this book, I have advocated these positions so far.
Given their mutual support of human rights and ecological duties, I
next conclude that Buddhism and Roman Catholicism, despite their
different theological systems, can offer a test case for a global ethic.

CHAPTER 5

A GLOBAL ETHIC

5.1: INTRODUCTION TO A GLOBAL ETHIC

A. A GLOBAL ETHIC: THE DECLARATION OF THE PARLIAMENT OF THE WORLD'S RELIGION

From August 28 to September 4, 1993, the Council of the Parliament of the World's Religions met in Chicago. Around 6,500 adherents from the world's religions approved and signed a joint *Declaration Toward a Global Ethic* (Küng and Kuschel 1995, 8). The Declaration and its Summary Statement state that "we condemn the poverty that stifles life's potential; the hunger that weakens the human body; the economic desparities that threaten so many families with ruin" (ibid. 13). It continues that "we affirm that a common set of core values is found in the teachings of the religions, and that these form the basis of a global ethic" (ibid. 14). This is a basic contention of this book as well. The document emphasizes that "we must not live for ourselves alone, but should also serve others, never forgetting the children, the aged, the poor, the suffering, the disabled, the refugees, and the lonely" (ibid. 15). It explains that "we must strive for a just social and economic order, in which everyone has an equal chance to reach full potential as a human being" (ibid.). Finally, it concludes that "every human being ... possesses an inalienable and *untouchable dignity*. And everyone, the individual as well as the state, is therefore obliged to honour this dignity and protect it" (ibid. 23).

The draft of this document presented to the Parliament was written by Hans Küng, after previous consultation with over a hundred scholars and representatives of the world's religions. (The English translation was prepared by Leonard Swidler.) It emphasizes Küng's assertion that there can be "no new global order without a new global ethic" (ibid. 18). Presented as a minimum ethical standard to which the world's religions agree, the approach also acknowledges that each of the traditions will also contain within themselves unique elements and higher ethical standards and expectations than the minimal global ethic. However, this minimal global ethic is seen as a major advance and a necessity for the emerging global village. In addition, Küng is quick to point out that this minimum ethic "does not of course mean an ethical minimalism," but rather is "what is now already common to the ethic of the religions of the world and which hopefully can be extended and deepened in the course of the process of communication" (ibid. 73).

Küng reflects on what a "global ethic" should and should not be. He explains that, while "a declaration on a global ethic should provide ethical support for the UN Declaration on Human Rights" (ibid. 56), which it does, he also emphasizes that "an ethic is more than rights" (ibid. 55). Küng elaborates that "an ethic is primarily concerned with the inner realm of a person, the sphere of conscience, of the 'heart,' which is not directly exposed to sanctions that can be imposed by political power" (ibid. 58). In addition, he notes that "for religions, an ethic has a religious foundation ... an ethic has to do with trust (quite rational trust) in an ultimate supreme reality" (ibid. 59 [see Küng 1978, 442-477, for his understanding of the concept of "trust" for his theology]). Küng also points out that the German 'Weltethos' should be translated 'world ethic' or 'global ethic' (ibid. 60), and "not 'Global Ethics,'" since "'ethic' means a basic human moral attitude, whereas 'ethics' denotes the philosophical or theological theory of moral attitudes, values and norms" (ibid. 59).

Küng recalls that there were three basic concepts which were never in question throughout the discussion of the document. He notes that "no side put in question the *need for* a Declaration Toward a Global Ethic and its *usefulness*," that "the basic ethical requirement that 'Every human being must be treated humanely' was accepted as a matter of course," and that "the second complementary basic demand, the Golden Rule, was similarly accepted as a matter of course" (ibid. 71 [italics mine]). Küng suggests that "the *Golden Rule* in particular, which is so fundamental, shows impressively that the *common global ethic* of the religions is *not a new invention* but *only a new discovery*" (ibid. [italics in original]).

While the initial Parliament in 1893 was a historic event, and the first major exposure of the Western public to some "exotic figures" of the Eastern religions, the mindset of that Parliament was radically different than the one a century later in 1993. Karl-Josef Kuschel explains that, at the end of the 19th Century, there were "the expectations of Christianity that it would become *the* dominant universal world religion in the twentieth century, in the wake of Eurocentric modernity," but of course these expectations "failed all along the line." Thus, he observes that "at the end of the twentieth century on the whole the other religions of humankind are stronger than they were at the beginning," and that "the world-view of Euro-centric Christian modernity has been replaced" (Kuschel in ibid. 88). That "polyreligious situation of our time" forms one key component of the "postmodern" era.

The concept of a "global ethic" is not a radically new idea. Other versions have been offered and have influenced Küng's thought on what an ethic should look like. Küng notes the World Conference of Religions for Peace in 1970 in Kyoto, Japan, which adopted a declaration which "expresses in exemplary fashion what a concrete, universal basic ethic, a world ethic of world religions, could be" (Küng 1990, 118). Some statements from that declaration resemble those contained in Küng's version for the Parliament. Leonard Swidler wrote his own global ethic, and translated the English draft of Küng's. In February, 1989, a colloquium in Paris was held at the invitation of the Goethe-Institute in Paris and UNESCO (Kuschel 1990, 97). There, Küng presented a paper which laid the groundwork for his later global ethic. The paper had the general title of "No world peace without religious peace. An ecumenical path between being fanatical for the truth and forgetting the truth" (ibid. 98). In it, Küng "put forward the following thesis: the *humanum*, that is to say, the truly human, is (together with the internal criteria of truth) an additional criterion of truth for religions." He argued that "only a religion which promotes humanity can be a true and good religion," and that "in so far as a religion spreads inhumanity, in so far as it impedes human beings' sense of identity, meaning and value, it is a false and bad religion" (ibid. 99).

Küng emphasizes the role that religion *should* play in regard to a global ethic. He points out that "one thing those without religion cannot do … is to justify the unconditionality and universality of ethical obligation" (Küng 1990, 113). Küng explains that "the categorical nature of the ethical demand, the unconditional nature of the 'thou shalt,' cannot find its justification in a human being who is conditioned in so many ways, but only in the unconditional: an absolute" (ibid. 114). Therefore, as I discussed earlier in Chapter One, religion offers the only ground which can truly justify "why should a human being do good and not evil?" (ibid. 102), even to the extreme extent that one may sacrifice one's own life (ibid. 110).

Küng emphasizes that a global ethic is necessary because, while the West has contributed much to a global culture, it has also left many hazardous omissions. For example, he contends that "the West has given:

> – *science*, but no wisdom in order to prevent the misuse of scientific research
> – *technology*, but no spiritual energy to bring the unforeseen risks of a highly efficient, major technology under control
> – *industry*, but no ecology to combat the ever-expanding economy
> – *democracy*, but no morality which could counteract the huge power interests of the various men of power and power groups.
> (ibid. 104 [italics in original]).

Hence, a global ethic acts as a check against the extremes of Western societies. It also works against the claim that it is a purely Western document, since it acknowledges the widespread criticism of non-Western countries against the West. As a global society continues to develop, the necessity of a global ethic, and the role of religions in it, is crucial.

B. A GLOBAL ETHIC AND HUMAN RIGHTS

Despite the observation that the Parliament's Global Ethic represents an agreement of primarily liberal constituents of the world's religions (see Juergensmeyer 1995, 48 and S. King 1998, 129-130), the fact remains that radically different worldviews *have* come to an agreement on practical matters that involve a global ethic. And, despite the critique that it is a mixed collection of minimal standards ("what is") and higher challenges ("what ought to be"),[1] the Global Ethic offers major contributions to two key areas of this study, the issues of universality and human rights.

Sallie King observes that "the Global Ethic has the potential to constitute a breakthrough on the question of universality and relativism

---

1 Sallie King points out this inconsistency, arguing that the Global Ethic's statement on the equality of males and females is an "ought" statement which can not possibly reflect "an ethic [that] already exists within the religious teachings of the world" (ibid. 132-133 [quotation from *A Global Ethic*, Küng and Kuschel 1995, 18]).

in ethics" and "provides important support for international human rights" (ibid. 138). Hence, I find it necessary to bring the concept of a "global ethic" into this study on human rights, for the concept of a global ethic logically flows from, and adds support to, that concept of human rights. And, both of these concepts imply a "universality" which stands in direct opposition to current claims of "cultural relativism."

King notes that "the Global Ethic has an important affinity with the U.N. Universal Declaration of Human Rights" and in places uses explicit "rights" language (ibid. 135). The Global Ethic itself states that:

> We recall the 1948 Universal Declaration of Human Rights of the United Nations. What it formally proclaimed on the level of *rights* we wish to confirm and deepen here from the perspective of an *ethic*: the full realization of the intrinsic dignity of the human person, the inalienable freedom and equality in principle of all humans, and the necessary solidarity and interdependence of all humans with each other (Küng and Kuschel 1995, 20).

King explains that "simply put, no one wants to be tortured, injured, killed, hated, discriminated against, 'cleansed,' exiled, or liquidated, and they do not want these things done to others they care about." She emphasizes that

> people all over the world recognize that if they don't want their own basic human rights violated, their best bet is to try to prevent all human rights violations. Hence, the nearly universal acceptance of the principles and language of human rights (S. King 1998, 137).

This is what Traer is referring to in saying that the concept of human rights represents a "universal faith," hence a "faith in human rights." Traer asserts that "this support for human rights is global, cutting across cultures as well as systems of belief and practice"(Traer 1991, 1 [see also 207-221]).

The necessity of the concept of human rights is apparent on two levels. In theory, the concept of human rights operates as a concept which upholds the belief in the dignity, value, and preciousness of each human being, a belief which is articulated in various ways by the world's religions. In practice, the concept of human rights is an agreed upon international concept which has political ramifications and enforcibility. Thus, it represents perhaps our best hope for political and ethical common ground while also challenging these areas to a higher standard.

Küng admits that "the international community cannot exist without common values," and observes that the implementation of human rights "cannot succeed against the religions but only with them" (Küng 1991, 89). He asserts that "religion can unambiguously provide reasons that politics cannot: as to why morality and ethics should be more than a matter of personal taste or political opportunism." Küng contends that "religion can unambiguously demonstrate why morality, ethical values and norms must be unconditionally binding. . . and thus universal" (ibid. 87). Küng also points out that "the sharpest criticism of any form of untruth in religions is immanent in the religions themselves" in the sense that they are reminded by their prophets and reformers that they have become unfaithful to their own 'nature' or origins (ibid. 84).

But, in the case of human rights, the universality of the concept necessarily leads to the need for a universality in practice. Paul Knitter acknowledges the claims and concerns of post-modern views against a moral common ground. However, he also admits that he cannot reconcile that relativist worldview with the amount of suffering which exists globally and which he argues places a moral imperative upon us. He states that "I see and hear a world in agony, torn by starvation, dehumanizing living conditions, unjust distribution of wealth, ecological deterioration – a world that calls for global, coordinated action based on commonly recognized values and truths." He reflects that "I cannot put the insights and admonitions of postmodern awareness together with the reality and the moral requirements of the world as it is" (Knitter 1995, 55). David Tracy observes that "such a pluralism masks a general confusion in which one tries to enjoy the pleasures of difference without ever *committing to any particular vision of resistance and hope*" (Tracy cited in ibid. [italics Knitter's]).

Knitter argues, correctly in my judgment, that "if there are no common criteria to be discovered or fashioned by nonviolent consensus, then ultimately what is 'true' will be decided by power – by who has the money or the guns." He suggests that "the common cause out of which we can fashion our common ground is all around us in the sufferings that rack and endanger our species and planet" (ibid. 56). Therefore, he contends that if there is one issue that we can agree on, "*it is this-the human and ecological suffering that now menaces our world*" (ibid. 57 [italics mine]).

* Knitter is pressing for a *pluralistic, liberative dialogue of religions*, but because he is leery of the theological baggage of those terms, he prefers the phrase *globally responsible, correlational dialogue of religions* (ibid. 15), borrowing terminology from Hans Küng. He explains that "in proposing a model for a 'globally responsible' dialogue or theology of religions, I will be urging that religious persons seek to understand and speak with each other on the basis of a *common commitment to human and ecological well being*." He notes that this global responsibility goes beyond traditional liberation theology in that it seeks "not just *social justice* but *eco-human justice* and well-being" (ibid. [italics mine]).

Knitter asserts that "any interfaith encounter is incomplete, perhaps even dangerous, if it does not include ... a concern for and an attempt to resolve the human and ecological suffering prevalent throughout the world" (ibid.). Earlier, in arguing that "a worldwide liberation movement needs a worldwide interreligious dialogue," Knitter went so far as to say that "religion that does not address, as a primary concern, the poverty and oppression that infest our world is not authentic religion" (Knitter 1987, 180). Dorothy Solle points out the limits of pluralism and tolerance, stating that "the limits of tolerance are manifest by the victims of society. Whenever human beings are crippled, deprived of their dignity, destroyed, raped, that is where tolerance ends" (Cited in ibid.).

Knitter continues by explaining that "we encounter other religions, not *primarily* to enjoy diversity and dialogue but to eliminate suffering and oppression – not only to practice charity but ... to work for justice" (ibid. 181). He observes that "without a commitment to and with the oppressed, our knowledge is deficient – our knowledge of self, others, [and] the Ultimate" (ibid. 185). The practice of bringing about justice and helping others is a vital part of what religion is, what God (however defined) is. Jay McDaniel sums this up by reminding us that "wherever there is suffering and victimization, of either human or nonhuman life, there is God. God is indeed a God of the oppressed" (McDaniel 1985, 694). Thus, the connection between human rights and ecological duties as contributing toward a global ethic is apparent.

5.2: BUDDHISM, ROMAN CATHOLICISM, AND A GLOBAL ETHIC

A. BUDDHIST AND ROMAN CATHOLIC PERSPECTIVES ON A GLOBAL ETHIC

Catholicism, even in its very name, has always advocated universal moral truths. However, Catholics are correct in being cautious about what is advocated as a universal norm, especially in light of the history of some Catholic teachings on sexual issues. In describing a Catholic feminist critique of the latter, for instance, Margaret Farley explains that "feminists resist theories of common morality primarily because they have been harmful to women" and "have inaccurately universalized a particular perspective" (Cited in S. King 1998, 128). Sallie King adds that "history gives ample evidence that when a powerful group manages a discussion in such a way that they declare their perspective to be the universally correct one, the less powerful may well suffer the consequences" (ibid.).

This is an important critique, and concern, and must be considered when trying to become too particular in advocating universal moral norms. However, given current human rights and ecological abuses, one cannot be too timid in arguing for some universal moral norms. This is where the global ethic is important. In shying away from it, some feminists and others may be bringing on a "relativity" which will ultimately be more harmful to women. Current abuses of human rights and the environment necessitate a stronger feminist stance, not a more relative one.

Catholic scholars involved in interreligious dialogue have played a major role in developing and advocating a global ethic, as is evidenced by Hans Küng's draft of "A Global Ethic" which the Parliament endorsed, Leonard Swidler's "Universal Declaration of a Global Ethic" and his support for Küng (see S. King 1998, 118-123, for a nice summary of Swidler's contribution), and Paul Knitter's emphasis on "global responsibility" toward the suffering. Although Catholicism has been late in accepting the modern idea of human rights (i.e., the past century), the development from *Rerum Novarum* (the rights of workers) to *Pacem in Terris* (full acceptance of human rights) to *Economic Justice for All* (human rights, the poor, and the economy) is significant.

In Chapter One, I dealt with the support of human rights within the Judaeo-Christian tradition, and that will not need to be reiterated here. Yet, the importance of its congruence with a global ethic cannot be overstated. In addition, Chapter Three emphasized Roman Catholicism's strong tradition of a concern for human dignity and its recent language of social justice and human rights advocacy. All of this reveals a strong alliance with the concept of a global ethic. As a global organization, one can say that, in a real sense, Catholicism has always supported a global ethic. Yet, historically, this "global ethic" was often viewed as a "Catholic ethic." Therefore today, Roman Catholicism needs to exercise some restraint in how it officially pursues a global ethic, and more openmindedness in how it actually dialogues with other religions. Yet, the theological groundwork for this dialogue has been laid with Vatican II, and the actual practice of dialogue by Catholic theologians and the laity in developing a global ethic and working for social justice exemplifies approaches in which this can operate.

Charles Curran argues that "the best of the Roman Catholic tradition has always been in favor of a global ethic," noting that the Catholic Church has always stressed universalism, although this was often at the cost of individualism. He points out that two key concepts of the Christian message are in resonance with a global ethic: the Christian belief in creation and the Christian understanding of love. In the belief in creation, every human being is seen as brother and sister to us, and the Christian understanding of love, or "love of neighbor," is universal and all inclusive. Curran asserts as well that Roman Catholicism has always insisted on a global ethic or universal morality by its ecclesiology ("our concerns are universal," not just about the Church, but society as well), by its natural law theory, and by its actual practice.

While admitting that the general Catholic problem historically was that "we were too certain about too many specifics, especially moral ones," he cautions that "in a global ethic, we'll never get agreement on specifics." Yet, Curran suggests that the Roman Catholic tradition offers a vision that is in line with a global ethic, an "inclusive communitarianism," which argues that the "human being is by nature social and political" (Thomas Aquinas from Aristotle). Curran concludes that while a global ethic may be difficult to achieve, we should still work on it in a spirit of hope, and that it is a demand of the needs of our times (Curran, 1999).

In Buddhism, the ecological implications of duty and interconnect-edness are apparent. Yet, despite the seemingly problematic concept of anatta (non-self), Sallie King argues that "Buddhism is squarely in the human rights camp" and that "it strongly supports the effort to define a global ethic" (S. King 1995b, 82). Aung San Suu Kyi, Nobel Peace Prize winner and Leader of the Opposition in Burma, wrote in a text for the UNESCO World Commission on Culture and Development that "the challenge we now face is for the different nations and peoples of the world to agree on a basic set of human values, which will serve as a unifying force in the development of a genuine global community" (Kyi 1996, 234).

Buddhism's support for human rights (as seen in Chapter Two) and its support for ecological duties (Chapter Four) form a strong support for a global ethic. Yet, another contribution toward the ac-tual Declaration Toward a Global Ethic was Buddhism's check on the Western concept of "God." Küng explains that when other par-ticipants continually used "God the Almighty" or "God the Creator" in their invocations, prayers and blessings, "leading Buddhists during the parliament felt called on to protest," and "complained about the lack of knowledge and sensitivity on the part of certain religious leaders" (Küng 1993, 64). A leader of the Zen Buddhist Temple in Chicago read a statement signed by other Buddhist leaders which stated that "Buddhism is not a religion of God. Buddhism is a religion of wis-dom, enlightenment and compassion." It continued that "unlike those who believe in God who is separate from us, Buddhists believe that Buddha which means 'one who is awake and enlightened' is inherent in us all as Buddhanature or Buddhamind" (ibid.).

Küng reflects that the lesson was a valuable one, in helping delegates to be more understanding of each other, yet also in showing that de-spite radical differences of belief, delegates could still come to a con-sensus on an ethic. He contends that "the Buddhist objections to the use of the name of God ... were already evidence that a consensus can be achieved in matters relating to a global ethic only if ... one leaves aside all differences of faith and 'dogma,' symbols and rites, and con-centrates on common guidelines for human conduct" (ibid. 65).

From within Buddhism, Sallie B. King offers four Principles of a Buddhist Proposal for a Global Ethic. These include 1) *Nonviolence to humans and the biosphere,* 2) *Economic justice,* 3) *Human rights and human equality,* and 4) *Truth and the free flow of information* (S. King

1995a, 130-134 [italics in original]). In regard to human rights, she points out that "in the Buddhist view all humans are equal insofar as all have the ability to become Buddha." She notes that "views, entertained for a while, that perhaps some had Buddha potential and some did not, die out," and that therefore "Buddhism is committed in principle to human equality"(ibid. 133).

King contends that "the ethic I have proffered as a Buddhist proposal for a global ethic is similar to the global ethic proposed by Hans Küng and Karl-Josef Kuschel," noting that "a number of the most distinguished and beloved leaders of the Buddhist world have signed that declaration [Küng's]." Therefore, she asserts that "Buddhists support human rights and will support the attempt to formulate a global ethic of the world's religions"(ibid. 135).

But why? King explains that "the five precepts of Buddhism ask Buddhists to place limitations on themselves in order to prevent suffering," and that she believes that "Buddhists would happily welcome a global ethic in which the human community pledged self-restraint in order to prevent suffering." In fact, she contends that "*it seems an extension of Buddhism itself to seek and embrace such a global ethic*"(ibid. [italics mine]).

Others could see the global ethic itself as resonating with the heart of Buddhism. Walpola Rahula wrote that "Buddhism arose in India as a spiritual force against social injustices, against degrading superstitious rites, ceremonies and sacrifices; it denounced the tyranny of the caste system and advocated the equality of all men; it emancipated woman and gave her complete spiritual freedom"(Cited K. Jones 1988, 65). He observed that the Buddha "did not recognize progress as real and true if it was only material, devoid of a spiritual and moral foundation." Rahula concluded that "Buddhism always lays great stress on the development of the moral and spiritual character for a happy, peaceful, and contented society"(Rahula 1988, 106), which is the contention of the global ethic as well. An example of a religion remaining true to its religious heritage yet advocating global responsibility in the spirit of the global ethic can be seen in the movement called Engaged Buddhism.

B. ENGAGED BUDDHISM: AN EXAMPLE OF TRADITION, TRANSITION, AND GLOBAL CONCERN

Chapter Two introduced the movement known as Engaged Buddhism, but I return to it here as an example of a religion transforming itself in light of global concerns yet remaining true to its tradition (at least in the eyes of its adherents). Three points are significant in this example:

1) It feels it has remained true to the fundamental beliefs and sources of its tradition. It does not see itself as a new religion.
2) It has been influenced from outside, in this case the West.
3) It has shifted the historical focus of the religion to so-cial-global action from the traditional focus on individual enlightenment/salvation.

Thus, it serves as a model of how a religion can seek to transform itself, in congruence with principles which are also contained within the global ethic, and yet still retain its unique character and identity as a religion.

One American Zen teacher explained that

> a major task for Buddhism in the West ... is to ally itself with reli-gious and other concerned organizations to forestall the potential catastrophes facing the human race: nuclear holocaust, irreversible pollution of the world's environment, and the continuing large-scale destruction of non-renewable resources. We also need to lend our physical and moral support to those who are fighting hunger, pov-erty, and oppression everywhere in the world (Cited in Kraft 1988, xii).

Kenneth Kraft explains that "the term 'engaged Buddhism' refers to this kind of active involvement by Buddhists in society and its prob-lems." He observes that "participants in this nascent movement seek to actualize Buddhism's traditional ideals of wisdom and compassion in today's world" (ibid.). Kraft points out that when current authors "re-examine Buddhism's 2,500-year-old heritage," they "find that the principles and even some of the techniques of an engaged Buddhism have been latent in the tradition since the time of its founder" (ibid.).

Kraft contends that "the touchstone for engaged Buddhists is a vi-sion of interdependence, in which the universe is experienced as an organic whole, every 'part' affecting every other 'part'"(ibid. xiii). He observes that this linkage of personal peace with world peace "is one of Buddhism's fresh contributions to politics" (ibid. xiv), and cites the writing of Vietnamese Zen teacher Thich Nhat Hanh:

> We need such a person to inspire us with calm confidence, to tell us what to do. Who is that person? The Mahayana Buddhist sutras tell us that you are that person. Only with such a person – calm, lucid, aware – will our situation improve (Cited in ibid.).

Christopher S. Queen points out that "the term 'engaged Buddhism' is attributed to Thich Nhat Hanh, who published a book by that title in 1963." He suggests that "it seems likely that the French term 'engagé,' meaning politically outspoken or involved, was common among activist intellectuals in French Indochina long before the 1960's." Queen observes that "the term 'socially engaged Buddhism' appeared in two titles in 1988," one of which was by Sulak Sivaraksa, and that "the term has achieved currency within the Buddhist Peace Fellowship, founded in 1978," and their publication *Turning Wheel*, "and the International Network of Engaged Buddhists, founded in 1989" (Queen 1996, 34 [see also Queen 2000, a companion volume]).

Another organization which some would include in this category is the Soka Gakkai International. Founded as the Soka Kyoiku Gakkai (Value-Creating Education Society) in Japan by Tsunesaburo Makiguchi in 1930 (Straus 1995, 201), this was originally an educational reform movement which evolved into an aggressive, modern and global style of Buddhism. Virginia Straus explains that SGI "supports the founding spirit of the United Nations" (ibid. 203), and is concerned with "applying Buddhist philosophy to the practical realities of international affairs." She observes that throughout all its proposals "can be seen an unrelenting opposition to war and violence, trust in the wisdom and peaceful instincts of the common people, compassion for the sufferings of all beings, and a courageous challenge against any force threatening to oppress people's humanity" (ibid. 204).

SGI's leader, Daisaku Ikeda, founded the Boston Research Center for the 21st Century in Cambridge, Massachusetts, which has been actively involved with scholarly conferences and publications related to the Global Ethic and the Earth Charter. Straus suggests that SGI is "one example of a Buddhist response to the Global Ethic" (ibid. 200). However, others argue that "Soka Gakkai is fundamentally unlike the liberation movements" called Engaged Buddhism because of its considerable wealth, its intolerance of other Buddhist sects, its aggressive outreach, the breakup of its historical ties with the orthodox Nichiren Shoshu priesthood, and the high-profile and energetic style of its leader Ikeda (Queen 1996, 4). Nevertheless, it does show a new style of Buddhism which has evolved in response to global ethical concerns.

Leaders most often associated with Engaged Buddhism are those like Buddhadasa Bhikkhu, Sulak Sivaraksa, Thich Nhat Hanh, and even the Dalai Lama, who "speak the universal language of human suffering, wisdom, compassion, and liberation [which] we associate with traditional Buddhist teachings" (ibid. 3). Queen observes that "the *liberation* that these leaders envision and articulate in their addresses and writings is consistently based on their own distinctive readings of traditional Buddhist doctrines, particularly those of selflessness, interdependence, the five precepts, the four noble truths, nondualism, and emptiness." Thus, all of them are concerned with "the contemporary application of traditional Buddhist teachings" (ibid. 8 [italics in original]).

Historically, however, other influences from outside of Buddhism seem to have been instrumental in the development of these liberation movements which are now called "Engaged Buddhism." Queen points out that "it is only in the late nineteenth-century revival of Buddhism in Sri Lanka-and particularly in its two principal figures, the American Theosophist, Col. Henry Steel Olcott (1832-1907) and his protege, the Sinhalese Anagarika Dharmapala (1864-1933)-that we first recognize the spirit and substance of the religious activism we call 'socially engaged Buddhism.'" He suggests that "it is only in this context that we first meet the missing ingredient ... the influence of European and American religious and political thought (and perhaps equally important, western methods of institutional development and public communication)" (ibid. 20). Queen contends that "we are forced to acknowledge and to trace the ways in which Buddhist and Christian – Asian, European, and American – traditions have become inextricably intertwined in the brief history of socially engaged Buddhism" (ibid. 21).

However, Queen asserts that acknowledging this does not discredit the authority of current Engaged Buddhism (ibid. 31). Rather, he argues that a criterion exists which validates these movements as truly Buddhist. He suggests that "the refuge formula, expressing homage to Buddha, Dharma, and Sangha, offers a standard for regarding a thinker or movement as 'Buddhist,' regardless of the presence

of non-Buddhist cultural elements, and regardless of the absence of
other traditional teachings"(ibid. 32). Hence, Engaged Buddhism can
be seen as authentically Buddhist, yet responding to current global
ethical issues which are the concern of the Global Ethic.

This example of Engaged Buddhism is noteworthy for these reasons. As religions rethink themselves in light of global issues, more
traditional and literalist adherents of those religions will reject the
kind of cross-cultural dialogue, advocacy, and appropriation of new
ideas which the perspective of the Global Ethic necessitates. However,
religions are not museum pieces, but are living traditions, and they can
evolve in light of global concerns and also remain true to their distinctive core beliefs. Engaged Buddhism is an example of this. Without
this type of development, little dialogue will be possible, and the
Global Ethic will fail.

C. BUDDHIST-CATHOLIC DIALOGUE AND A GLOBAL ETHIC

Cardinal Francis Arinze, then of the Pontifical Council for
Interreligious Dialogue, pointed out that, of the many "signs of hope"
in the world today, there is "a particular sign of hope, which Pope John
Paul II has underlined-namely, interreligious dialogue" (Arinze 1999,
199). Buddhist-Catholic dialogue has operated on a number of levels.
One of these is the concern with meditation. Arinze noted that "ongo-
ing dialogue between Buddhists and Christians is distinguished by efforts to meet at the level of religious experience," observing that "both
Buddhism and Christianity emphasize the 'contemplative dimension'
in their practice of religion" (ibid.). More specifically, though, as Jay
B. McDaniel suggests, since meditation techniques have "often been
viewed with suspicion by Protestants," therefore "it is no accident that
most of the Christians experimenting with various forms of Buddhist
meditation have been Roman Catholic and Orthodox, not Protestant"
(McDaniel 1990, 244). Given Roman Catholicism's tradition, which
includes a history of mysticism and an appreciation for this experiential and affective side of religion, it is not surprising that that aspect of
Buddhist-Christian dialogue is largely a Buddhist-Catholic dialogue.

However, a growing dimension of Buddhist-Catholic dialogue is
concerned with those elements which are contained in the Global
Ethic, issues involving social justice and liberation, including human
rights and duties toward the environment. These common concerns
form parallels, for example, between Engaged Buddhism and Roman

Catholic Liberation Theology, although some would argue that Engaged Buddhism is more "universal" in its approach and strategy, while Liberation Theology is more cognizant of the unique settings from which each type of liberation theology emerges (Queen 1996, 5). Nevertheless, they are still similar in that, while not the "traditional" and "formal" expression of their religions, they have invigorated those religions in their approach and their concerns, which are also concerns of the Global Ethic.

As Arinze pointed out, among the other "signs of hope" are "the growing solidarity among people in our time, especially with the poor and destitute, the desire for justice and peace, voluntary service, the return of the search for transcendence, an awareness of human dignity and the rights that flow from it, [and] attention to the environment" (Arinze 1999, 199). While concerns of Engaged Buddhism and Roman Catholic Liberation Theology, these elements now form central elements within Buddhist-Catholic dialogue in general. The Jesuits' 34th General Congregation issued a statement on its mission and interreligious dialogue in the Spring of 1995 which observed that "dialogue seeks to bring out the unifying and liberating potential of all religions, thus showing the relevance of religions for human well-being, justice and world peace." In addition, it affirmed that "above all we need to relate positively to believers of other religions because they are our neighbors, and the common elements of our religious heritages and our human concerns force us to establish ever closer ties *based on universally accepted ethical values*" (Cited in "Catholic-Buddhist Dialogue" 1995, 222 [italics mine]).

From July 31-August 4 in 1995, a Catholic-Buddhist colloquium in Taiwan was organized by the Pontifical Council for Interreligious Dialogue and hosted by the Fo Kuang Shan Buddhist order at Kaohsiung. Participants there acknowledged in a statement that "in the spirit of the Buddha's teachings, in detachment and compassion, contemporary Buddhists engage in new forms of social service and spiritual service in practice," and that "in the recent history of Christianity there has been a renewal of the traditional commitment toward social justice, which is seen to be inseparable from the life of faith" (ibid.). Admitting that they were gathering "in a world torn by division and strife, poverty and injustice, violence and war, erosion of spiritual values and destruction of nature," the participants also "reaffirmed the need for religions today to promote both personal and social transformation leading to a more peaceful world" (ibid. 224).

An additional area of dialogue is theological. While much of this is not within the scope of this study, it should be noted that some of this dialogue is fueled by or influential to ethical concerns. For example, dialogue on the topic of Sunyata (Emptiness) as the "ultimate principle" in Buddhism is seen by many Christians to shed light on the relational aspects of a Trinitarian God, which has implications for our own ethical relationships with God and each other (see, for example, von Bruck 1990). As another example, Charles Strain suggests that "just as Christian teaching situates all ethical discourse about the self within the broader understanding of the kingdom of God, so many engaged Buddhists resort to the teaching of dependent co-arising as providing the broadest context within which ethical issues can be framed" (Strain 1998, 164). Thus, Strain sees "the Catholic model of a transcendent kingdom of God which creates a sacred discontent with all existing social institutions and the engaged Buddhist model of an immanent Order of Interbeing grounded in compassion as complementary models" (ibid. 169).

In addition, he maintains that there are certain concepts which operate as better "bridge concepts" between the religions than others. For example, he contends that "Catholicism in focusing upon human dignity and solidarity as the principles upon which to build its teachings about human rights deliberately chose terms that might work as bridge concepts to other communities rather than the more specifically theological concepts (e.g., *imago Dei*)" (ibid. 165), and that in Buddhism, dependent co-arising "might work better as a bridge concept than concepts like Buddha Nature" (ibid. 166). In any case, diverse theological concepts within Buddhism and Roman Catholicism often find common ground when approaching current ethical and global concerns.

Conflicts do exist between Buddhism and Christianity, and in this study I do not intend to understate those. The non-theism of much of Buddhism vs. the personal theism of Christianity, the concept of non-self vs. the concept of a unique person in God's image, and the perception by some Christians that Buddhism has traditionally held a passivity in the face of suffering, especially regarding social concerns, are all examples of the radically different structures of these belief systems. However, in this text I have shown that despite some radical theological differences between Buddhism and Roman Catholicism,

A MOUNTING EAST–WEST TENSION

a growing dialogue does exist. And, much of this dialogue recognizes the fact that many of the beliefs within one tradition *do* resonate with beliefs in the other. Many of these commonalities are ethical, and these in turn resonate with the statements and concerns of the Global Ethic. As Cardinal Arinze affirmed, "we Christians and Buddhists, embarked on our respective spiritual paths, can work together to give increased hope to humanity" (Arinze 1999, 200). Current Buddhist-Catholic dialogue is strong in affirming and advocating the Global Ethic.

5.3: CONCLUSION ON A GLOBAL ETHIC

A Global Ethic: The Declaration of the Parliament of the World's Religions stands as a testament to the fact that religions can put aside their fundamental doctrinal differences and come to agreement on common ethical values. In addition, it shows that the world's religions can refocus themselves to address global concerns, concerns involving human values which will not be adequately addressed if the religions themselves are not involved. It is the realization that there will be "no new global order without a new global ethic" (Küng and Kuschel 1995, 18), and that religions must play a role in this. As the Dalai Lama states: "Today we have become so interdependent and so closely connected with each other that without a sense of universal responsibility, irrespective of different ideologies and faiths, our very existence or survival would be difficult" (Cited in Jones 1988, 79).

The Global Ethic itself focuses on strong social justice concerns. Its recognition of global interdependence acknowledges ecological duties which we all have, and its stress on the value of every human being is a strong endorsement of human rights. Buddhism and Roman Catholicism, which strongly support human rights and ecological duties, are strong supporters of the Global Ethic. As such, they offer an example of how two radically diverse sets of beliefs can come to terms with the Global Ethic and support it on a world scale.

The Global Ethic also speaks to the concept of universality. Buddhism and Roman Catholicism both support the conception that there are universal moral values, and that as human beings we have certain obligations to each other. In addition, the spirit of the Parliament is instructive, since it incorporated a wide variety of adherents, not only official representatives of the religions' hierarchies. As Robert Thurman argues, religious believers should "take back the definition and analysis of the world religions from the dominant elites"

(Cited in Straus 1995, 210), and according to Virginia Straus, "with support from secular human rights advocates and religious scholars, return to the original teachings of their founders, which share a spirit of kindness" (ibid.). The Global Ethic stands as an example of this process and spirit.

The Global Ethic offers an example of religions at their best, working in dialogue and addressing global concerns. Buddhism and Roman Catholicism both endorse and support the Global Ethic, which includes the social justice and liberation issues of human rights and ecological duties. As such, it stands as a strong endorsement of the role of religions in human rights advocacy on a global scale.

CONCLUSION

Much has changed in the world over the past century, and Roman Catholicism has been a part of that change. A religion which viewed human rights as an enemy of religion and a threat to the social order became a major proponent of human rights on a global scale. And, while Roman Catholicism has always recognized the existence of truth everywhere,[1] a new openness to its presence in other religions has developed since Vatican II. While it often historically saw itself as an adversary with other religions, it has more recently acknowledged that it must work with these religions. And, while Western Christians initially viewed Buddhists suspiciously as possible "atheists," now Catholic scholars are among the major contributors to Buddhist-Christian dialogue.

As the new century develops, religions are still fighting against each other, and fundamentalist and terrorist adherents are a shrill reminder of the negative and ugly sides of religion. But more often than not, mainstream and more liberal adherents are also working together against a growing secular mindset and culture. On the negative side, part of this culture embraces an economy which views humans as a commodity, as cogs in a machine, to fuel a growing consumer/materialist worldview which runs roughshod over traditional religious and ethical values. Religions, as classical belief and value systems which advocate the value of the human person and the goodness and purposefulness of life and creation, offer a check against a completely secular/materialist mindset which, when unchecked, can justify for its own gain the abuse of human beings and the environment.

I have examined the concepts of human rights and ecological duties within religions, focusing particularly on Buddhism and Roman Catholicism, and have argued that human rights is a concept which belongs in, and can be grounded by, religious traditions. I also maintain that the concept of human rights is currently supported by Buddhism and Roman Catholicism despite their radically different

---

1   For example, the Jesuits, and they were not the first, were respecting the truth in other religions centuries before Vatican II. (My appreciation to Fr. Raymond Gawronski at Marquette University for this insight.)

belief systems, including their different views of the individual human being, and have emphasized that human rights is currently viewed within Catholicism as a key expression of faith, not as a side issue. I have also argued that much can be learned from these two traditions in the formulation of the concept of human rights. One of these contributions is the notion of duty and the importance of ecological duties as a correlate to human rights. Thus, the ego-centeredness of *human* rights has been tempered with a concern for duties toward other living creatures and the environment, without negating the unique status of humans in the larger cosmological scheme.

In addition, given current human rights and ecological abuses, I have argued for the necessity of a global ethic to counteract a global economy and technology which is often exploitive, and have asserted that religions can and must play a key role in this global ethic.[2] Despite the often radically different beliefs of Buddhism and Roman Catholicism, I have shown in this study that the concepts of human rights and ecological duties are seen in both traditions to express common aspirations and ethical values. Both traditions currently have segments among their faithful who are strong advocates for human rights and ecological duties on a global scale. In addition, I have contended that the fact that such diverse traditions can find agreement and value in the concept of human rights and ecological duties can serve as a test case for a global ethic, where less diverse traditions would also find agreement.

Both Buddhism and Roman Catholicism view the human being as uniquely valuable and precious, view life as purposeful, and emphasize the interconnectedness of humans with other living beings and the environment. As such, they are major proponents today of human rights, ecological duties, and a global ethic. Having argued such, I also suggest that as global religions, Buddhism and Roman Catholicism, as well as all religions East and West, must continue to work as advocates for global justice.

The concepts of human rights and ecological duties are key concepts in the development of a global ethic, in the work for global justice, and

---

2   Dirk Ficca of the Council for the Parliament of the World's Religions emphasizes that the Global Ethic is "not ethical reductionism, but ethical convergence." In addition, he observes that "one can only approach the global ethic through one's own tradition," thereby keeping and taking seriously the particularity within individual religious traditions (Ficca 2001).

in the advocacy of true liberation. They offer key contributions of religions toward the modern world in overcoming greed, consumption,
materialism, and militarism. In addition, they offer a practical and
compassionate hope for religion to contribute to and to be in dialogue
with modern society, in working for the rights of all human beings.
This beacon of hope offers a shining alternative to the dark failure of
the fundamentalist worldview in religion and politics, and also stands
in contrast to a secular, relativist culture which denies our common
humanity and our responsibilities toward the earth.

WORKS CITED

Abbott, Walter M. ed. *The Documents of Vatican II*, America Press, 1966.

Abe, Masao. "A Buddhist Response to Mohammed Talbi." In *Religious Liberty and Human Rights*, ed. Leonard Swidler. Philadelphia: Ecumenical Press, 1986.

——. "The Buddhist View of Human Rights." In *Human Rights and Religious Values: An Uneasy Relationship*, ed. Abdullahi A. An-Naim, Jerald D. Gort, Henry Jansen and Hendrik M. Vroom. Grand Rapids: Eerdman's Publishing, 1995.

——. "God, Emptiness, and the True Self." In *The Buddha Eye*, ed. Frederick Franck. N.Y.: Crossroad, 1982.

——. "Man and Nature in Christianity and Buddhism." In *The Buddha Eye*, ed. Frederick Franck. N.Y.: Crossroad, 1982.

——. "Religious Tolerance and Human Rights: A Buddhist Perspective." In *Religious Liberty and Human Rights in Nations and Religions*, ed. Leonard Swidler. Philadelphia: Ecumenical Press, 1986.

An-Na'im, Abdullahi Ahmed. "Qur'an, Shari'a and Human Rights: Foundations, Deficiencies and Prospects." In *The Ethics of World Religions and Human Rights*, ed. Hans Küng and Jürgen Moltmann. London: SCM Press, 1990.

Arinze, Cardinal Francis. "Christians and Buddhists: Together in Hope," *Buddhist-Christian Studies* 19 (1999): 199-200.

Ashcraft, Richard. "Religion and Lockean Natural Rights." In *Religious Diversity and Human Rights*, ed. Irene Bloom, J. Paul Martin and Wayne L. Proudfoot. New York: Columbia University Press, 1996.

Awn, Peter. "The World's Religions: Prospects for a Global Ethic in Support of Human Rights." Panel #3 presentation in *The United Nations and the World's Religions: Prospects for a Global Ethic*, ed. Nancy Hodes and Michael Hays. Cambridge, MA: Boston Research Center for the 21st Century, 1995.

Batchelor, Stephen. "The Sands of the Ganges: Notes Towards A Buddhist Ecological Philosophy." In *Buddhism and Ecology*, ed. Martine Batchelor and Kerry Brown. London: Cassell Publishers, 1992.

Bellah, Robert. "Faith Communities Challenge – And Are Challenged By – The Changing World Order." In *World Faiths and the New World Order: A*

Muslim-Jewish-Christian Search Begins, ed. Joseph Gremillion and William Ryan. Washington D.C.: Interreligious Peace Colloquium, 1978.

Berry, Thomas. "Ecology and the Future of Catholicism." In *Embracing Earth: Catholic Approaches to Ecology,* ed. Albert J. La Chance and John E. Carroll. Maryknoll, NY: Orbis, 1994.

Boff, Leonardo. *Cry of the Earth, Cry of the Poor.* Maryknoll, NY: Orbis, 1997.

Burford, Grace G. "Hope, Desire, and Right Livelihood: A Buddhist View on the Earth Charter." In *Buddhist Perspectives on the Earth Charter,* ed. Amy Morgante. Cambridge: Boston Research Center for the 21st Century, 1997.

Burtt, E.A., ed. *The Teachings of the Compassionate Buddha.* N.Y.: Mentor, 1982.

Cabezon, Jose Ignacio, ed. *Buddhism, Sexuality and Gender.* New York: State University of New York Press, 1992.

Carman, John B. "Duties and Rights in Hindu Society." In *Human Rights and the World's Religions,* ed. Leroy S. Rouner. Notre Dame: University of Notre Dame Press, 1988.

Casey, Helen Marie. "Consultation Works to Evolve Integrated Human Rights-Environmental Action Strategy." *Boston Research Center for the 21st Century Newsletter* (Summer/Fall 1998): 1, 8-9, 15.

"Catholic-Buddhist Dialogue: Two World Religions Examine Points of Shared Concern," *Origins* 25 (September 21, 1995): 222-24.

Cerna, Christina M. "Universality of Human Rights and Cultural Diversity: Implementation of Human Rights in Different Socio-Cultural Contexts." *Human Rights Quarterly* 16 (November 1994): 740-52.

Chatterjee, Margaret. *Gandhi's Religious Thought.* Notre Dame: University of Notre Dame Press, 1983.

Christiansen, Drew. "Ecology and the Common Good: Catholic Social Teaching and Environmental Responsibility." In *"And God Saw That It Was Good": Catholic Theology and the Environment,* ed. Drew Christiansen and Walter Grazer. Washington, D.C.: United States Catholic Conference, 1996.

Clasquin, Michel. "Buddhism and Human Rights." *Journal for the Study of Religion* 6 (S 1993): 91-101.

Cobb, John B., Jr. "The Role of Theology of Nature in the Church." In *Liberating Life: Contemporary Approaches to Ecological Theology,* ed. Charles Birch, William Eakin, and Jay B. McDaniel. Maryknoll, NY: Orbis, 1990.

Collins, Steven. "Self and Non-Self in Early Buddhism." *Numen* 29 (December 1982): 250-71.

Coward, Harold. "New Theology on Population, Consumption, and Ecology." *Journal of the American Academy of Religion* 65 (Summer 1997): 259-73.

Cox, Harvey, and Arvind Sharma. "Positive Resources of Religion for Human Rights." In *Religion and Human Rights*, ed. John Kelsay and Sumner B. Twiss. New York: Project on Religion and Human Rights, 1994.

Crahan, Margaret E. "Catholicism and Human Rights in Latin America." In *Religious Diversity and Human Rights*, ed. Irene Bloom, J. Paul Martin, and Wayne L. Proudfoot. N.Y.: Columbia University Press, 1996.

Crim, Keith, ed. *The Perennial Dictionary of World Religions*. San Francisco: Harper, 1981. S.v. "Hinduism," by P.H. Ashby, "Buddhism," by K.K.S. Chen, and "Anatta," by Winston L. King.

Curran, Charles E. "The Global Ethic and the Catholic Moral Tradition." Presentation at the Call To Action National Conference, Milwaukee, WI, Nov. 6, 1999.

————. *Toward An American Catholic Moral Theology*. Notre Dame, IN: University of Notre Dame Press, 1987.

Dalton, James S. "Human Dignity, Human Rights and Ecology: Christian, Buddhist and Native American Perspectives." In *Made In God's Image: The Catholic Vision of Human Dignity*. ed. Regis Duffy and Angelus Gambatese. N.Y.: Paulist Press, 1999.

de Silva, Lily. "The Hills Wherein My Soul Delights: Exploring the Stories and Teachings." In *Buddhism and Ecology*, ed. Martine Batchelor and Kerry Brown. London: Cassell Publishers, 1992.

————. "Man and Nature in a Mutual Causal Relationship: Buddhist Scriptural Insights." In *Man in Nature: Guest or Engineer?*, ed. S.J. Samartha and Lynn de Silva. Colombo, Sri Lanka: Ecumenical Institute for Study and Dialogue, 1979.

de Silva, Lynn A. "Religious Dimensions in Humanity's Relation to Nature: Christian Scriptural Insights." In *Man in Nature: Guest or Engineer?* ed. S.J. Samartha and Lynn de Silva. Colombo, Sri Lanka: Ecumenical Institute for Study and Dialogue, 1979.

de Silva, Padmasiri. "Human Rights in Buddhist Perspective." In *Human Rights and Religious Values: An Uneasy Relationship*, ed. Abdullahi A. An-Naim, Jerald D. Gort, Henry Jansen and Hendrik M. Vroom. Grand Rapids: Eerdman's Publishing, 1995.

de Waart, P.J.I.M. "International Order and Human Rights: A Matter of Good Governance." In *Human Rights and Religious Values: An Uneasy Relationship*, ed. Abdullahi A. An-Naim, Jerald D. Gort, Henry Jansen and Hendrik M. Vroom. Grand Rapids: Eerdman's Publishing, 1995.

DeBary, W. Theodore. "Neo-Confucianism and Human Rights." In *Human Rights and the World's Religions*, ed. Leroy S. Rouner. Notre Dame: University of Notre Dame Press, 1988.

Declaration of Interdependence. In *Buddhism and Human Rights*, ed. Damien V. Keown, Charles S. Prebish, and Wayne R. Husted. Great Britain: Curzon, 1998.

Donovan, Peter. "Do Different Religions Share Moral Common Ground?" *Religious Studies* 22 (S-D 1986): 367-75.

Dorr, Donal. *The Social Justice Agenda: Justice, Ecology, Power and the Church.* Maryknoll, N.Y.: Orbis, 1991.

Drummond, Richard Henry. *A Broader Vision: Perspectives on the Buddha and the Christ.* Virginia Beach, Virginia: A.R.E. Press, 1995.

The Earth Charter. Pamphlet distributed at the Society for Christian Ethics Annual Meeting, Chicago, IL, Jan. 5-7, 2001. www.earthcharter.org.

The Earth Charter Benchmark Draft (18 March 1997). Insert in *Boston Research Center for the 21st Century Newsletter* (Spring 1997): EC1-4.

Eden, Philip M. "Anatta: The Linchpin of Buddhist Teaching." *The Middle Way: Journal of the Buddhist Society* 70 (Fall 1996): 267-70.

Edwards, Denis. *Jesus the Wisdom of God: An Ecological Theology.* Maryknoll, NY: Orbis, 1995.

Eliade, Mircea, ed. *The Encyclopedia of Religion*, Vol. 2. N.Y.: Macmillan Publishing, 1987. S.v. "Buddhist Ethics," by Frank E. Reynolds and Robert Campany.

Farhang, Mansour. "Fundamentalism and Civil Rights in Contemporary Middle Eastern Politics." In *Human Rights and the World's Religions*, ed. Leroy S. Rouner. Notre Dame: University of Notre Dame Press, 1988.

Fernando, Anthony, with Leonard Swidler. *Buddhism Made Plain: An Introduction for Christians and Jews.* Maryknoll, NY: Orbis, 1985.

Ficca, Dirk. "Religions and Ethics: Integral Relationships." Closing Plenary at the Society of Christian Ethics Annual Meeting, Chicago, January 7, 2001.

Firer Hinze, Christine. "Catholic Social Teaching and Ecological Ethics." In *"And God Saw That It Was Good": Catholic Theology and the Environment*, ed. Drew Christiansen and Walter Grazer. Washington, D.C.: United States Catholic Conference, 1996.

Fishbane, Michael. "The Image of the Human and the Rights of the Individual in Jewish Tradition." In *Human Rights and the World's Religions*, ed. Leroy S. Rouner. Notre Dame: University of Notre Dame Press, 1988.

Formicola, Jo Renee. *The Catholic Church and Human Rights: Its Role in the Formulation of U.S. Policy 1945-1980.* N.Y.: Garland Publishing, 1988.

Gandhi, Mahatma. *All Men Are Brothers: Autobiographical Reflections.* ed. Krishna Kripalani. New York: Continuum, 1995.

Garaudy, Roger. "Human Rights and Islam: Foundation, Tradition, Violation." In *The Ethics of World Religions and Human Rights,* ed. Hans Küng and Jürgen Moltmann. London: SCM Press, 1990.

Garfield, Jay L. "Human Rights and Compassion: Towards A Unified Moral Framework." In *Buddhism and Human Rights*, ed. Damien V. Keown, Charles S. Prebish, and Wayne R. Husted. Great Britain: Curzon, 1998.

Garrett, William R. "Liberation Theology and the Concept of Human Rights." In *The Politics of Religion and Social Change: Religion and the Political Order,Vol. II*, ed. Anson Shupe and Jeffrey K. Hadden. N.Y.: Paragon House, 1988.

George, William P. "Looking for a Global Ethic? Try International Law." *Journal of Religion* 76 (July 1996): 359-82.

Gomez, Luis O. "Emptiness and Moral Perfection." *Philosophy East and West* 23 (1973): 362-73.

Graef, Sunyana. "The Foundations of Ecology in Zen Buddhism." *Religious Education* 85 (Winter 1990): 42-50.

Gross, Rita. "Toward a Buddhist Environmental Ethic." *Journal of the American Academy of Religion* 65 (Summer 1997): 333-53.

Gunaratne, Neville. "An Evaluation by a Buddhist of Mother Teresa's Boundless Compassion and Voluntary Poverty." *Dialogue* (Colombo, Sri Lanka) 8 (1981): 100-104.

Habito, Ruben L.F. "Mountains and Rivers and the Great Earth: Zen and Ecology." In *Buddhism and Ecology: The Interconnection of Dharma and Deeds,* ed. Mary Evelyn Tucker and Duncan Ryuken Williams. Cambridge, Massachusetts: Harvard University Press, 1997.

Hamilton, Sue. "Anatta: A Different Approach." *The Middle Way: Journal of the Buddhist Society* 70 (May 1995): 47-60.

Harakas, Stanley. "Human Rights: An Eastern Orthodox Perspective." In *Human Rights in Religious Traditions*, ed. Arlene Swidler. New York: Pilgrim Press, 1982.

Harrelson, Walter. *The Ten Commandments and Human Rights*. Philadelphia: Fortress Press, 1980.

Harris, Ian. "Buddhism." In *Attitudes to Nature*, ed. Jean Holm. N.Y.: Pinter Publishers, 1994.

Hassan, Riffat. "On Human Rights and the Qur'anic Perspective." In *Human Rights in Religious Traditions*, ed. Arlene Swidler. New York: Pilgrim Press, 1982.

Hehir, J. Bryan. "Human Rights and U.S. Foreign Policy: A Perspective from Theological Ethics." In *The Moral Imperatives of Human Rights: A World Survey*, ed. Kenneth W. Thompson. New York: University Press of America, 1980.

————. "Religion and International Human Rights: A Catholic Perspective." In *Formation of Social Policy in the Catholic and Jewish Traditions*, ed. Eugene J. Fisher and Daniel F. Polish. Notre Dame, Indiana: University of Notre Dame Press, 1980.

————. "Religious Activism for Human Rights: A Christian Case Study." In *Religious Human Rights in Global Perspective: Religious Perspectives*, ed. John Witte, Jr. and Johan D. Van der Vyver. The Hague: Martinus Nijhoff Publishers, 1996.

————. "Why is the Church Involved?" In *Human Rights, Human Needs: An Unfinished Agenda*. Washington, D.C.: U. S. Catholic Conference, 1978.

Henkin, Louis. "The Universal Declaration of Human Rights: The Framers and Their Visions." Panel #1 Presentation in *The United Nations and the World's Religions: Prospects for a Global Ethic* , ed. Nancy Hodes and Michael Hays. Cambridge, MA: Boston Research Center for the 21st Century, 1995.

Henle, R.J. "A Catholic View of Human Rights: A Thomistic Reflection." In *The Philosophy of Human Rights: International Perspectives*, ed. Alan S. Rosenbaum. Westport, Conn.: Greenwood Press, 1980.

Henriot, Peter J., Edward P. DeBerri, and Michael J. Schultheis, eds. *Catholic Social Teaching: Our Best Kept Secret*. Maryknoll, NY: Orbis, 1997.

Henry, Carl F. H. "The Judeo-Christian Heritage and Human Rights." In *Religious Beliefs, Human Rights and the Moral Foundation of Western Democracy*, ed. Carl H. Esbeck. Columbia: University of Missouri, 1986.

Hewage, Lankaputra. "A Buddhist Response." In *World Faiths and the New World Order: A Muslim-Jewish-Christian Search Begins*, ed. Joseph Gremillion and William Ryan. Washington, D.C.: Interreligious Peace Colloquium, 1978.

Hick, John. "The Universality of the Golden Rule." In *Ethics, Religion, and the Good Society*, ed. Joseph Runzo. Louisville: Westminster/John Knox Press, 1992.

Hill, Brennan R. *Christian Faith and the Environment: Making Vital Connections*. Maryknoll, NY: Orbis, 1998.

Hollenbach, David. *Claims in Conflict: Retrieving and Renewing the Catholic Human Rights Tradition*. N.Y.: Paulist Press, 1979.

———. "Global Human Rights: An Interpretation of the Contemporary Catholic Understanding." In *Readings in Moral Theology, No. 5: Official Catholic Social Teaching*, ed. Charles E. Curran and Richard A. McCormick. N.Y.: Paulist Press, 1986.

———. *Justice, Peace, and Human Rights: American Catholic Social Ethics in a Pluralistic World*. N.Y.: Crossroad, 1988.

Hug, James E. "Preface." In *Catholic Social Teaching: Our Best Kept Secret*, ed. Peter J. Henriot, Edward P. DeBerri, and Michael J. Schultheis. Maryknoll, NY: Orbis, 1997.

Human Rights, Human Needs: An Unfinished Agenda. Washington, D.C.: United States Catholic Conference, 1978.

Ihara, Craig K. "Why There Are No Rights in Buddhism: A Reply to Damien Keown." In *Buddhism and Human Rights*, ed. Damien V. Keown, Charles S. Prebish, and Wayne R. Husted. Great Britain: Curzon, 1998.

Inada, Kenneth. "The Buddhist Perspective on Human Rights." In *Human Rights in Religious Traditions*, ed. Arlene Swidler. New York: Pilgrim Press, 1982.

Ingram, Paul O. "The Jewelled Net of Nature." In *Buddhism and Ecology: The Interconnection of Dharma and Deeds*, ed. Mary Evelyn Tucker and Duncan Ryuken Williams. Cambridge, Mass.: Harvard University Press, 1997.

Jennings, James R. ed., "Introduction." In *Human Rights, A Question of Conscience: A Catholic Perspective on International Human Rights in an American Context*. Washington, D.C.: United States Catholic Conference, 1974.

John XXIII. *Pacem in Terris: Peace on Earth*. In *Catholic Social Thought: The Documentary Heritage*. ed. David J. O'Brien and Thomas A. Shannon. Maryknoll, NY: Orbis, 1998.

John Paul II. *The Ecological Crisis: A Common Responsibility*. In *"And God Saw That It Was Good": Catholic Theology and the Environment*, ed. Drew Christiansen and Walter Grazer. Washington, D.C.: United States Catholic Conference, 1996.

Jones, Ken. "Buddhism and Social Action: An Exploration." In *The Path of Compassion: Writings on Socially Engaged Buddhism*, ed. Fred Eppsteiner. Berkeley, CA: Parallax Press, 1988.

———. *The Social Face of Buddhism: An Approach to Political and Social Activism*. London: Wisdom Publications, 1989.

Juergensmeyer, Mark. "Perspectives on a Global Ethic and Common Values." Panel #2 Presentation in *The United Nations and the World's Religions: Prospects for a Global Ethic* , ed. Nancy Hodes and Michael Hays. Cambridge, MA: Boston Research Center for the 21st Century, 1995.

Jung, Hwa Yol. "Ecology, Zen, and Western Religious Thought," *Christian Century* 89 (Nov. 15, 1972): 1153-56.

Junger, Peter D. "Why the Buddha Has No Rights." In *Buddhism and Human Rights*, ed. Damien V. Keown, Charles S. Prebish, and Wayne R. Husted. Great Britain: Curzon, 1998.

Kasper, Walter. "The Theological Foundations of Human Rights." *The Jurist* 50 (1990): 148-66.

Kaza, Stephanie. "Acting with Compassion: Buddhism, Feminism, and the Environmental Crisis." In *Ecofeminism and the Sacred*, ed. Carol J. Adams. N.Y.: Continuum, 1993.

Kelsay, John. "Islamic Tradition(s) and Freedom of Religion: Intracommunal Differences and International Human Rights." Paper presentation at the Annual Meeting of the American Academy of Religion, San Francisco, CA, November, 1997.

Kelsay, John, and Sumner B. Twiss, eds. *Religion and Human Rights*. New York: Project on Religion and Human Rights, 1994.

Keown, Damien. "Are There Human Rights in Buddhism." In *Buddhism and Human Rights*, ed. Damien V. Keown, Charles S. Prebish, and Wayne R. Husted. Great Britain: Curzon, 1998.

King, Sallie B. *Buddha Nature*. Albany: State University of N.Y. Press, 1991.

———. "The Buddha Nature: True Self As Action." *Religious Studies* 20 (June 1984): 255-67.

———. "A Buddhist Perspective on a Global Ethic and Human Rights." *Journal of Dharma* 20 (April-June 1995): 122-35.

———. "A Global Ethic in the Light of Comparative Religious Ethics." In *Explorations in Global Ethics: Comparative Religious Ethics and Interreligious Dialogue*, ed. Sumner B. Twiss and Bruce Grelle. Boulder, Colorado: Westview Press, 1998.

————. "The World's Religions: Prospects for a Global Ethic in Support of Human Rights." Panel #3 Presentation in *The United Nations and the World's Religions: Prospects for a Global Ethic* , ed. Nancy Hodes and Michael Hays. Cambridge, MA: Boston Research Center for the 21st Century, 1995.

King, Winston L. *In the Hope of Nibbana: An Essay on Theravada Buddhist Ethics*. LaSalle, Ill.: Open Court Pub., 1964.

————. "No-Self, No-Mind, and Emptiness Revisited." In *Buddhist-Christian Dialogue: Mutual Renewal and Transformation*, ed. Paul O. Ingram and Frederick J. Streng. Honolulu: University of Hawaii Press, 1986.

————. "Sunyata as a Master-Symbol." *Numen* 17 (August 1970): 95-104.

Kittel, Gerhard, and Gerhard Friedrich, eds. *Theological Dictionary of the New Testament, Vol. 6*. Grand Rapids, Mich.: William B. Eerdman's Publishing, 1968. S.v. "πτωχος in the Greek World," by Friedrich Hauck, and "The New Testament" and "The Poor in the Old Testament," by Ernst Bammel.

Knitter, Paul F. *One Earth Many Religions: Multifaith Dialogue and Global Responsibility*. Maryknoll, NY: Orbis, 1995.

————. "Toward a Liberation Theology of Religions." In *The Myth of Christian Uniqueness: Toward a Pluralistic Theology of Religions*, ed. John Hick and Paul F. Knitter. Maryknoll, NY: Orbis, 1987.

Kraft, Kenneth. "Engaged Buddhism: An Introduction." In *The Path of Compassion: Writings on Socially Engaged Buddhism*, ed. Fred Eppsteiner. Berkeley, CA: Parallax Press, 1988.

Küng, Hans. *Does God Exist?* Translated by Edward Quinn. New York: Crossroad, 1978.

————. *Global Responsibility: In Search of A New World Ethic*. New York: Continuum, 1991.

————. "The History, Significance and Method of the Declaration Toward A Global Ethic." In *A Global Ethic: The Declaration of the Parliament of the World's Religions*, ed. Hans Küng and Karl-Josef Kuschel. New York: Continuum, 1995.

————. "Towards a World Ethic of World Religions." In *The Ethics of World Religions and Human Rights*, ed. Hans Küng and Jürgen Moltmann. London: SCM Press, 1990.

Küng, Hans and Karl-Josef Kuschel, eds. *A Global Ethic: The Declaration of the Parliament of the World's Religions*. New York: Continuum, 1995.

Kuschel, Karl-Josef. "The Parliament of the World's Religions, 1893-1993." In *A Global Ethic: The Declaration of the Parliament of the World's Religions,* ed. Hans Küng and Karl-Josef Kuschel. New York: Continuum, 1995.

———. "World Religions, Human Rights and the Humanum: Report on a Symposium in Paris." In *The Ethics of World Religions and Human Rights,* ed. Hans Küng and Jürgen Moltmann. London: SCM Press, 1990.

Kyi, Aung San Suu. "Towards a Culture of Peace and Development." In *Yes to a Global Ethic: Voices from Religion and Politics,* ed. Hans Küng. New York: Continuum, 1996.

Lancaster, Lewis. "Buddhism and Ecology: Collective Cultural Perceptions." In *Buddhism and Ecology: The Interconnection of Dharma and Deeds,* ed. Mary Evelyn Tucker and Duncan Ryuken Williams. Cambridge, Massachusetts: Harvard University Press, 1997.

Langan, John. "Human Rights in Roman Catholicism." In *Readings in Moral Theology, No. 5: Official Catholic Social Teaching.* ed. Charles E. Curran and Richard A. McCormick. N.Y.: Paulist Press, 1986.

———. "Human Rights Theory: A Basis for Pluralism Open to Christian Ethics." In *Cities of Gods: Faith, Politics and Pluralism in Judaism, Christianity and Islam,* ed. Nigel Biggar, Jamie S. Scott, and William Schweiker. Westport, Conn.: Greenwood Press, 1986.

Leo XIII. *Rerum Novarum: The Condition of Labor.* In *Catholic Social Thought: The Documentary Heritage.* ed. David J. O'Brien and Thomas A. Shannon. Maryknoll, NY: Orbis, 1998.

Little, David. "The Development in the West of the Right to Freedom of Religion and Conscience: A Basis for Comparison with Islam." In *Human Rights and the Conflict of Cultures: Western and Islamic Perspectives on Religious Liberty,* ed. David Little, John Kelsay and Abdulaziz A. Sachedina. Columbia, S.C.: University of South Carolina Press, 1988.

Locke, John. *Two Treatises of Government.* ed. P. Laslett. Cambridge, 1963.

Lovin, Robin W. "Ethics, Wealth and Eschatology: Buddhist and Christian Strategies of Change." In *Ethics, Wealth and Salvation: A Study in Buddhist Social Ethics,* ed. Russell F. Sizemore and Donald K. Swearer. Columbia S.C.: University of South Carolina Press, 1990.

Loy, David R. "The Religion of the Market." *Journal of the American Academy of Religion* 62 (Summer 1997): 275-90.

Macy, Joanna Rogers. "Dependent Co-arising: The Distinctiveness of Buddhist Ethics." *Journal of Religious Ethics* 7 (1979): 38-52.

————. "The Ecological Self: Postmodern Ground for Right Action." In *Sacred Interconnections*, ed. David Ray Giffin. New York: State University of New York Press, 1990.

Maguire, Daniel C. *A Case for Affirmative Action*. Dubuque, Iowa: Shepherd, 1992.

————. "Introduction." In *Visions of A New Earth: Religious Perspectives on Population, Consumption, and Ecology*, ed. Harold Coward and Daniel C. Maguire. Albany: State University of New York Press, 2000.

————. *The Moral Core of Judaism and Christianity: Reclaiming the Revolution*. Minneapolis: Fortress Press, 1993.

————. "More People: Less Earth, The Shadow of Mankind." Chap. in *Ethics for a Small Planet: New Horizons on Population, Consumption, and Ecology*, Daniel C. Maguire and Larry L. Rasmussen. Albany, NY: State University of New York Press, 1998.

Mahoney, Jack. "The Basis of Human Rights." In *Moral Theology: Challenges for the Future*, ed. Charles E. Curran. New York: Paulist Press, 1990.

Mahoney, John. *The Making of Moral Theology: A Study of the Roman Catholic Tradition*. Oxford: Clarendon Press, 1989.

Maritain, Jacques. *Man and the State*. Chicago: University of Chicago Press, 1951.

————. *The Rights of Man and Natural Law*. N.Y.: Charles Scribner's Sons, 1943.

Marty, Martin E. "Religious Dimensions of Human Rights." In *Religious Human Rights in Global Perspective: Religious Perspectives*, ed. John Witte, Jr. and Johan D. Van der Vyver. The Hague: Martinus Nijhoff Publishers, 1996.

Massingale, Bryan. "An Ethical Reflection Upon 'Environmental Racism' in the Light of Catholic Social Teaching." In *The Challenge of Global Stewardship: Roman Catholic Responses*, ed. Maura A. Ryan and Todd David Whitmore. Notre Dame, Ind.: University of Notre Dame Press, 1997.

May, John D'Arcy. "Zen with Teeth: The Contributions of Buddhists and Christians to Preserving the Earth." *Buddhist-Christian Studies* 18 (1998): 213-15.

Mayer, Ann Elizabeth. "The Dilemmas of Islamic Identity." In *Human Rights and the World's Religions*, ed. Leroy S. Rouner. Notre Dame: University of Notre Dame Press, 1988.

McBrien, Richard P., ed. *The Harper Collins Encyclopedia of Catholicism*. San Francisco: Harper, 1995. S.v. "Human Rights," by Todd D. Whitmore.

A MOUNTING EAST—WEST TENSION

McDaniel, Jay. "The God of the Oppressed and the God Who is Empty."
Journal of Ecumenical Studies 22 (Fall 1985): 687-702.

————. "Revisioning God and the Self: Lessons from Buddhism." In
Liberating Life: Contemporary Approaches to Ecological Theology, ed. Charles
Birch, William Eakin and Jay B. McDaniel. Maryknoll, NY: Orbis, 1990.

McKeon, Joseph. "Zen Master Dogen: The Articulation of the Enlightenment
Experience." Paper presented at the annual meeting of the College Theology
Society, DePere, WI, June 5, 1999.

Mealand, David L.*Poverty and Expectation in the Gospels*. London: SPCK,

Mich, Marvin L. Krier. *Catholic Social Teaching and Movements*. Mystic, CT:
Twenty-Third Publications, 1998.

Mitra, Kana. "Human Rights in Hinduism." In *Human Rights in Religious
Traditions*, ed. Arlene Swidler. New York: Pilgrim Press, 1982.

Moltmann, Jürgen. *Creating a Just Future: The Politics of Peace and the Ethics of
Creation in a Threatened World*. Philadelphia: Trinity Press, 1989.

————. *On Human Dignity: Political Theology and Ethics*. Translated by M.
Douglas Meeks. Philadelphia: Fortress Press, 1984.

Moniz, John. *"Liberated Society": Gandhian and Christian Vision Comparative
Study, Documenta Missionalia* 23. Rome: Editrice Pontificia Universita

Munera, Alberto. "New Theology on Population, Ecology, and
Overconsumption from the Catholic Perspective." In *Visions of a New
Earth: Religious Perspectives on Population, Consumption, and Ecology*, ed.
Harold Coward and Daniel C. Maguire. Albany: State University of New

Murray, John Courtney. Commentary in *The Documents of Vatican II*, ed.
Walter M. Abbot. America Press, 1966.

————. *We Hold These Truths: Catholic Reflections on the American
Proposition*. Kansas City: Sheed and Ward, 1960.

Narayanan, Vasudha. "'One Tree is Equal to Ten Sons': Hindu Responses
to the Problems of Ecology, Population, and Consumption." *Journal of the
American Academy of Religion* 65 (Summer 1997): 291-332.

Nash, James A. *Loving Nature: Ecological Integrity and Christian Responsibility*.
Nashville: Abingdon Press, 1991.

Nishitani, Keiji. "The Awakening of Self in Buddhism." *Eastern Buddhist* 1

O'Brien, David J., and Thomas A. Shannon, eds. "Introduction." In *Catholic Social Thought: The Documentary Heritage*. Maryknoll, NY: Orbis, 1998.

Ojo, Bamidele. *Human Rights and the New World Order: Universality, Acceptability and Human Diversity*. New York: Nova Science Publishers, 1997.

Otto, Rudolf. *The Idea of the Holy*. Translated by John W. Harvey. London: Oxford University Press, 1923; Oxford Paperbacks, 1958.

Panikkar, Raimundo. "Is the Notion of Human Rights a Western Concept?" *Diogenes* 120 (Winter 1982): 75-102.

Pastoral Constitution on the Church in the Modern World, no. 12. In *The Documents of Vatican II*, ed. Walter M. Abbott. America Press, 1966.

Paul, Diana Y. *Women in Buddhism: Images of the Feminine in the Mahayana Tradition*. Berkeley: University of California Press, 1985.

Pedersen, Kusumita P. "Environmental Ethics in Interreligious Perspective." In *Explorations in Global Ethics: Comparative Religious Ethics and Interreligious Dialogue*, ed. Sumner B. Twiss and Bruce Grelle. Boulder, Colorado: Westview Press, 1998.

Pilgrim, Walter. *Good News to the Poor: Wealth and Poverty in Luke-Acts*. Minneapolis: Augsburg, 1981.

Polish, Daniel F. "Judaism and Human Rights." In *Human Rights in Religious Traditions*, ed. Arlene Swidler. New York: Pilgrim Press, 1982.

Prozesky, Martin. "Is the Concept of Human Rights Logically Permissible in Theistic Religion?" *Journal for the Study of Religion* 2 (S 1989): 17-26.

Pushparajan, A. "Harijans and the Prospects of Their Human Rights." *Journal of Dharma* 8 (Oct.-Dec. 1983): 391-405.

Putuwar, Bhikkhu Sunanda. "The Buddhist Outlook on Poverty and Human Rights." In *The Wisdom of Faith: Essays in Honor of Dr. Sebastian Alexander Matczak*, ed. Henry O. Thompson. Lanham, MD: University Press of America, 1989.

Queen, Christopher S. "Introduction: The Shapes and Sources of Engaged Buddhism." In *Engaged Buddhism: Buddhist Liberation Movements in Asia*, ed. Christopher S. Queen and Sallie B. King. Albany: State University of New York Press, 1996.

————, ed. *Engaged Buddhism in the West*. Somerville, MA: Wisdom Publications, 2000.

Rahula, Walpola. "The Social Teachings of the Buddha." In *The Path of Compassion: Writings on Socially Engaged Buddhism*, ed. Fred Eppsteiner. Berkeley, CA: Parallax Press, 1988.

Rajavaramuni, Phra. "Foundations of Buddhist Social Ethics." In *Ethics, Wealth and Salvation: A Study in Buddhist Social Ethics*, ed. Russel F. Sizemore and Donald K. Swearer. Columbia, S.C.: University of South Carolina Press, 1990.

Rasmussen, Larry L. *Earth Community, Earth Ethics.* Maryknoll, NY: Orbis, 1996.

Refoule, Francois. "Efforts Made on Behalf of Human Rights by the Supreme Authority of the Church." In *The Church and the Rights of Man*, ed. Alois Muller and Norbert Greinacher. N.Y.: Seabury Press, 1979.

Rendtorff, Trutz. "Christian Concepts of the Responsible Self." In *Human Rights and the World's Religions*, ed. Leroy S. Rouner. Notre Dame: University of Notre Dame Press, 1988.

Rockefeller, Steven C. "Buddhism, Global Ethics, and the Earth Charter." In *Buddhism and Ecology: The Interconnection of Dharma and Deeds*, ed. Mary Evelyn Tucker and Duncan Ryuken Williams. Cambridge, Massachusetts: Harvard University Press, 1997.

Sachs, Aaron. *Eco-Justice: Linking Human Rights and the Environment*, Worldwatch Paper 127. Washington D.C.: Worldwatch Institute, 1995.

Saddhatissa, Hammalawa. *Buddhist Ethics.* Boston: Wisdom Publications, 1997.

Schaefer, Jame Ehegartner. "Ethical Implications of Applying Aquinas' Notions of the Unity and Diversity of Creation to Human Functioning in Ecosystems." Ph.D. diss., Marquette University, 1994.

Schaeffer, Pamela. "Restoring the Sacred in Nature: Bishops Face Tough Issues in Bringing Moral Order to Environmental Debate." *National Catholic Reporter* , 4 June 1999, 14-16.

Schelling, Andrew. "Jataka Mind: Cross-species Compassion from Ancient India to Earth First! Activists." *Tricycle: The Buddhist Review* 1(Fall 1991): 10-19.

Schuhmacher, Stephan, and Gert Woerner, eds. *The Encyclopedia of Eastern Philosophy and Religion.* Boston: Shambhala, 1994.

Schumann, Hans Wolfgang. *Buddhism: An Outline of Its Teachings and Schools.* Wheaton, Ill.: Theosophical Publishing House, 1974.

Scullion, James P. "Creation-Incarnation: God's Affirmation of Human Worth." In *Made in God's Image: The Catholic Vision of Human Dignity*, ed. Regis Duffy and Angelus Gambatese. New York: Paulist Press, 1999.

Sivaraksa, Sulak. "Buddhism and Development – A Thai Perspective." *Ching Feng* 26 (August 1983): 123-33.

———. "Buddhism and Human Freedom." *Buddhist-Christian Studies* 18 (1998): 63-68.

———. "Engaged Buddhism: Liberation from a Buddhist Perspective." In *World Religions and Human Liberation*, ed. Dan Cohn-Sherbok. Maryknoll, NY: Orbis, 1992.

———. "Human Rights in the Context of Global Problem Solving: A Buddhist Perspective." In *The Ethics of World Religions and Human Rights*, ed. Hans Küng and Jürgen Moltmann. London: SCM Press, 1990.

Smith, Jonathan Z., ed. *The Harper Collins Dictionary of Religion*. San Francisco: Harper, 1995. S.v. "Buddhism (thought and ethics)."

Smith, Pamela. *What Are They Saying About Environmental Ethics*. N.Y.: Paulist Press, 1997.

Sobrino, Jon. "Eastern Religions and Liberation: Reflections on an Encounter." In *World Religions and Human Liberation*, ed. Dan Cohn-Sherbok. Maryknoll, NY: Orbis, 1992.

Stackhouse, Max. *Creeds, Society, and Human Rights: A Study in Three Cultures*. Grand Rapids: William B. Eerdmans Publishing, 1984.

Stackhouse, Max L., and Stephen E. Healey. "Religion and Human Rights: A Theological Apologetic." In *Religious Human Rights in Global Perspective: Religious Perspectives*, ed. John Witte, Jr. and Johan D. Van der Vyver. The Hague: Martinus Nijhoff Publishers, 1996.

Strain, Charles R. "Socially Engaged Buddhism's Contribution to the Transformation of Catholic Social Teachings on Human Rights." In *Buddhism and Human Rights*, ed. Damien V. Keown, Charles S. Prebish, and Wayne R. Husted. Great Britain: Curzon, 1998.

Straus, Virginia. "Peace, Culture, and Education Activities: A Buddhist Response to the Global Ethic." *Buddhist–Christian Studies* 15 (1995): 199-211.

Swearer, Donald K. "'Rights' Because of Intrinsic Nature or 'Responsibilities' Because of Mutual Interdependence?" In *Buddhist Perspectives on the Earth Charter*, ed. Amy Morgante. Cambridge: Boston Research Center for the 21st Century, 1997.

Swidler, Arlene, ed. *Human Rights in Religious Traditions*. New York: Pilgrim Press, 1982.

Swidler, Leonard. "Human Rights: A Historical Overview." In *The Ethics of World Religions and Human Rights*, ed. Hans Küng and Jürgen Moltmann. London: SCM Press, 1990.

Teltsch, Kathleen. *The United Nations, the Human Rights Covenants, and the United States.* New York: Public Affairs Committee, 1981.

Thera, K. Anuruddha. "The Buddhist Attitude to Poverty." *Dialogue* (Colombo, Sri Lanka) 7 (1980): 99-103.

Thomas Aquinas, "*Summa theologiae*: Question 94. Of the Natural Law." In *Readings in Moral Theology, No. 7: Natural Law and Theology,* ed. Charles E. Curran and Richard A. McCormick. N.Y.: Paulist Press, 1991.

Thurman, Robert A. F. "Human Rights and Human Responsibilities: Buddhist Views on Individualism and Altruism." In *Religious Diversity and Human Rights,* ed. Irene Bloom, J. Paul Martin, and Wayne L. Proudfoot. N.Y.: Columbia University Press, 1996.

――――. "Social and Cultural Rights in Buddhism." In *Human Rights and the World's Religions,* ed. Leroy S. Rouner. Notre Dame: University of Notre Dame Press, 1988.

Tierney, Brian. *The Idea of Natural Rights: Studies on Natural Rights, Natural Law and Church Law 1150-1625.* Atlanta: Scholars Press, 1997.

Tillich, Paul. *Dynamics of Faith.* New York: Harper & Row, 1957.

Traer, Robert. "Buddhist Affirmations of Human Rights," *Buddhist-Christian Studies* 8 (1988): 13-19.

――――. *Faith in Human Rights: Support in Religious Traditions for a Global Struggle.* Washington, D.C.: Georgetown University Press, 1991.

Twiss, Sumner B. "Comparative Ethics and Intercultural Human-Rights Dialogues: A Programmatic Inquiry." In *Christian Ethics: Problems and Prospects,* ed. Lisa Sowle Cahill and James F. Childress. Cleveland: Pilgrim Press, 1996.

United Nations. *Universal Declaration of Human Rights.* In *Human Rights: The International Bill of Human Rights.* New York: United Nations, 1993.

United States Catholic Conference. *Economic Justice for All: Pastoral Letter on Catholic Social Teaching and the U.S. Economy.* Washington, D.C.: United States Catholic Conference, 1986.

――――. *Renewing the Earth: An Invitation to Reflection and Action on Environment in Light of Catholic Social Teaching.* In *"And God Saw That It Was Good": Catholic Theology and the Environment,* ed. Drew Christiansen and Walter Grazer. Washington, D.C.: United States Catholic Conference, 1996.

Unno, Taitetsu. "Personal Rights and Contemporary Buddhism." In *Human Rights and the World's Religions,* ed. Leroy S. Rouner. Notre Dame: University of Notre Dame Press, 1988.

von Bruck, Michael. "Buddhist Shunyata and the Christian Trinity: The Emerging Holistic Paradigm." In *Buddhist Emptiness and Christian Trinity*, ed. Roger Corless and Paul F. Knitter. N.Y.: Paulist Press, 1990.

Wackenheim, Charles. "The Theological Meaning of the Rights of Man." In *The Church and the Rights of Man*, ed. Alois Muller and Norbert Greinacher. N.Y.: Seabury Press, 1979.

Walf, Knut. "Gospel, Church Law and Human Rights: Foundations and Deficiencies." In *The Ethics of World Religions and Human Rights*, ed. Hans Küng and Jürgen Moltmann. London: SCM Press, 1990.

Warner, Keith. "Was St. Francis A Deep Ecologist?" In *Embracing Earth: Catholic Approaches to Ecology*, ed. Albert J. LaChance and John E. Carroll. Maryknoll, NY: Orbis, 1994.

Wayman, Alex. "Human Rights in Buddhism." In *Studia Missionalia*, Vol. 39. Rome: Editrice Pontificia Universita Gregoriana, 1990.

Williams, Cyril G. "Selflessness in the Pattern of Salvation," *Religious Studies* 7 (June 1971): 153-67.

Wilson, Andrew, ed. *World Scripture: A Comparative Anthology of Sacred Texts*. New York: Paragon House, 1995.

INDEX

U

V